Domestic Georgic

# Domestic Georgic

LABORS OF PRESERVATION FROM
RABELAIS TO MILTON

*Katie Kadue*

*The University of Chicago Press   Chicago and London*

The University of Chicago Press, Chicago 60637
The University of Chicago Press, Ltd., London
© 2021 by The University of Chicago
Published 2021
Printed in the United States of America

30  29  28  27  26  25  24  23  22  21      1  2  3  4  5

ISBN-13: 978-0-226-79735-9 (cloth)
ISBN-13: 978-0-226-79749-6 (paper)
ISBN-13: 978-0-226-79752-6 (e-book)
DOI: https://doi.org/10.7208/chicago/9780226797526.001.0001

The University of Chicago Press gratefully acknowledges the
generous support of the Society of Fellows at the University of
Chicago toward the publication of this book.

Library of Congress Cataloging-in-Publication Data

Names: Kadue, Katie, author.
Title: Domestic georgic : labors of preservation from Rabelais
to Milton / Katie Kadue.
Description: Chicago ; London : The University of Chicago, 2021. |
Includes bibliographical references and index.
Identifiers: LCCN 2021009505 | ISBN 9780226797359 (cloth) |
ISBN 9780226797496 (paperback) | ISBN 9780226797526 (e-book)
Subjects: LCSH: European literature—Renaissance, 1450–1600—
History and criticism. | Literature, Modern—15th and
16th centuries—History and criticism. | English literature—
Early modern, 1500–1700—History and criticism. | Literature,
Modern—17th century—History and criticism. | Work in literature. |
Housekeeping in literature.
Classification: LCC PN721.K33 2021 | DDC 809/.031—dc23
LC record available at https://lccn.loc.gov/2021009505

⊗ This paper meets the requirements of ANSI/NISO Z39.48-1992
(Permanence of Paper).

# CONTENTS

# Introduction

## THE PRIVATE LABORS OF PUBLIC MEN

*The protection and preservation of the world against natural processes are among the toils which need the monotonous performance of daily repeated chores. . . . However, the daily fight in which the human body is engaged to keep the world clean and prevent its decay bears little resemblance to heroic deeds; the endurance it needs to repair every day anew the waste of yesterday is not courage, and what makes the effort painful is not danger but its relentless repetition.*

HANNAH ARENDT, *The Human Condition*

*It is good for all infirmities of the Body, and driveth out all Corruption, and inward Bruises; if it be drunk with Wine moderately, it killeth Worms in the Body; whosoever drinketh much of it, shall live so long as Nature shall continue in him.*

*Finally, if you have any Wine that is turned, put in a little Viol or Glass full of it, and keep it close stopped, and within four days it will come to it self again.*

HANNAH WOOLLEY, recipe for "Walnut water, or the Water of Life," *The queen-like closet; or, Rich cabinet stored with all manner of rare receipts for preserving, candying & cookery*

*For Books are not absolutely dead things, but doe contain a potencie of life in them to be as active as that soule was whose progeny they are; nay they do preserve as in a violl the purest efficacie and extraction of that living intellect that bred them. . . . We should be wary therefore what persecution we raise against the living labours of publick men, how we spill that season'd life of man preserv'd and stor'd up in Books.*

JOHN MILTON, *Areopagitica*

In Francis Bacon's utopian fiction *New Atlantis* (1626), the Father of Salomon's House proudly introduces his institution as one committed to "the enlarging of the bounds of Human Empire, to the effecting of all things possible." But when he begins describing the actual operations of this palace of learning, things take a jarring turn. Grand gestures toward limitless progress suddenly shift to inventories of "coagulations, indurations, refrigerations, and conservations," materials that the experimenters "lay there for many years," containers devoted to "isolation, refrigeration, conservation," and a spa stocked with "Water of Paradise," a liquid "very sovereign for health, and prolongation of life." "I will not hold you long with recounting our brewhouses, bakehouses, and kitchens" containing "mixtures with honey, sugar, manna, and fruits dried and decocted," the Father assures his auditor, before launching into a lengthy list of "flesh and fish dried," "divers kinds of leavenings and seasonings," "mortified" meats, and medicines "of divers ages, and long fermentations," prepared in "all manner of exquisite distillations and separations."[1] These cabinets of curiously preserved fishes and delicately distilled vapors have the ultimate goal of temporarily protracting the lives of already existing individuals, and if anything new is created it is to that indefinitely deferred end; innovation is subordinated to preservation. Though Bacon and his acolytes never tired of trumpeting about scientific advancements to come, here his wildest fantasies of knowledge production are almost entirely limited to the field of preservation technology.

To borrow from Hannah Arendt's schema of the *vita activa*, despite the Father's claims to the public realm of "action"—characterized for Arendt by "unique deeds or achievements" and "the highest and greatest activities of man"—Salomon's House is devoted to what Arendt calls "labor," "the lowest, most despised" rung on the trichotomous ladder of human activity: "the protection and preservation of the world against natural processes."[2] This mythical house is structured like any ordinary house: it is a site of repetitive, metabolic, reconstitutive microoperations organized around the perpetuation of biological life. Such operations are both the techniques and the desired outcomes of many of the recipes contained in early modern collections like Hannah Woolley's of 1670, which instructed housewives in how to preserve or revive existing material—seasonal meats, nuts, and fruits, fragile medicinal herbs, wine on the verge of souring—in order to preserve or revive ailing or simply mortal human bodies. Woolley's recipe for "Walnut water, or the Water of Life"—included alongside "A very Soveraign Water" presumably as "sovereign" as Bacon's "Water of Paradise," as well as dozens of similar recipes for distillates—concludes with a promise that the result will cure various illnesses, prolong human life, and, "finally," undo the over-fermentation of wine and restore it to its proper form: "If you have any Wine that is turned, put in a little Viol or Glass full of it, and keep it close stopped, and within four days it will come to it self again."[3] Less resurrection than correction, this process is still a quasi-miraculous, if minor, reversal of the course of nature, at once impressive in its efficacy and tedious in its execution: the preserver needs to plan for multiple harvests across several weeks and prepare multiple distillations of the walnuts before the product is ready to use and to "keep."[4]

Bacon does not immediately strike us as a figure who could easily be brought home to the domestic sphere. The project of modernity, as understood by a diverse group of what we might call self-identified "early moderns" ranging from Petrarch to Erasmus to Bacon, involved creating a virtual, cosmopolitan community of minds and building immortal monuments to the arts and sciences.[5] Housewives, by contrast, were parochial, materialistic, and incapable of thinking beyond immediate bodily needs. In the terms of classical rhetoric, women were concerned not with *koinoi topoi*—topics of common interest, appropriate for public discussion—but with the irrelevant *idioi topoi* of "private places," literalized by the domestic interior.[6] As the French humanist Estienne Pasquier puts it, describing the division of labor in his own household, "Ses vins sont aux cuves sur le point d'être pressurez, les miens cuvent dans ma tête" (Her wines are in the vats, ready to press; mine are fermenting in my head).[7] What men did metaphorically and spiritually—seasoning raw material into something of value through sheer brainpower—their wives did only literally and mechanically, in a process about as interesting as watching grapes dry.

Narrow-minded and confined to narrow rooms, piling up provisions, mindlessly spinning on their wheels, early modern housewives were scorned in humanist polemic in terms resembling those applied to the cloistered, unimaginative monks of a bygone era. According to that polemic, medieval men of letters did no more than hoard material in enclosed, quasi-domestic spaces, constraining knowledge with their botched attempts at scholarship. These constraints not only impeded the productive growth of knowledge but also created breeding grounds for its contamination. Bacon blames the putrefied, "vermiculate" learning of the schoolmen on "their wits being shut up in the cells of a few authors" just "as their persons were shut up in the cells of monasteries and colleges," describing their "infinite agitation" in terms that evoke the labor of spinsters as well as spiders: "It is endless, and brings forth indeed cobwebs of learning, admirable for the fineness of the thread and work, but of no substance or profit."[8] When Edmund Spenser's

teacher, Richard Mulcaster, extols the pedagogical virtues of the public and denigrates the privations of the private—"the one in nature a
rowmy *pallace* full of most varietie to content the minde, the other a
close *prison,* tedious to be tied to, where the sense is shakled: the one in
her kinde, a *libertie,* a broade *feild,* an open *aire,* the other in the contra-
rie kinde, a *pinfold,* a *cage,* a *cloister"*—he does so in explicitly gendered
terms: young gentlemen who prefer private confines, where education
"is corrupted it selfe by a degenerate forme," are "liker to maidens."[9]
And when, in *Pantagruel,* François Rabelais's hero derides an over-
glossed classical compendium as "une belle robbe d'or triomphante et
precieuse à merveilles, qui feust brodée de merde" (a beautiful golden
robe, triumphant and wondrously precious, which had been hemmed
with shit), casting overzealous medieval commentary as a kind of ex-
cretory embroidery, he laments the defilement of a grand and glorious
tradition by a bodily secretion, the contamination of spiritual yearning
with a materiality both grossly natural and the product of effeminately
artificial labor.[10]

Yet even though many humanists and their heirs defined their work
against that of both women and monks, this book argues that sixteenth-
and seventeenth-century French and English authors were intently focused on the interior work and housewifely task of merely, laboriously,
and not always successfully preserving the materials of life and culture,
a process that often involved wading through waste, or at least tedium
and a nagging feeling of irrelevance.[11] Wearisome, incessant, and necessary, this work in some ways fits the category of "georgic," a mode derived from Virgil's four-book didactic poem that is part pseudo–farming
manual, part panegyric of the civilizing power of labor. Marking the
middle stage in Virgil's career and written against the backdrop of civil
war, the *Georgics* were less explicitly imitated in the Renaissance than
the more popular *Eclogues* and *Aeneid,* but their emphasis on work, as
opposed to pastoral leisure or epic battle, nonetheless exerted a powerful influence on early modern authors as a medium for the message that
man's obligation to till the soil marks the end of an idyllic Golden Age
but the beginning of a glorious civilization.[12] This was a useful narrative
for authors living through uncertain times who were both nostalgic for
the classical past and confident in their own progress toward enlightenment, a founding myth of sorts for modernity. Petrarch uses the Virgilian motto "labor omnia vincit improbus" (adapted from *Georgics* 1.145–
46) to mark two momentous, epoch-breaking occasions: his ascent of
Mont Ventoux and his 1341 poet laureate coronation oration, both frequently read as symbolic of the shift from the Middle Ages to the Renaissance.[13] "Labor omnia vincit," with Virgil's preterit *vicit* modified to

a timeless present tense, has since been taken by many commentators as the georgic rallying cry: unrelenting, all-conquering labor will reliably achieve both personal glory and a fruitful future for a society long beset by ignorance or political violence.[14]

But what I call *domestic* georgic falls short of, and sometimes even expresses indifference to, the triumphant optimism associated with early modern literary and philosophical engagements with georgic. In effect domesticating that georgic ethos, the authors studied in this book perform and describe a form of labor that—because it focuses on preservation more than the production of anything really new, or because it achieves results that are at best temporary—formally resembles the mundane maintenance work of housewives and domestic laborers rather than the trailblazing feats of modern and modernizing heroes. Pickling, preserving, storing, and organizing are not usually considered the province of the literary powerhouses this book considers: François Rabelais, Michel de Montaigne, Edmund Spenser, Andrew Marvell, and John Milton. But an attention to the role these activities played in the mentalities of those authors, in their attitudes toward their own writing processes and toward cultural production more generally, reveals a shared and surprising preoccupation with the repetitive, uneventful labors necessary to preserve life, and with how those labors inform the metabolic processes of thinking and writing.

## Humanist Fieldwork

At least according to the most vocal propagandists for the new cultural and intellectual paradigms, the medieval mausoleum of imperfectly embalmed texts was to be blasted open and replaced by the high-yield, well-tended Renaissance garden of letters. In the new, modern world, writers like Erasmus and Bacon proclaimed, mere and provisional preservation—the physical and intellectual hoarding of inherited material without regard for either its improvement or its permanence—would prove unviable. Erasmus would teach students not to "pile up a meaningless heap of words and expressions without any discrimination" (congesta vocum et sententiarum turba), the effect of which was "silly and offensive" (inani) and instead to master "the abundant style" (copia).[15] This exhortation aimed to restore *copia*, degraded by medieval textual practices to mean mere repetitive "copies," to its classical definition of material and rhetorical wealth, or "copiousness."[16] Defenses of vernacular literatures, like Joachim Du Bellay's 1549 *Défense et Illustration de la Langue française*—"illustration" in the sense of "adding of luster to"—expressed frustration with the impoverishment of con-

temporary discourse, often extending the metaphor of the desired rhetorical cornucopia to an explicit agricultural idiom. Du Bellay's mani-
festo participates heavily in this idiom, which was consistent with the
humanist commonplace of the "garden of letters." Just as Latin authors,
like good farmers ("en guise de bons agriculteurs"), discarded weak aspects of their language and grafted Greek scions onto their own rootstock, so too should Du Bellay's readers splice ancient literary forms
with French to create a hybridized poetry productive of healthy flowers and fruits of rhetoric, "ces fleurs et ces fruits colorés de cette grande
éloquence."[17]

In a similarly georgic vein, Baconian new science made vigorous use
of agricultural metaphors to outline how it would clear new ground
and improve the intellectual soil to produce prodigious harvests. Bacon begins the section of *The Advancement of Learning* entitled "De cultura animi" by collapsing agriculture and culture, declaring the life of
the mind as good as dead ("without life and motion") if deprived of
"husbandry."[18] Thomas Sprat opined "that wisdom, which they fetch'd
from the ashes of the dead, is something of the same nature, with Ashes
themselves: which, if they are kept up in heaps together, will be useless:
But if they are scattred upon Living ground, they will make it more
fertile, in the bringing forth of various sorts of Fruits."[19] This optimiza-
tion of dead wisdom to fertilize living ground was a more literal goal of
the Royal Society's Georgicall Committee, convened in 1664 to glean
what it could from "Georgicall Authors" of the past, from which "inqui-
ries should be collected, and digested," and sent out to farmers across
the country for answers, with the aim of circulating widely what had
been merely local knowledge so that "every place be enrich'd with the
aides, that are found in any place" and agricultural practices across the
nation could improve.[20] In short, approaching their intellectual labors
with a desire to bolster individual and common reserves of cultural,
political, and economic capital, writers called for the augmentation
and enhancement of their national languages, literatures, and stores of
knowledge through a collective commitment to what Bacon called a
"Georgics of the mind, concerning the husbandry and tillage thereof,"
a project "no less worthy than the heroical descriptions of virtue, duty,
and felicity": an agro-intellectual revolution that, through innovative
technologies, would coax surplus harvests from native soil that had for
too long lain fallow.[21]

Such exultant sentiments are typical of early modern versions of
georgic, even if, as some classicists have persuasively argued, the original *Georgics* should be read much more pessimistically.[22] The familiar
narrative of a heroic (or aspirationally so) georgic humanism, put for-

ward by scholars from Jacob Burckhardt to Thomas Greene to Leonard Barkan and still a tacit basis for periodization, imagines the first modern men, Petrarch foremost among them, digging up the glorious classical past to bring it, and us, into the light with an energy their anemic forebears lacked.[23] Greene, for example, emphasizes the Renaissance's "archaeological, necromantic metaphor of *disinterment*": the humanist-adventurer was on a quest to excavate lost treasures, sometimes literally unearthing ancient manuscripts and artworks from beneath layers of sediment accumulated by time and medieval incuriosity.[24] The figure of the groundbreaking humanist has been a subject of fascination—and identification—for scholars and critics into the twenty-first century. Stephen Greenblatt's 2011 popular history *The Swerve: How the World Became Modern* tells the story of how the intrepid library raider Poggio Bracciolini thwacked his way through a thicket of moldy manuscripts in 1417 to discover a copy of Lucretius's long-lost Epicurean poem, *De rerum natura*, whose powerful account of materialism and defense of pleasure would liberate Europe from fear, flagellation, and general backwardness.[25] Where would we be, Greenblatt asks, without the work of brave individuals who bring our cultural heritage to light to defeat the forces of darkness, then or now? In a controversial essay, Stephen Best and Sharon Marcus identify a variation of this fantasy: the "image of the critic as wresting meaning from a resisting text or inserting it into a lifeless one," an image that perhaps became so influential "because it presented professional literary criticism as a strenuous and heroic endeavor, one more akin to activism and labor than to leisure, and therefore fully deserving of remuneration."[26] This response to the declining prestige of the humanities in the late twentieth century in some ways echoes early modern humanists' response to the economic and political crises that came with the decline of the aristocracy, the beginnings of market capitalism, and the deep fault lines generated by the civil wars in sixteenth-century France and seventeenth-century England.[27]

And yet even some of early modernity's strongest apparent advocates of making literature and knowledge public and monumental also offer a different model for valuing literary and intellectual work. These authors returned repeatedly to private chambers, towers, cabinets, and closets to perform and describe labor that was georgic in character but domestic in scope, an intellectual husbandry tempered by intellectual housewifery. Complicating a set of overlapping oppositions integral to our understanding of the early modern period—private and public, *vita contemplativa* and *vita activa*, idleness and productivity, medieval and modern, feminine and masculine—these authors' poetics and the practices they describe evoke the labor undertaken in early modern domestic sites, labor most immediately concerned with the organization, reproduction, hygiene, and preservation of material rather than with progress, production, profit, or improvement.

Like Bacon's life- and fruit-preserving "refrigerations" or Woolley's elixir that could coax an ailing human body or soured wine to "come to it self again," the figures for textual production chosen by these five authors—Rabelais's frozen words that have crystallized as if in sugar, Montaigne's haphazardly collected bundle of kindling, Spenser's recipes for preserving and reviving men from death, Marvell's sewing kits and jam-making techniques, Milton's vials of seasoned and preserved life—evoke a kitchen cabinet, storage closet, or medicine chest rather than a collective advancement of learning. Rather than offering georgic visions of labor's conquering power or empire's inevitable expansion, Rabelais devotes his prose project to organizing the waste of the ancient and contemporary world, Montaigne blurs constant and inefficient household management with his writing process, Spenser allegorizes the brain as an attic full of decaying documents, Marvell imagines a future housewife candying the world like fruit, and Milton has his indomitable Son of God mark his historic triumph over Satan by going home to his mother's house. In other words, these authors, best known for strategic self-fashioning, innovative self-styling, or triumphant self-crowning—authors we often see as marking the end of the era of mere monkish retention and the beginning of an age of free thinking where the power of language and learning would liberate humanity—spent a lot of time thinking about housework.

## Humanist Housework

I refer to these authors' preoccupation with "housework" to describe not so much a set of activities as a mode of performing them: a mode that is confined, repetitive, and often at least implicitly feminized.[28] This imaginative interest in housework was supported by the actual work of housewives and domestic staffs who maintained the conditions for intellectual labor as well as all other labor, as Marxist feminists like Mariarosa Dalla Costa, Silvia Federici, Selma James, and Leopoldina Fortunati have shown in mostly more modern but also transhistorical contexts.[29] As circumscribed as her official role may have been, confined to an entirely interior sphere of influence, the *femme* of the Renaissance *homme de lettres* was charged with the important tasks of keeping track of the household's stores, managing servants, personally performing culinary or medicinal labor (distilling and candying, if nothing else), and safeguarding her husband's confidences.[30] Early modern men might also have called upon their wives, daughters, and domestic servants to contribute to their intellectual labor more directly as secretaries, amanuenses, and research assistants.[31] A wife's responsibilities in particular—sometimes only nominal, but sometimes substantial—could offer women surprising opportunities to impose their wills on their households, especially Protestant ones, and the relative independence of housewives could chafe against the accepted Christian doctrine of wifely subordination.[32]

My argument, though, takes a different point of departure: not the lived realities of women, but the imaginations of male authors who repeatedly returned to rhythms of domestic labor in the form and content of their work. While female authors like Louise Labé and Margaret Cavendish drew connections between domestic and literary or intellectual spheres precisely to distance themselves from the former and claim a place in the latter—replacing distaffs with pens, using cooking as a metaphor for poetic composition—elite male authors had no clear reason to refer to domestic work at all.[33] Insofar as scholars have noticed male authors' identification with women's reproductive labor, they have focused on the creative work of pregnancy, as when poets like Pierre de Ronsard and Philip Sidney figure themselves birthing a poem like a child and bringing something new and singular into the world.[34] And yet the male authors studied here imagined their literary activities as intimately involved with forms of reproductive labor that were, by contrast, repetitive, mundane, and oriented toward the maintenance of bodies that already existed. These authors understood poetic "housework" as a mode of labor that was usually confined to physically enclosed and private spaces, that was often only temporary in its effectiveness and that might never emerge from the fermenting vat at all.[35] This work was not only painstaking, slow, and menial but also, rather than clearly and directly contributing to the progress of public projects, often did little more—for the foreseeable future, anyway—than maintain the basic fabric of local and domestic life and materials, preserving the "living labours of publick men," as Milton puts it, in enclosed containers, "that season'd life of man preserv'd and stor'd up in Books" for uncertain future use.[36]

The rhetoric of such preservation encompassed not only putting up seasoned spirits in vials but also a more intangible kind of "keeping." The job description of the ideal housewife is perhaps articulated most clearly in John Dod and Robert Cleaver's popular *A godlie forme of householde gouernment* (1598)—based, like many other English and French domestic manuals, on Xenophon's *Oeconomicus*—which declares, "The dutie of the husband is to get goods: and of the wife to gather them together, to saue them."[37] Other wifely duties, similarly symmetrically opposed to the husband's, included "to keep the house," "not vainly to spend" the money and provisions acquired by her husband, "to be a sauer," and "to ouersee and giue order for all things within the house."[38] Mary Astell, in her 1696 *Essay in Defence of the Female Sex*, shows how such keeping is also a safeguard against ontological slippage: without it, things simply cannot remain what they are. Objecting to men's contempt for women's preoccupation with trivial "*Houshold Affairs*," she reminds her readers that "without our Care of 'em . . . their Houses wou'd be meer *Bedlams*; their most luxurious Treats, but a rude Confusion of ill digested, ill mix'd, Scents and Relishes; and the fine Furniture they bestow so much Cost on, but an expensive Heap of glittering *Rubbish*."[39] Astell describes domestic labor's capacity to make meaning in terms similar to those Arendt uses for the human condition itself: "Things would be a heap of unrelated articles, a non-world, if they were not the conditioners of human existence"; "Without being talked about by men and without housing them, the world would not be a human artifice but a heap of unrelated things."[40] As Olivier de Serres recognized in his 1600 estate management manual *Le théâtre de l'agriculture*, a man wastes his time implementing effective farming practices if the resulting fruits, once secured in the granary, are not wisely governed by the wife ("serrés dans les greniers, ne sont par la femme gouvernés avec raison"). For this Serres provides a pithy proverbial gloss: "On dict bien vrai, qu'en chacune saison / La femme fait ou defait la maison" (It is true that each and every season, the wife makes or breaks the household).[41] Domestic labor maintains the most local infrastructure, preserving households from disintegration, keeping the furniture as furniture, and this preservation needs to be regularly renewed: in every season, the household must be remade. An attention to the processes and effects of activities that look like nothing—because they seem to do no more than reproduce existing local conditions, even when this reproduction involves transformation—invites us to expand our ideas of what, potentially, can come from the "nothing" of preservative labor and maintenance work.[42]

The writers considered in this book understood intellectual work as domestic labor, in a strongly figurative and sometimes literal sense, while still maintaining the possibility of its relevance to the public. The difficulty in this rhetorical positioning is that the more successful the figure, the more it risks being taken too literally. To put a laureate and a housewife in parallel recalls rhetoric manuals' guidelines for *dispositio*, or the careful arrangement of arguments, and their casting of the *imitatio* of classical texts as a form of "domestication"; domestic economy, or *oikonomia*, conceptually structured ancient and early modern rhetorical discourse.[43] At the same time, the analogy comes close to collapsing supposedly sublime, transcendent, high-value intellectual production into the merely material and the temporally bound.[44] As Richard Helgerson puts it, "A laureate could not be a timeserver. Rather he was the servant of eternity."[45] For the authors studied in this book, however, literary production was real, temporally bound labor—and yet not quite the honest, hard, and potentially dangerous labor evoked by writers like Ben Jonson, whose writing philosophy was "that he / Who casts to write a living line, must sweat, / . . . and strike the second heat / Upon the Muses' anvil," with a typically contemporary georgic enthusiasm for transforming matter through Vulcanic toil in the "mines of knowledge."[46] But nor was it the self-effacing labor that went into the construction of an aristocratic literary culture of pastoral, valued for its appearance of idleness and purely natural bounty.[47] It was instead more like the labor performed and supervised by women within the confines of the early modern home, often invisible in its operations but necessary in its sustaining effects. This labor made the household—repeatedly, "each and every season"—by preventing it from breaking. *Domestic Georgic* thus diverges from other scholarly accounts of labor and literature in its focus on literary labor that was neither muscular enough to be straightforwardly valued *as* meaningful labor nor rarefied enough to be effectively dissolved into leisure or passed off as a spiritual pursuit.

In her recent study of early modern recipes, Wendy Wall argues that "seasoning," "preserving," and "distilling" "not only named specific technical practices but also underwrote the philosophical categories through which people theorized their work."[48] For Wall, the goal of these domestic practices was "nothing short of the elimination and transcendence of elements that corrupted matter."[49] Patricia Fumerton similarly distills her own discussion of seventeenth-century confectionery's medical and spiritual benefits: "What sugar and spice really cured, in a word, was mortality."[50] The ability of preserved foods to resist or reverse degeneration—both their own and of the bodies they nourish—is of course limited, and they are never preserved perfectly: salt, sugar, dehydration, and distillation necessarily transform matter in order to preserve it. And yet preservation promises a kind of paradise, where seasons are abolished as a regularly replenished store of preserves grants immortality, or something close to it, to cherries, quinces, roses, and walnuts. Many recipes for preserves in English and French collections end with instructions that testify to how their products can last until the next harvest or longer, ensuring an unending, Edenic supply: "then box it up and keepe it all the yeare"; "et la se gardera la rose toute l'année" (and there the rose will keep all year); "and so you may keep them all the yeare"; "elles se pourront garder deux ans" (they can keep for two years); "so may you keepe them a whole yeare without shrinking"; "pickle to keep six months or longer"; "will keep many a year"; "then take them up & pot them, and you may keepe them all the yeare."[51] Beyond any given incarnation of a conserve, recipes (or "receipts") were passed down and received through generations, often on pages interleaved with genealogies and other family records, both to endure and to be repeated.[52]

Many scholars who have studied the translation of the domestic to the literary in the English context have focused their attentions on drama, where what otherwise seem like trivial domestic concerns can literally take center stage.[53] Studies of domesticity in drama also seek to elevate offstage activities we usually think of as mundane, playing up their more spectacular aspects. Disabusing readers of any anachronistic ideas of domestic affairs, Wall suggests that a day in an early modern housewife's life might involve, along with more expected tasks, disemboweling a rabbit, cleaning up spilled blood from a freshly decapitated capon with a urine-based astringent, and scavenging for human bones to grind with snails to make hemorrhoid cream.[54] Throughout her work on both literary and practical texts, Wall portrays early modern housewifery as fast paced, bloody, and always ripe for drama, providing a welcome corrective to modern notions of housework as sanitary prudishness or soul-killing boredom. At the same time, as Kim Hall has pointed out, the English housewife was tasked with effacing and "refining" the violence endemic to the production of the colonial imports on which preservation and other culinary feats depended, notably the sugar that by the mid-seventeenth century was beginning to be primarily cultivated and processed by enslaved Africans in the West Indies.[55] By focusing on nondramatic writers who took decidedly nondramatic stances on housework, I do not mean to dispute early modern housework's potential for danger or excitement or its imbrication in large, oppressive political systems. But I do mean to suggest that this labor deserves our attention not only because of the ways in which it was sensationally interesting or globally important but also because of the ways in which it was not. In her skewering of the modern housewife in *The Second Sex*, Simone de Beauvoir mocks the pretensions to Promethean power that scholars like Wall and Fumerton would associate with preservative culinary labor:

Women writers have particularly celebrated the poetry of making preserves: it is a grand undertaking, marrying pure solid sugar and the soft pulp of fruit in a copper preserving pan; foaming, viscous, boiling, the substance being made is dangerous: it is a bubbling lava the housewife proudly captures and pours into jars. When she covers them with parchment paper and inscribes the date of her victory, it is a triumph over time itself: she has captured the passage of time in the snare of sugar; she has put life into jars.[56]

Beauvoir deflates this spectacular image of taming molten lava and freezing time with a deadening reality check: "Women and men writers can lyrically exalt these triumphs because they never or rarely do housework. Done every day, this work becomes monotonous and mechanical."[57] And yet Beauvoir acknowledges that this work, even when done every day, is not merely mechanical; if only. Even though housework is "too rudimentary, too monotonous" to qualify as "a technical activity," it is unscientific precisely because of how erratic it is:

> Besides, even in this area, things are capricious: there is material that "revives" and material that does not "revive" in the wash, spots that come out and others that persist, objects that break on their own, dust that grows like plants. Woman's mentality perpetuates that of agricultural civilizations that worship the earth's magical qualities: she believes in magic.[58]

Beauvoir's frustration with the simultaneous repetitiveness and unpredictability of housework, at once as unsurprising and as mystical as agricultural cycles, is the defining affective mode of domestic georgic. It is both the ineffable mystery *and* the repressive ordinariness of domestic labor—its constant necessity *and* its inconstancy, its dullness *and* its intensity—that structured the imaginations of the authors studied in this book, whose lyrical exultations of housework can sometimes sound like laundry lists. Preserving fruit and producing literary works are both like putting life into jars: an extraordinary feat from one perspective, but a boring chore from another.

## Tempering Georgic

The interest my authors took in the slow and minor processes that make literal and figurative domestic economies run was both literary and moral, an interest both in the compositional practice of tempering and in the ethical and affective practice of temperance.[59] Rabelais,

Spenser, Montaigne, Marvell, and Milton complicate apparent stances of disavowal and self-denial by converting static and negative (and often traditionally feminine) virtues into the active and positive (but only barely legibly so) operations by which a poetic and moral subject can be sustained, and literary and economic value can (if only indirectly) be suggested. Both the process and the product of this conversion could be described as temperance, understood to mean not simple abstinence or restraint but rather, borrowing from Milton's definition in *Areopagitica*—and borrowing, too, from a central activity of early modern housewives—the active collection of "usefull drugs and materialls wherewith to temper and compose effective and strong med'cins, which mans life cannot want."[60]

Tempering akin to that performed by housewives will emerge throughout this book as a central practice of domestic georgic. That Renaissance commentators found the *Georgics* to be primarily defined by thematic and stylistic variety underscores how the careful tempering of materials can be seen as equally important in that poem as the theme of labor is.[61] At the same time, the selection and management of various ingredients is a particular kind of labor: it is perhaps no wonder Virgil was said to have written his poem at the excruciating rate of one line per day.[62] Such tempering, like housework in Beauvoir's description, can be at once mind-numbingly tedious and so rarefied as to seem mystical or nonexistent, at once boring and precarious. As much as progressive improvement was the explicit aim of much georgic labor, the georgic mode on which I focus, and that can be traced back to Virgil's poem, is shot through with an anxious uncertainty, and sometimes an outright pessimism, about the future of any of its proposed projects: some material revives in the wash, other material does not, and nothing can stop the linens from eventually discoloring permanently.[63] Farming, like cooking, preserving, and other housewifely tasks, is subject to both predictable cycles and unpredictable anomalies. In book 1 of the *Georgics*, after extended praise of human ingenuity in the face of drought or flood, its power to mitigate or even overpower natural forces, Virgil concedes,

> But though both men and cattle do their work,
> And do it well, there are the mischievous geese
> And Strymonian cranes, and choking fibrous weeds,
> And overshading trees, to trouble the crops.[64]

Given such annoying obstacles, labor is necessary but not sufficient to human thriving, and the poem soon launches into a catalog of pests and blights that threaten to derail even the most vigilant agriculturalist, ending with a warning:

> Unless you take up your hoe, attacking
> The enemy weeds over and over again,
> And over and over again shout at the birds
> To scare them away, and use your pruning knife
> To keep on cutting back the overgrowth
> That threatens your plants with shade, you will, alas,
> End up, defeated, staring at your neighbor's
> Granary full of corn, and in the woods
> You'll shake the oak tree, frantic for something to eat.[65]

Here a helpful checklist of chores is folded into a threat: anything less than the assiduous upkeep of crops will lead to disaster. In this context, "labor conquered all"—which, to early modern readers like Petrarch and Bacon and twentieth-century commentators like Anthony Low, has rung out like a triumphant declaration of victory over nature—is more like a life sentence: "everything / Was toil, relentless toil, urged on by need."[66]

The contingency of georgic, as opposed to its inevitably conquering power, has been ably analyzed by Melissa Schoenberger, who contrasts confidently imperial georgic English poets of the long eighteenth century with those who, picking up on the halting ambivalence of Virgil's poem, grappled with the fragility of political stability and the necessity of its constant cultivation.[67] Kevis Goodman frames georgic uncertainty more explicitly in terms of affect, arguing that despite georgic's reputation for burying history in nature or plowing it into the ground, georgic does more than mystify power and property relations and thus demands additional critical responses besides demystification. Claiming that "historical presentness is often 'turned up' by georgic as *unpleasurable* feeling: as sensory discomfort, as a disturbance in affect," Goodman accentuates georgic's role as a mediating mode, one that draws attention to its own uneasy conversion of reality into art.[68] For the authors I consider here, unpleasurable feeling turned up by domestic georgic usually takes the form of boredom with the monotony of intellectual and domestic labor, irritation with that labor's simultaneous relentlessness and triviality, and anxiety about its management—what Sianne Ngai calls "ugly feelings," affects so minor they barely show up on the radar.[69] While this book's chapter on Montaigne engages with affect theory most directly, a concern with affect stubbornly and sometimes imperceptibly asserts itself in all the chapters.

A domestic georgic ethos is what allows textual production to sig-
nify as both private and open, both natural process and cultural artifice,
both mere conservation of value and source of surplus value, both self-
consuming spiritual exercise and durable material product, both rote-
produced copy and plenitudinous *copia*. In turning to Erasmus in the
following section, I aim to explore more fully how one of the most emblematic figures of the Renaissance reconciled, or failed to reconcile,
some of these contradictions. What does it mean when the most public
face of humanism consigns himself to housework?

## The Labors of Erasmus

In a 1523 letter, Erasmus asks his friend John Botzheim to entertain a
thought experiment: what if Erasmus had died after finishing the first
edition of his annotated collection of Greek and Latin adages, only to
come back to life, bringing "a better and fuller version" of the book
with him, presumably having had some blessedly undisturbed time to
improve on it in the afterlife? Surely Botzheim would not resent the
money he had spent on the first edition of the *Adages* and would mostly
be preoccupied with his gratitude at seeing his friend restored to life.
Erasmus presents the whole hypothetical situation in his typical copious style, expanding and contracting its terms as it progresses, regulat-
ing his own questions, and obliquely discounting the proposition's own
validity:

> Suppose I had produced the *Adages* and died at once, as soon as
> the work came out; would you regret having spent money on it? I
> don't think so. Now suppose further that I had come to life again
> a few years later [*post annos aliquot reuiuiscere*], and that the book
> was born again with me [*mecum renasci*], in a better and fuller ver-
> sion; would you groan about the expense, or would you receive joy-
> fully both your friend and your friend's achievement [*monumento*]?
> I know quite well what you will say: "I should certainly rejoice with
> the friend who was alive again—but all this is imagination." But
> which do you think the happier fate, to come back from the dead or
> not to die at all? If it is a matter of congratulation to be resurrected,
> it is a greater one to have survived [*multo magis gratulare superstiti*].[70]

The conclusion to this friendly circumlocution, then, is that mere survival is a greater accomplishment than resurrection. This is an unexpected affirmation, however rhetorical, from a man who seems to have
prided himself on resurrecting the entire body of ancient knowledge. In

this letter, Erasmus does not dismiss singularly miraculous events as beyond his modest scope; Christlike resurrection seems to be an option on the table. But what he finds most extraordinary about his augmentation of the *Adages* is that their growth is attributable to something as ordinary as survival.

Erasmus's stated ambition, in the encyclopedic *Adages* he first published in 1500 and continued to expand until his death in 1536, is no less than the "restoration of learning," and he is not slow, in his long entry on the classical trope of "The Labors of Hercules," to compare his own works to the deeds of the legendary hero himself. "But if any human toils deserve to be awarded the epithet 'Herculean,'" he interjects into his description of the twelve legendary labors, "it seems to belong in the highest degree to those at least who devote their efforts [*elaborant*] to restoring [*restituendis*] the monuments of ancient and true literature."[71] On one of these monuments, the complete letters of St. Jerome, Erasmus claims to have worked even harder than their author, it having "cost Jerome less to write his works than it has cost me to restore and explain them."[72] Simon Goldhill, after quoting this boast, goes on to marvel jocoseriously at Erasmus's anachronistic idea that a Renaissance humanist skill set was a defining aspect of early Christian asceticism, translating Jerome's "smelly, painful, lonely sufferings" into laudatory linguistic faculties and a flawless memory. If the motivation of Jerome's trip to the desert was really "to 're-read his entire library' and systematically to collect references and citations for later use," it was, Goldhill quips, "more sabbatical than mortification."[73] But understanding scholarship as a form of everyday "mortification," or what one character in Rabelais calls "maceration"—a process that both damages and reconstitutes the body in a preservative way—is central to how Erasmus complicates his narrative, and our own, of a heroic forward march into the future. In this book, that understanding will be as relevant for literary production as it is for scholarly conservation efforts.

The edition of Jerome's letters became an important accessory for the scholar-hero so carefully constructed, as Lisa Jardine's influential account elucidates, by Erasmus himself: an iconic portrait he sent to his favorite patron portrays Erasmus sitting regally with his edition of the letters, emblazoned with the title *Herakleou Ponoi* (labors of Hercules). For Jardine, Erasmus exemplifies the successful self-fashioning to which so many Renaissance writers aspired. His self-presentation, "ostentatiously no model of cloistered selflessness," fits Jardine's narrative of the emergence of an autonomous author who "strives for visibility rather than invisibility," who sees public heroism rather than private drudgery as the scholar's due.[74]

But as Erasmus goes on, in his Herculean adage, to explain his meth-
odology, the scholar's heroic toils begin to sound more like the stuff
of mock epic, more suited to a lady's cabinet than a foreign battlefield.
The Hydra's many heads are replaced by a swarm of "monstrous scribal
errors," and it is not superhuman strength but myopic squinting that
is required to decode corrupt texts and unearth buried gems, for "adages, like jewels, are small things, and sometimes escape your eye as
you hunt for them."[75] As a result of having to "wear out [*conteras*] your
eyes on crumbling [*cariosis*] volumes covered with mould, torn, mutilated, gnawed all round by worms and beetles," any compiler can expect
to age prematurely, and this at the expense of doing more meaningful
work in those more expansive fields where "there is often scope for using one's wits [*ingenio*], so that there is some pleasure to be gained from
creative and original thought [*inveniendi*], and in any context and at any
moment you may be able by nimbleness of mind [*mentis agitatione*] to
polish off [*absolvere*] some portion of your task."[76] But nimbleness will
get Erasmus nowhere here. "Who can make an adequate estimate of
the infinite labor [*infiniti laboris*] required to seek out such small things
[*res tam minutulas*] everywhere?" our Hercules asks, complaining that
even his well-meaning predecessors have only made his job more hopelessly difficult: "An almost larger army of commentators . . . , some of
whom by their idleness and inaccuracy and a certain number by pure
ignorance (for they too must be worked through, in hopes of course of
one day picking some gold off the dunghill [*legas aurum e stercore*]),
have added not a little [*non mediocrem*] to the burden [*sarcinam*] of
my labors."[77]

The humanist scholar's task, then, is both infinite and infinitesimal.
On the one hand, such a paradox is a familiar one in Christian humanism, preoccupied as writers were not only with their own accommodation of pagan culture to familiar Christian narratives but also with the
more fundamental accommodation of Christ's divinity to his humanity. This twofold movement of domestication receives complex treatment in Erasmus's commentary on the "Sileni of Alcibiades," unassum-
ing wooden figurines with statues of Greek gods hidden inside: a lesson
in how humble looks can be deceiving.[78] But while the scriptural comparison of the kingdom of heaven to a little mustard seed and the widespread self-deprecation of humanist letters as mere toys and trifles are
conventional formulations of a certain relationship between the infinitesimal and the infinite, they suggest the decorous humility of restraint
rather than the abject humiliation of interminably wading through a
dunghill.[79]

The restoration of learning seems to involve the scholar's success in proving his work to be not only apparently insignificant, but, more to the point, menial, ceaseless, and poorly compensated beyond the common reader's imagination—not wispily immaterial, but weighed down by banality. Erasmus casts his Herculean task as less a Christianized heroic struggle than a misuse of human resources: a great intellectual, who could have been putting his talents to more productive use, is confined to dusty archives and degraded to secretarial status for a public who will never appreciate him. This contrasts not only with the neatly transvaluing Pauline inversion of worldly weakness into otherworldly strength but also, to return to Arendt's schema of the *vita activa*, with classical conceptions of the hierarchy of human activity. In this schema, the domestic laborer, as opposed to the worldly producer of works or the public-minded hero, could never achieve any significance outside the *oikos*, even if public life depended, indirectly and invisibly, on home economics. This point is made explicit in a sixteenth-century home-economics-themed dialogue where a complaining wife is finally forced to admit that her absent husband has good reason to spend so much time doing business out in the world: "I knowe that he dyd more wyth one worde, then I can do in a hole day."[80] According to Arendt as well as to this fictional shrew, no amount of labor, limited as it is to the preservation and never the ennobling of life, can ever achieve the world-changing effects of public speech.

Arendt, after acknowledging that Hercules was both an archetypal hero and temporarily a laborer, clarifies that his famous labors can be called heroic only because they were singular events, taking place in the preterit rather than the present progressive. By contrast,

> The daily fight in which the human body is engaged to keep the world clean and prevent its decay bears little resemblance to heroic deeds; the endurance it needs to repair every day anew the waste of yesterday is not courage, and what makes the effort painful is not danger but its relentless repetition. The Herculean "labors" share with all great deeds that they are unique; but unfortunately it is only the mythological Augean stable that will remain clean once the effort is made and the task achieved.[81]

And yet intellectual and poetic labor, with the process of constant correction and revision undermining the finality of the published work, can leave behind products that both are publicly significant and stand in need of continuous maintenance and repair, or what Erasmus calls, in reference to his own work, "the unpopular and unvarying [*odiosum illum ac semper eundem*] toil of collecting, of sweeping together [*con-*

*verrendi*], explaining, and translating."⁸² If Erasmus's goal is to clean up completely the Augean mess that medieval commentators and the ravages of time have left behind, and to do this once and for all, one might think he would stress the singularity of his accomplishment rather than its relentless seriality.

Thus Erasmus virtually—and with a somewhat hyperbolic self-deflation—situates himself, avant la lettre, among those men of letters whom Adam Smith includes in his famous list of "unproductive laborers," which spans from the sovereign himself to government officials and the armed forces to "churchmen, lawyers, physicians, men of letters of all kinds" and finally down to "players, buffoons, musicians, opera-singers, opera-dancers" and household servants.⁸³ Richard Halpern calls this roll call a "mock-epic catalog" that replaces Homeric feats with menial services, casting the king's official acts as just as worthless, in the terms of political economy, as those of a servant or a clown: as Smith puts it, "The work of all of them perishes in the very instant of its production."⁸⁴ If Erasmus maintained the hope that his emendations might leave a mark far into the future—or at least lay the groundwork on which others could build—that hope does little to mollify his sense that his labors, no matter how noble in their aspirations for public service, are fundamentally service work, destined for an evaporation almost as instant as what Smith describes, absorbed by his readers without notice. Chained to his texts like a laborer "bound to the mill [*alligatus pistrino*]," constrained to "repeat the same things three thousand times [*sed ter millies eadem illa repetenda fuerunt*]," Erasmus figures himself as just as condemned to relentless cycles of production and feeding as a menial servant or a housewife, sustaining the survival of others.⁸⁵

To understand Erasmus's self-identification as with a "housewife" is to draw attention to the difference between labor specific to the production and consumption cycles of a household, and usually performed or supervised by women, and the forms of unproductive, servile, or menial labor that were considered respectable in early modernity. Spenser worked for much of his life as a secretary; Marvell was a tutor; and authors frequently referred to themselves as the "humble servants" of their patrons or monarchs in ways that were not merely rhetorical. The status of the secretary in particular was a privileged one: the job involved not only administrative grunt work but also access to sensitive information—secrets—that had to be closely guarded.⁸⁶ At the same time, even before the point Lawrence Stone has identified at the turn of the seventeenth century when young gentlemen began to find service to aristocrats of higher rank "socially humiliating," many of these subject positions and activities were at constant risk of sliding into the category of femininity and women's work; wives, too, were trusted keepers of men's secrets.[87] In his 1570 pedagogical treatise *The Scholemaster*, Roger Ascham takes pains to distinguish between the noble "scholehouse" and the base "larder house":

> Every man sees, (as I sayd before) new wax is best for printyng: new claie, fittest for working: new shorne woll, aptest for sone and surest dying: new fresh flesh, for good and durable salting. And this similitude is not rude, nor borowed of the larder house, but out of his scholehouse, of whom, the wisest of England, neede not be ashamed to learne.[88]

Of course, this clarification that the subject at hand has nothing to do with food preservation is required only because Ascham's examples have slipped from the intellectually oriented, if ephemeral, task of "printyng" on wax to the domestic activity of meat-salting, revealing that the clear separation of respectable from unrespectable unproductive labor is not, after all, so clear.

My argument, again, hinges more on such rhetoric of housewifery than on its reality, and as much as Erasmus elsewhere discounts the opinions of "silly women [*mulierculas*]" and "men very much like women [*mulierculis simillimos*]," the figure he cuts for himself in this commentary resonates strikingly with a role rhetorically cast as feminine.[89] He could, after all, have chosen to focus on some of the challenges that more obviously tested Hercules's muscular mettle, like the slaying of the Nemean lion or the capture of the Erymanthian boar. Instead, we get perpetually dirty stables and unending scribal errors, tiresome trials that must be met with what Arendt calls "relentless repetition" rather than "courage," with the housewife's patience rather than the hero's audacity. Expanding, however aspirationally, on Arendt's conception of domestic labor, Erasmus's cleanup project does aim to do something more than "keep the world clean and prevent its decay": namely, to organize messy textual material in order to make it available, hopefully, for others to use for their own sustenance and preservation. In this, too, he fills a crucial role of the early modern housewife as defined by Dod and Cleaver and other authors of household manuals: to maintain, through unproductive or minimally productive labor, a store of resources.

Taking the poetics of household activity seriously if not quite liter-

ally, this book aims to temper the understanding of early modern intellectual labor as innovative and sweepingly transformative down to
a smaller scale. This involves reading early modern writing as sometimes primarily preservative or corrective, and only in minor ways, even
as it claimed to make a definitive and dramatic break with the medieval past. Thomas Greene, in his argument for such a break, claims that
"the medieval writer works within a system of texts that are all equally
available for extension, completion, higher realization," making medieval intertextuality "metonymic," as opposed to the more dramatically
"metaphoric" intertextuality of the Renaissance.[90] Greene goes on to
quote Gerald L. Bruns's claim that "for the medieval writer, the inherited text is tacitly unfinished: 'it is never fully present but is always available to a later hand to bring it more completely into the open,'" a sense
of continuous labor that was displaced by the once-and-for-all triumph
of archaeological discovery, the "resurrection of literary texts . . . by
the humanist necromancer-scholar" that Greene associates with the
Renaissance.[91] Erasmus's version of Hercules's Augean toils troubles
Greene's distinction: his is less a resurrection than a means of survival,
or life support, for ancient texts, a prosaic, continuous, laborious, and
metonymic endeavor.

   It should not surprise us that Erasmus, no stranger to paradox, could
illustrate the master narrative of the Renaissance as a heroic, once-and-
for-all revival that paved the way for authors' personal and cultural self-
aggrandizement while also dragging that narrative through the mud.
But the sediment of drudgery in his writing is often ignored in favor
of the more vibrant (if, by scholars' admission, artificial) glow of heroism. Jardine includes in her portrait of Erasmus as self-fashioning hero
a note on his commitment to constantly revising previous editions, to
"vigorously keeping his printed text open and alive, trying to prevent
the living text from sliding back into a dead textbook."[92] This incessant
attempt to ensure survival, which for Jardine appears as a supporting
detail of Erasmus's construction of a heroic image, is, by my account, a
crucially deflating complication of it. Erasmus's fight for textual (and,
by extension, personal) survival did not rise to the level of what Terence Cave identifies as a struggle to make plenitudinous *copia* victori-
ous against the emptiness of mere "copy."[93] It was radically more mundane: an insistence on the convergence of *copia* and copy, with the
awareness that, like early modern domestic labor and unlike any heroic
feat classically understood, the scholar's activity of correcting, copying,
editing, translating, and transcribing can seek only to *maintain* original
materials—and to only uncertain ends.

## Recipe for the Book

Chapter 1, "Rabelais in a Pickle," shifts from the dank mire of Erasmus's textual practices to what may seem the more festive world of François Rabelais, whose association with humanist exuberance and carnivalesque pleasure in textual production has, since Bakhtin, become the basis of a critical consensus in Rabelais scholarship. This chapter radically moderates that consensus by locating a deep concern about the fragility of culture and community at the heart of textual excess in Rabelais's *Tiers Livre* (1546) and *Quart Livre* (1552), reading that excess as a crisis to be managed. I shift the critical focus from Rabelais's famously flowing wine to the moments of tempering, pickling, fermentation, and maceration that emerge as creative strategies of textual control, both formal and figurative. Rabelais's books constantly arrest forward progress by attending to microscopic operations of alteration, lingering on meticulous descriptions of confectionary practices (the proper way to process and store a mythical herb, the proposal to preserve frozen words in straw, the praxis of pickling oneself to avoid being swept up by passions—practices often described in narration-suspending parentheticals). These modes of moderate, transformative preservation inform both Rabelais's constantly self-correcting style and his concern for the correction and maintenance of his readers' collective health at a historical moment when French national identity was threatened by the first fissures of civil war.

Chapter 2, "Spenser's Secret Recipes," centers on the male hero's dependence on the labor of women and servants in Spenser's *Faerie Queene* (1590). Far from showcasing the autonomy of his virtue-personifying knights, Spenser reveals how much heroic action not only relies on support but is fundamentally undermined by it. Tedious descriptions of domestic drudgery rule out a clean equivalence of self-mastery and heroic conquest while dispensing with any illusions of the aristocratic self's autonomy. The nursing staff of the House of Holiness in book I, the sweaty and frazzled workers in the Castle of Alma in book II, and Venus's home remedies in the Garden of Adonis in book III make clear how much the reproduction of the aristocratic self depends on laborers who do not always remain under the control of either the poem's allegorical method or the hierarchy of power it might at first seem to reinforce.

In chapter 3, "Correcting Montaigne," the book shifts to the outright civil unrest of Montaigne's late sixteenth-century France. I show that Montaigne reconciles himself to political degeneration by defining progress (*progrez*) not as inevitable improvement over time but as a domestic rhythm of constant alteration and inadequate correction: the "staggering, dizzy, wobbling" motion of a drunkard, the incessant "pinpricks" of his household cares and the intermittent recurrence of his kidney stones, and the parentheticals, self-interruptions, and—in the latter two editions of the *Essais* (1580, 1588, 1595), meticulous mid-sentence edits—of his text.[94] For Montaigne, who claimed to write only for "domestic and private" ends, only "for few men and for few years," microcorrecting his own text in technical and tangential ways provides an alternative to expected paths of historical development and channels of genealogical transmission.[95] My readings of "De la vanité" (Of vanity) and "De la ressemblance des enfans aux peres" (Of the resemblance of children to their fathers) show how the constant need for local and domestic adjustment informs Montaigne's commitment to the preservation of both his household and his legacy.

The book then turns back to England, where the fragility and laboriousness of self-reproduction exposed by Spenser has been further dramatized in a world destabilized, like Montaigne's, by civil war. Chapter 4, "Marvell in the Meantime," shows how Marvell's *Upon Appleton House* (1651) negotiates the shaky relationships of both the poet and his patron—who had made an embarrassing retreat to his rural estate and had failed to produce a male heir—to heterosexual norms and public life. The poem's deviation from the heteronormative conventions of the country house poem has prompted some readers to pronounce it "queer." By contrast, I draw on discourses of domestic labor, particularly food preservation, to argue that Marvell's apparently subversive tendencies sustain heterosexual norms by renovating them, not out of an unequivocal attachment to heterosexuality but out of an urgent desire to sustain present conditions and future potential. Marvell's poetic techniques show how the suspension of futurity can be as easily conservative as transformative.

Chapter 5, "Milton's Storehouses," focuses on the centrality of reproductive labor both to Milton's Eden and to his political hopes. After showing Milton's interest in preservation in *Areopagitica* (1644), where books contain "that season'd life of man preserv'd and stor'd up," I turn to *Paradise Lost* (1667), where Adam and Eve "reform" Eden merely by maintaining it, through constant pruning of the garden and (in Eve's case) culinary labor. The chapter ends anticlimactically with *Paradise Regain'd* (1671), where Milton presents the regaining of paradise not as the spectacle of crucifixion and resurrection but as the mundane, metabolic process of the exemplary Son, whose repeated and continuously reproductive consumption provides a model for cultivating political possibilities.

The book concludes with a brief coda on two later poems written by women that formalize the repetition inherent to preservative labor. In Mary Collier's "The Woman's Labour" (1739), the working woman's second shift as wife and mother precludes the idyllic (if brief) breaks that allow male laborers the space for poetic meditation, as in Stephen Duck's "The Thresher's Labour" (1730), to which Collier explicitly responds. Collier's poem, with its packed schedule of ceaseless labors, describes conditions that would seem to make poetry impossible, and yet, she suggests, composing and reading poetry can be coterminous with manual labor. Alice Oswald's *Memorial* (2011), a rewriting of the *Iliad*, reduces Homer's epic to an itinerary of deaths: the names of all the fatalities described in the poem are first listed, then repeated in vignettes, interspersed with similes describing rural activities. Both poems refigure masculine glory—whether through georgic labor or epic feats—as underpinned by, and reducible to, the repetitive labors that preserve them as men.

CHAPTER 1

# Rabelais in a Pickle

FIXING FLUX IN *LE QUART LIVRE*

*Je suys, moiennant un peu de Pantagruelisme (vous entendez que c'est
certaine gayeté d'esprit conficte en mespris des choses fortuites), sain et
degourt, prest à boire si voulez. (I am, by means of a little pantagruelism
[that is, you know, a certain merriness of mind pickled in contempt for
things fortuitous] well and sprightly and ready for drink if you are.)*

RABELAIS, *Le Quart Livre*

*Ce n'est pas tout de cultiver l'arbre fruictier, & bien l'avoir entretenu, qui
n'en sçait garder & conserver le fruict. (It's not enough to cultivate a fruit
tree and to have maintained it well if you don't know how to keep and
conserve its fruit.)*

CHARLES ESTIENNE, *L'agriculture et maison rustique*

If any early modern French figure is thought to have had his eyes fixed
on the far-off future, it would perhaps be Michel de Nostredame, better
known as Nostradamus, the astrologer whose *Les Prophéties* (1555) have
been credited with foreseeing world-historical events centuries later.
But Nostradamus was also a physician, an apothecary, and the author
of a two-part treatise on cosmetics and confitures, also first published
in 1555, that aimed to prevent rather than predict disasters, to keep the
ordinary catastrophes of aging and decay at bay. Addressed primarily
to female readers eager to learn the best ways to preserve their beauty,
their harvests, and their health, the *Excellent & moult utile opuscule à
touts necessaire, qui desirent avoir cognoissance de plusieurs exquises receptes* begins its second section with a recipe for candying lemon peel.
The process is very long and very boring: you must precisely chop the
lemon, slice the peels at a certain thickness, wash them, soak them in
salted water for two days, change the water to fresh water and change it

again every day for nine days, boil the mixture, remove the peels from the pot and dry them, place them in a quantity of honey or sugar syrup (to be prepared separately), leave them overnight, boil them again in the syrup, remove them from the syrup while it boils again, put them back in the syrup for three days, boil them again, and only a month later will you find out if your labors succeeded ("au bout d'un moys aviseres sil va bien"). Mind-numbing as this repetitive work seems to be, it also requires constant surveillance and judgment. Nostradamus frequently interrupts himself with anxious parenthetical reminders, warning the reader of potential pitfalls as much as providing positive instruction. Don't throw away the seeds; don't forget this important step; be careful so it doesn't break; watch out so it doesn't burn.[1]

It is unlikely that Rabelais had this particular preparation of *écorces de citron confites* in mind when in the prologue to the *Quart Livre* (1552) he defined the ethical stance of Pantagruelism as "a certain merriness of mind pickled [*conficte*] in contempt for things fortuitous," though perhaps Nostradamus shared his recipe while the two men were both students at the Montpellier medical school in 1530.[2] And yet the logic of culinary preservation, in some ways more than that of heavy-drinking hedonism, informs both the ethics and the style of Rabelais's four books, particularly the last two. Rabelais has long been considered a celebrant of fluidity, fecundity, and flux, the creator of a world of permeable boundaries, mutating bodies, and interminable outpourings of wine and words. Yet this chapter will argue that an attention to the periodic *suspension* of that famous Rabelaisian flow is as important to understanding Rabelais and his humanism as a celebration of the flow itself. Echoing the rhythms of preservative domestic labor on both stylistic and thematic levels, Rabelais's prose evokes and embodies a domestic georgic ethos that aims not at the breaking of new ground or the boundless progress of human imagination but at the constant management, or tempering, of material and intellectual life through periodic suspensions of its activity, as in the pickling of "merriness of mind" with an acerbic agent like "contempt." What Michel Jeanneret, discussing the famous "frozen words" episode with which this chapter concludes, pejoratively calls the "tombeau pétrifié" (petrified tomb) of the printed book is better understood, in Rabelais's textual world, as a temporary and potentially salutary petrification.[3]

## Dead Stones: Cultivating Petrification

To begin again in another state of suspension: in the opening pages of the *Quart Livre*, just when the prologue's story is getting started, we are abruptly taken to Olympus, where we find Jupiter's faculty of judgment paralyzed. Having recently and conclusively resolved a series of geopolitical conflicts, the king of the gods finds himself at a loss, "en grande perplexité," when it comes to the quarrel between two scholars at the University of Paris, Pierre Rameau and Pierre Galland.[4] The solution to this standstill, proposed by Priapus, is for Jupiter to do what he did the last time he found himself faced with such an aporia: to turn both parties into stone, thus suspending the question indefinitely. This method worked well then—when a fox, fated to be caught by no other animal, encountered a dog, fated to catch any other animal it came across— and seems especially fitting here, as Jupiter has just compared the pair of Pierres to a howling dog and a crafty fox. This sense of coincidence solidifies into poetic justice when Priapus reminds Jupiter that both men to be made into *pierres* are already Pierres in name, and they could conveniently join a third troublemaking homonym, the so-called Pierre de Coingnet, already a fixture in the corner of the walls of Notre Dame de Paris, in a triangular coterie of "trois pierres mortes" (551). Though Jupiter rejects this advice—such a literally monumental memorial is just what these narcissistic academics want—the outcome still, in a way, leaves the two Pierres petrified into perpetuity. Distracted first by the general state of human affairs and the related problem of Olympus's shortage of thunderbolts and then by the shouts from earth of the woodcutter at the center of the prologue's narrative, both Jupiter and the narrator abandon the question altogether, leaving Rameau and Galland stuck in their standoff indefinitely.

If these proposed dead stones, the bloodless remains of bitter factionalism, have been thought to fit anywhere in the Rabelaisian edifice, it is as negative exempla. Edwin Duval has argued that these imagined monuments to intramural incivility, wedged into the walls of an "anticommunity" built on "anticaritas," are the antithesis of the cheerfully reasonable Pantagruelist spirit we have come to know and love over the course of the previous books. By bringing civil war into the heart of humanism—once thought to be France's best hope *against* civil war— the factions of the University of Paris *petromachie* stand in opposition to the living stones (*lapides vivi*) with which Peter, that rock on which the church was built, would have Christians construct a living house for God. Duval finds these stony threats met throughout Rabelais's books by the author's call for literal life, pointing to Panurge's promise in the *Tiers Livre* to produce *pierres vives*, or children, in lieu of sterile stone buildings, and more generally to Rabelais's emphasis on sexual union as the half-serious answer to all threats of division.[5] Lawrence Kritzman, writing from a psychoanalytic perspective, finds Priapus's petrification proposal "inauthentic" and "artificial," an improper "immobilization and reification" of movement that wants to be free.[6] Kritzman extends his diagnosis to the author, describing Rabelais's polysemic play on the word *pierre* and "petrification" as an expression of his "fear of choosing" that leaves him stuck "between ideological extremes, the unfortunate victim of repression."[7]

But petrification and its domestic cousins—pickling, preserving, and other forms of culinary and medicinal suspension—are, in Rabelais's case, neither simply symptoms of pathological indecision nor heresies to be quickly and simply stamped out. As this chapter will show, provisional or indefinite immobilizations are central to the ethics and aesthetics of a writer usually associated with irrepressible life. Life is frequently and undramatically repressed—pickled—in Rabelais, on the level of the sentence as well as of the narrative. The indeterminacy of meaning in his work is thus not only the result of a delightful polysemy. It also comes from a deep sense of the contingency of the future and of the maintenance work needed to sustain both the basic conditions for linguistic and literary production and the potential for local and collective transformation.

For Duval, the deadening specter of "anticaritas" cast by the *pierres mortes* crucially sets the *Quart Livre* apart from the hopeful humanist vision that came before, and others have located similar shifts from celebrations of vital energies to ominous spectacles of calcification in Rabelais's books. Jeanneret finds Mikhail Bakhtin's famous account of Rabelais's empowering excess, which he agrees is a fair characterization of *Pantagruel* (1532) and *Gargantua* (1534), to ring false for the *Tiers Livre* (1546) and the *Quart Livre* (1552), where Victor Hugo's almost equally famous view of Rabelaisian debauchery as didactically disgusting might make for a more valid interpretation.[8] In the *Tiers Livre*, published at a moment when lively debate over the future of Christianity was giving way to uncompromising entrenchments and the early signs of civil war, Rabelais's previously joyous excess, Jeanneret observes, begins to take on a different hue. The uncomplicated embrace of material and intellectual abundance of the first two books—what Jeanneret calls the euphoric mode of "*très*"—gives way to the sinister tone of "*trop*," the nagging sense in the last two of the authentic books, often insinuated by the grown-up Pantagruel, that there is indeed such a thing as "too much."[9]

Given that the *Quart Livre* ends with Panurge covered in his own excrement, ignoring Pantagruel's pleas to clean himself up, and inviting everyone to drink, Jeanneret takes as a foregone conclusion that Pantagruel's mature role as the voice of moderate reason ends up doing little to keep the messiness of the body in check. Even if the last two authentic books defend "mediocrité"—variously understood as *mediocritas, sophrosune,* temperance, modesty, or the charitable inclusivity of "Pantagruelism"—as a virtue, their author's excessive style (the never-ending descriptions, the bloated lists) undermines any nominal commitment to that virtue.[10] Ultimately, Jeanneret concludes, excess always triumphs: the body's appetites will not be controlled, and if food, wine, and sex are no longer available for innocent and unlimited enjoyment, excess will instead come out verbally, producing text with inexhaustible significations and defying those who would reduce Rabelais's "polyphonique" text to a museum of determinate meanings.[11] In interpretations like these, Rabelais holds onto his literary reputation as irrepressible, boundary breaking, infinitely productive, and infinitely capacious, an author whose work could be described, as in Jules Michelet's influential estimation, as "the sphinx or the chimera, a monster with a hundred heads, with a hundred tongues, a harmonious chaos, a farce of infinite range, a marvelously lucid drunkenness, a profoundly wise folly."[12]

However much his philosophical interests moved to moderation, Rabelais's artistic spirit would thus still seem far afield of the domestic georgic concern with temperance and the mundane maintenance work of "tempering" the materials of life, preserving them by temporarily suspending them.[13] A cosmopolitan humanism would seem to drift far from domestic cares; a comical approach to menial labor, as when Epistémon enjoys the spectacle of Homeric heroes doing scullery work in the underworld, would not suggest a respect for its value; and readers have often found in Rabelais a purely pastoral fantasy of a natural economy that renews itself perfectly automatically, through passive or reflexive verbs, with no active maintenance, intervention, or culturing required. As Jeanneret puts it, channeling Bakhtin, "excess is recycled in the regenerative process of natural energies," so that "everything circulates and is transformed."[14] But acknowledging the great pleasure Renaissance humanists took in the novel abundance of textual material and the playful manipulation of language does not require denying that they also found importance, and even pleasure, in the (even if only provisional, and even if precisely through play) ordering and fixing of that material.[15] Even though organic processes and bodily functions are natural, and even though Rabelais is inclined to celebrate them, he approaches these processes and functions as contingent on management and control. That control, however, often goes unnoticed, the more so the more one is swept up in the celebration. Jeanneret's approving reading of the famous *torche-cul* episode in *Gargantua* as an unembarrassed embrace of the body's natural processes, for example, ignores that the young giant's experiments are engineered entirely toward managing the results of defecation after the fact, rather than taking pure immediate pleasure in the activity.[16] Grandgousier's pride in his son, however exuberant, is due not to his profligate production of waste but to his superlative hygiene. After hearing of the number of innovative methods—rose petals, a basket, pearls, a pigeon—Gargantua has found by laborious and painful (and, yes, humorous) experimentation to clean up after himself, his father marvels that his son had so well ordered things ("avoit donné tel ordre") that he was the cleanest boy in all the land ("en tout le pays n'estoit guarson plus nect que luy" [65]).

Rabelais operates stylistically and affectively as well as ethically and philosophically under the sign of economical order, rather than that of wasteful excess, and the domestic georgic labor of tempering operates as a cultural form that bridges material and textual practices of organizing, altering, preserving, and moderating. Maintaining Rabelais's textual economy often involves the temporary freezing and fixing of meaning and material in ways that recall the freezing and fixing techniques of domestic labor, tasks typically designated for women as among the small matters ("menues affaires") of the house.[17] When the abstract concept of moderation is refined into a materially grounded practice of temperance—the tempering of materials, like confected lemon peels, through labor, sweetener or salt, and time—the relevant question becomes not how much is too much but rather the more basic question of what to *do* about superfluous material, whether *très* or *trop*, abundant or excessive, textual or otherwise.[18] Whether having more than one needs at a given time is a blessing or a curse, those extra resources need to be managed, and this process often involves freezing, pickling, and other mortifying operations. Though the question of resource management emerges periodically throughout the four books, it is most urgent in the *Tiers* and *Quart Livre*, where the consumption of food and wine becomes increasingly tempered, in quality if not in quantity: the processing of food and other organic material by maceration, fermentation, and careful storage becomes more important than its simple consumption, in a way that draws attention to Rabelais's careful management— rather than gleeful explosion—of language.[19] This management occurs on the level of the sentence, on a microscopic and contingent level. Using contemporary conceptions of medicinal and culinary preservation to temper existing scholarly accounts, I find Rabelais's careful, local management of his text to result in the cultivation of specific potentials rather than either the revelation of oracular truth or the opening of Pandora's box.

## Pickled Gaiety: Preserving Alteration

Though we never quite emerge from the *petromachie* of the *Quart Livre* prologue—the two Pierres may not have been sentenced to a stony immortality, but they have been indefinitely suspended between life and death, between *pierres vives* and *pierres mortes*—readers of Rabelais would have already received a long training in perplexity in the previous book. Despite the manic pace of the *Tiers Livre*, centered around Panurge's quest to answer the question of whether to marry and moving restlessly from one "expert" consultation to the next, the end result of the volume is suspension. Panurge's tendency to endless deferral has been read as pathological; as reluctant to marry as he is to drink, preferring in both cases to talk rather than act, he fails to participate properly in the Pantagruelian economy of consumption and consummation.[20] By the end of the *Tiers Livre*, neither he nor the reader emerge from paralyzing indecision, and both are sent instead on a potentially interminable voyage.

In that volume's prologue, as in the following one, we are thrust into a bustle of activity that ends up leading nowhere. Citing the example of Aeschylus, who drank while writing and wrote while drinking ("beuvoit composant, beuvant composoit"), the narrator announces that he has put himself on a similarly circular regimen of drinking, deliberating, resolving, concluding, laughing, writing, composing, and more drinking (347). Near the end of the prologue, with the rolling metaphorical wine barrel gaining momentum, he addresses all good drinkers and gout sufferers who happen to be "altéréz." Already altered, they are invited to alter themselves further by partaking of the copious barrel of wine ("le tonneau inexpuisible") that is Rabelais's text, in a seeming continuation of the Bakhtinian, euphoric mode of *très* (349).

Yet Rabelais's incitement to alteration is, at bottom, a call for maintenance: bodies—whether biological, textual, or communal—need to be altered not to reach new heights of intoxication but in order to remain themselves. "Altération," as the ancient medical writer Galen's *alloiosis* was usually translated into French, refers to the state of a body whose humors are out of balance; it could also simply mean thirst, a relatively minor maladjustment and one that can usually easily be corrected, unless one's thirst is, like some of Rabelais's characters, insatiable. In the *Quart Livre* prologue, we learn that the Olympian assembly, hopelessly and collectively perplexed by the aporia of the uncatchable fox and all-catching dog, was afflicted by an "altération mirifique" (551), a thirst so wondrous as to be unslaked by seventy-eight barrels of nectar and abated only with the solution of the petrifying alteration of the animals in question into stone. Even in less dramatic circumstances, the correction to alteration is itself understood as an "altération," the disease linguistically indistinguishable from the remedy.[21]

The preservation of the body's health thus requires the corrective alteration, or minor transformation, of its state, with the same logic extending to the wider community. Discussing how Pantagruel, from the moment of his birth during a severe drought, is figured as both a dipsetic scourge and a "restorative hero," Thomas Greene concludes that the giant's salvific nativity along with a procession of salt-bearing mules "*alters* as it provokes us to alter our own insufficient world," reminding us that our thirst will not be miraculously satisfied once and for all.[22] The etymology of Pantagruel's name—*panta* meaning "all" in Greek, *gruel* meaning "thirsty" in Hagarene (Arabic)—refers to both a character and a world that are entirely "altérés," and alteration proves crucial to Pantagruel's ethical proximity to Christ, who also came to save and restore humanity under the sign of life-altering, soul-reforming wine.[23]

Pantagruel's altering effects attest to the role of remedial transformation in even the earlier books, but the *Tiers Livre* and *Quart Livre* most explicitly frame the issue of moderation through a culinary or medicinal model of tempered alteration.[24] This is not, as we have seen, how moderation is usually understood in Rabelais. It is also not how the related epistemological concern of perplexity has been understood. "The riddle of the future is the philosophical question that underlies the quest of Panurge" is Greene's apt gloss of the *Tiers Livre*, Panurge's narcissistic obsession with the possibility of being cuckolded inspiring lofty questions "of foreknowledge, of divination, of freedom and determination, of history, of providence, of human action and human prudence": "Panurge's dilemma is the predicament of the conditional and the contingent, the unforeseen, the enigmatic ground of our condition."[25] But the attempt to manage futurity, to unpack carefully if not to solve its "riddle," is also the primary concern of the much more mundane practices of culinary preservation and domestic healing.

Following the perplexities of the *Tiers Livre*, the *Quart Livre* prologue opens in more temperate tones, with our reckless barrel roller suddenly concerned with the maintenance and care of himself and his readers.[26] Congratulating his audience, no longer thirsty and poxed, on finding a remedy "contre toutes altérations," our author-physician attributes his own healthy state to his moderate consumption of a certain pickled product:

Vous avez remède trouvé infinable contre toutes altérations? C'est vertueusement opéré. Vous, vos femmes, enfans, parens et familles

estez en santé desirée? Cela va bien, cela est bon, cela me plaist.
Dieu, le bon Dieu en soit éternellement loué et (si telle est sa sacre
volunté) y soiez longuement maintenuz. Quant est de moy, par sa
saincte bénignité j'en suys là et me recommande. Je suys, moiennant
un peu de Pantagruelisme (vous entendez que c'est certaine gayeté
d'esprit conficte en mespris des choses fortuites), sain et degourt,
prest à boire si voulez. (545)

(You've found an infallible remedy against all thirsts and distempers?
That's worthily done. You, your wives, children, family and kinsfolk
are all in the health you desire? Things are going well. That's good.
I'm pleased. God, our good God, be eternally praised for it and [if
such be his holy will] may you long be maintained in it. As for me,
by his holy loving-kindness I'm still here and pay you my respects.
I am, by means of a little *pantagruelism* [that is, you know, a certain
merriness of mind pickled in contempt for things fortuitous] well
and sprightly and ready for drink if you are. [650])

Partaking "un peu" from the pickle barrel—with the explanation of
this figurative pickling process held in a parenthetical suspension—
sounds less conducive to linguistic and narrative production than
a continuous flow of wine, and certainly less promising for the reader's pleasure. Early modern dietetics often prescribed the use of pickles for "correction"—to improve digestion and balance the humors—
more than for direct nutritional or gustatory value, though confitures
could taste good too: Nostradamus recommends his pickled pumpkin
for heart and liver problems ("pour mitiguer la chaleur exuberante du
cœur & du foye"), but it's also simply "bonne pour manger."[27] Pickling—a term encompassing various methods of preserving food with
vinegar, salt, honey, sugar, or must—was a mode of gradually transforming foods and the people that consumed them in order to stave off
their deterioration. As Nostradamus puts it, anyone who tries to store
fruits just as they are ("ainsi qu'ilz sont") will soon find themselves with
rotten fruit: it won't be long before an untreated harvest succumbs to
"corruption, ou alteration." The only way to avoid such "alteration," to
preserve fruits indefinitely ("conseruer aucuns fruitz en une perpetu-
elle duration"), is to alter them in another way, changing their form
("leurs changeant . . . la forme"), removing the natural bitterness from
their flavor and replacing it with an artificial sweetness ("luy faisant ac-
querir . . . une doulceur qui fait esuanouir leur naturelle amaritude").[28]

Even accepting that Rabelais's exuberance had long begun to sub-
side by 1552, maintenance and preservation might go against the guid-

ing principles of even the most abstemious chronicler: the metonymic displacements of alteration are necessary to drive any narrative forward. If Panurge spends most of the *Tiers Livre* mired in indecision, his hand-wringing is at least energetic. A story of a healthy person who simply, calmly, and quietly remains healthy would be no story at all.[29] Yet health for Rabelais, as for ancient and early modern medical writers, is defined not as completely static sufficiency but as a slight imbalance, or open-ness to imbalance, an alteration presented only as an afterthought but that nonetheless invites, "si voulez," an alteration in turn. This chain of alterations paradoxically stabilizes and preserves both health and nar-rative coherence.[30] If our narrator has abstained from writing drunk, it is not because he is completely cured of all "altérations." He is, if his readers will allow it, "prest à boire," ready to drink and be altered anew.

The prologue goes on to alter a straightforward parable of moder-ate desire fulfilled—a reasonable prayer for a lost hatchet results in the hatchet regained—into an extended Aesopic fable of immoderate re-turns. Couillatris, a simple woodcutter, loses the means of his liveli-hood, and his wish for its return is answered by the gods with a choice of his own lost hatchet, a silver hatchet, or a gold hatchet. When he moderately chooses his own, he is rewarded with the silver and gold as well, capital with which he buys enough land and livestock to become the richest man around. When the minor nobility of the neighborhood hear about Couillatris, they try to replicate his success, with disastrous results: they choose the gold hatchet and are punished for their greed with decapitation. As Terence Cave's reading of the episode elucidates, this elaborate story—stocked with semantic and material wealth, in-terrupted with Olympic wordplay, and ending with disproportionate punishment—is an exercise in excess. The temperate and tempering pickled gaiety with which this prologue begins stimulates a mode of linguistic production perhaps less festive, but no less prolific, than the Bacchic barrel-rolling of the *Tiers Livre* prologue. Cave reminds us that, however copious this production is, it gets us nowhere fast—a simu-lation of superficial abundance that does little or nothing, in Cave's understanding, but mask an emptiness beneath.[31] I argue, however, for reading Rabelais's text not as a dizzying interplay of plenitude and lack but as a healthy, modestly maintained mechanism, a carefully regulated body that finds imperfect but sustainable ways to alter its own altera-tion, transformative preservation or "pickling" foremost among them. The results of these constant, minor alterations are relatively stable, but never completely certain, and no less stressful for being ordinary, or even boring.

As Rabelais boldly predicts in his parodic *Pantagrueline Prognosti-*

*cation* (a riff on popular prophesying almanacs like Nostradamus's), in the year to come blind men will experience difficulty seeing, the rich will enjoy a higher status than the poor, and the summer will be warm. But these seemingly obvious eventualities all depend, Rabelais feels the need to point out, on God, who "par sa divine parolle tout régist et modère . . . et sans la maintenance et gouvernement duquel toutes choses seroient en un moment réduictes à neant" (920) (rules and directs all things through his holy Word . . . and without whose preservation and control all things would in a moment be reduced to nothing [174–75]). In more mundane terms, such *gouvernement* is also the task of the housewife, who for Olivier de Serres "en chacune saison . . . fait ou defait la maison," overseeing and transforming spaces and materials so that they can remain themselves. A recipe in *Le Menagier de Paris*, a 1393 household manual reprinted numerous times in the sixteenth century and narrated by a fictional husband instructing his young wife on the affairs of the home, emphasizes how much close human observation and regulation are required even of products primarily confected by the simple passage of time. Like Nostradamus's recipe for candied lemon peel, this *confiture de noix* requires a tempering or moderating judgment in several senses on the part of the preserver, including remembering to renew periodically the conditions for confection. She must select the nuts at the right season, make sure the shell is neither too hard nor too soft, painstakingly peel all five hundred of them, change their soaking water every day for ten to twelve days until they blacken and can be determined to have lost their bitterness, and boil them either for the length of a prayer or until, again according to judgment, they are neither too hard nor too soft. This method may also be applied, the author goes on to suggest, to parboiled turnips, carrots, unripe peaches, and squashes, which should be "gouvernez" just like the others, no more or less ("ne plus ne moins").[32] This is a reminder both not to deviate from the moderate range of times and methods prescribed by the other recipes and to moderate—*gouverner*—within that range, fine-tuning according to individual judgment: Randle Cotgrave's 1611 French-English dictionary lists "to guide, order, direct, conduct, looke vnto, haue the charge of; also, to temper, moderate, restraine" alongside "to gouerne, rule, commaund, maister, sway" as English translations for *gouverner*.[33] The primary agent of culinary preservation is time, but this temporal action must be moderated—tempered or governed—by minor and intermittent human intervention.

As Nostradamus laments, much can go wrong in preservative processes like this: an overconfident and careless *confiseur* too often spoils the confection ("gaste la confiture") by burning the sugar or honey,

so that one is constrained to throw it out ("l'on est contrient de jet-
ter la confiture à mal").[34] And in his *Prognastication*, Rabelais suggests that everyday events we easily take for granted are, in a very real
sense, granted by God, "sans la maintenance et gouvernement duquel
toutes choses seroient en un moment réduictes à neant," providence
expressed in terms of contingency. If Rabelais's almanac is a clear mock-
ery of Nostradamus, it also articulates a real concern of that bombastic
fortune teller for the fragility of preservative plans that all too easily
fall through. This awareness of the necessity of constant and invisible
intervention—whether divine, human, or accidental—informs Rabelais's interest in moderation and maintenance that extends beyond the
textual body to the bodies of its author, its readers, and the larger Christian community.[35]

As a technology of moderation and preservation that involves excess
and waste in its process, pickling wedges a solid if provisional middle
ground into Cave's unstable binary of emptiness and plenitude, a possible location of that elusive Rabelaisian moderation. In the midst of
Panurge's perplexity in the *Tiers Livre*, he is thrilled to learn that the answer to sexual excess is not total abstinence but the recasting of excess
as a moderate regime. After citing scripture's imperative to "be fruitful
and multiply," frere Jan instructs Panurge to void his reserves of sperm
as a prudent, pious expenditure, and the chapter closes by valorizing
moderate rather than multiple returns: the genetic material of a death-
sentenced man should not be foolishly wasted ("ne doibt estre folle-
ment perdue"); he should die "laissant home pour home" (447), leaving man for man, hatchet gained for hatchet lost, a simple reproductive
projection into the future of conditions that exist in the present. Later,
when the doctor Rondibilis, after deferring for a while with alternative
solutions, finally informs a delighted Panurge that he can temper his
immoderate sexual desire simply by having sex, frere Jan adds his own
gloss: this must be what they call the "macération de la chair" (465),
the mortification—or the pickling, the tempering, the confecting—of
the flesh. The way to cure the unhealthy alteration caused by passions
of the body and restore its balance is—moderately enough—by satisfying them; the most efficient way to control bodily appetite is to pickle
it, frere Jan instructs, twenty-five or thirty times daily.

Whether presented comically or seriously, the preservation of self
and virtue promised by "macération" or "gayeté . . . conficte" requires
maintenance. The promise of an unalterably preserved product must be
constantly renewed, like the soaking water of lemon peels or walnuts
as they are prepared for pickling. Rabelais's text rephrases the ostensible inalterability of preserved products in alternative forms, resulting

in an increase in semantic value so imperceptible that it could easily be confused with, or potentially amount to, loss, decay, or stagnancy. The *Tiers Livre* closes with the narrator offering advice on the preparation of the miraculous superherb Pantagruelion in the manner of an entry in a contemporary household manual, herbal, or book of secrets: the recipe is attributed to an authority on the matter, encompasses proper actions from growing practices all the way through preparation and preservation, and includes a sprinkling of botany and casual anthropology.[36] Harvested during the "temps de altération"—the dry season in which Pantagruel was born (528)—Pantagruelion must, according to its namesake's master recipe, be steeped ("macérer") in standing water (with variations according to season and water temperature) and sun dried, followed by removal of the mostly useless woody parts (523). Only after being altered into a "conficte" form can the herb be put to its proper use. In one remarkable instance, it is not used up by use, remaining unalterable under fire. When applied around a corpse undergoing cremation, it cleanly separates human- from plant-based ash, and will be extracted from the flames "plus beau, plus blanc et plus net," more beautiful, whiter, and cleaner than before, improved in value and yet remaining fundamentally "sans altération" (533). What François Rigolot has called Rabelais's progressive "transmutation poétique" of the hemp described in Pliny's *Natural History* into the mythical Pantagruelion is thus mirrored in the narrative account of the plant's minor metamorphosis: Pantagruelion increases in value by being used, improving, paradoxically, by becoming more properly itself.[37]

The main justification the narrator provides for the herb's name is that Pantagruel is its "inventeur": the discoverer not (the narrator quickly clarifies) of the plant itself, but of a certain use of it, the strategic stopping up of the oral passageway usually traversed by exiting words and entering foods, "bons motz" and "bons morseaulx" (528). At the close of the volume, the narrator celebrates not the natural growth of a plant but the variety of uses to which it can be put, including a wide array of cultural references: Penelope, apparently, wove her daily text with precisely this textile (524). Pantagruel's deliberate culturing of the herb is what makes Pantagruelion Pantagruelion. And it is Pantagruelion, with its many uses in housekeeping and manufacturing, that makes many other everyday things what they are:

Sans elle, seroient les cuisines infâmes, les tables détestables, quoyque couvertes feussent de toutes viandes exquises; les lictz sans délices, quoyque y feust en abondance or, argent, electre, ivoyre et porphyre. Sans elle, ne porteroient les meusniers bled au moulin, n'en rapporteroient farine. (529)

(Without *pantagruelion* our kitchens would be shocking and our tables repellent even when laden with every kind of delicacy; our beds would be without charm, even though bedecked with gold, silver, amber, ivory, and porphyry. Without it the miller could bring no corn to the mill and take home no flour. [607])

And the eulogistic list goes on: tasks like drawing water from the well, carrying plaster to the workshop, and dressing clerics would no longer be possible; lawyers, secretaries, and printers—of, perhaps, the book containing these words—would no longer have professions ("Ne periroient le noble art d'imprimerie?" [529]). God forbid, in other words, that Pantagruelion should ever be scarce, and this is precisely the point of this extended *eloge*. By making human life possible, Pantagruelion is a sign that God still "tout régist et modère" by his divine word, as the *Prognostication* not entirely unseriously hoped, not neglecting "la maintenance et gouvernement" that prevent the things of the world from becoming reduced to nothing.

In Rigolot's account, the lengthy encyclopedia entry on the herb is Rabelais's way of forcing us, and himself, to eat our greens before we can have dessert. Only after two dry and dreary scientific chapters can our author get to the good stuff: the fun of distorting dimensions, unsettling categories, and subverting any sense of coherence.[38] And yet for Rabelais such disruption is not the ultimate goal, either: Pantagruelion is praised not for breaking boundaries but for providing the glue of society, on levels local and literal—working as a binding agent—as well as vast and figurative, as the condition for the functioning of vital human industries. When Rabelais mixes myth and fantasy with natural science and distracts us with digressions, he suggests that disruption is central to the preservation of the world as it is, complete with its inequalities and its injustices. As our Pantagrueline Prognosticator reminds us, this year, like every year, with God's constantly intervening "maintenance et gouvernement," relations will stand: the rich will be a bit better off ("se porteront un peu miuelx") than the poor, the healthy better than the sick (921). By touting the civilization-preserving properties of a miracle of agricultural technology that itself requires preservation, Rabelais suggests that transformation might not change anything at all.

The slippage, illustrated by Pantagruelion, between preservation and transformation—this suggestion that mere preservation is at once

threatening to, integral to, and potentially indistinguishable from transformation and human progress—is central to this book's account of
early modern poetic labor. If many humanists were at pains to distinguish retrograde and unproductive textual activities from original literary creation and scholarly innovation, they were plagued by a creeping suspicion that these modes were perhaps not so different. This
tension was perhaps most visible in the practice of translation. That
books translated into French were conventionally introduced as *réduit
en français* implies, as "reduction" does in cooking, an intensifying concentration even while it suggests a diminishment, a regression that is
also a return to a proper origin.[39] Jean Nicot's dictionary definition of
"reduction" emphasizes the word's connotations of a return to an original state: a "ramenement . . . d'une chose à son premier lieu et estat."[40]
Nicot thus anticipates Jacques Derrida, who in "What Is a 'Relevant'
Translation?" explains how the alteration of a food by seasoning, like
that of a word by translation, can make it more itself:

> *Relever* first conveys the sense of cooking . . . , like *assaisonner*. It is a
> question of giving taste, a different taste that is blended with the first
> taste, now dulled, remaining the same while altering it, while chang
> ing it, while undoubtedly removing something of its native, original,
> idiomatic taste, but also while adding to it, and in the very process,
> *more* taste, while cultivating its natural taste, while giving it *still more
> of its own taste*, its own, natural flavor—this is what we call "relever"
> in French cooking.[41]

Just as Derrida repeatedly translates himself, constantly putting his
ideas in alternative terms, adjusting the seasoning on his prose, keeping his idea the same while avowedly altering it, Rabelais takes to copious paraphrase, to altering his terms, even when describing the very
quality—Pantagruelism—associated with inalterability. "Je vous ay jà
dict et encores rediz," the narrator says of Pantagruel, saying it again
because having said it once is not enough:

> Toutes choses prenoit en bonne partie, tout acte interprétoit à bien;
> jamais ne se tourmentait, jamais ne se scandalizoit: aussi eust il esté
> bien forissu du déificque manoir de raison, si aultrement se feust
> contristé ou altéré, car tous les biens que le Ciel couvre et que la
> Terre contient en toutes ses dimensions: haulteur, profondité, lon
> gitude et latitude, ne sont dignes d'esmouvoir nos affections et trou
> bler nos sens et espritz. (357)

(He took everything in good part: every deed he interpreted to the
good. He never tormented himself: he never took offence. He would
moreover have quitted the God-made mansion of Reason if he had
been otherwise saddened or upset: for all the goods which the heav-
ens cover and this earth contains in all its dimensions—height,
depth, length or breadth—are not worth stirring our emotions or
troubling our wits or our minds. [418, translation modified])

Pantagruelism, in this formulation, involves both the appreciation
in value that comes with charitable reading—the interpretation of
everything "à bien"—and a radical indifference to "tous les biens" that
earthly life has to offer, even to the idea of appreciation itself. Written
into the description of Pantagruel's inalterable state is the admission
that it could be otherwise: "si aultrement" he was "altéré," he would
be evicted from the manor of reason, with his imperviousness from alteration conditional, tautologically, on his not ever becoming upset, or
"altered." A definition of inalterability is never sufficient in itself, always
requiring an alternate, supplemental evocation of another possible state
of affairs.

    In the *Quart Livre*, where this philosophy is alternatively defined as a
"gayeté" fortunately "conficte" in scorn for fortunate things, the necessity and sufficiency of health and moderation is deemed to be in need
of repeated restatement. As if a reader could not infer herself that the
ancients' comparison of moderation to gold meant they deemed it valuable, Rabelais translates it into more literal terms, only for Couillatris to
refiguralize it later: "Médiocrité a esté par les saiges anciens dicte aurée,
c'est à dire précieuse, de tous louée, en tous endroictz agréable" (547)
(By the sages of Antiquity the Mean was called Golden, that is to say,
precious, praised by all, and everywhere delightful [652]). The moderate Couillatris is rewarded with gold for choosing not gold but the
"golden mean": something only *like* gold, both equivalent to and (only
eventually, potentially) more valuable than gold.

    When the neighbors try to lose their hatchets and get riches in re-
turn, they choose gold—the golden hatchets Mercury offers them—
instead of moderation (their own hatchets). In return, they get their
heads chopped off. In the narrator's accounting, "feut des testes coup-
pées le nombre équal et correspondent aux coignées perdues. Voylà
que c'est! Voylà qu'advient à ceulx qui en simplicité soubhaitent et op-
tent chose mediocres" (558) (And the severed heads were equal and
equivalent in number to the axes which were lost. Well: there it is.
There you have what happens to those who innocently wish and opt

for things within the Mean [661]). A formal order has been preserved, as if nothing has been altered, as if, as in the directly preceding biblical lost-hatchet narrative, the hatchet gained were equal to the hatchet lost and value had been perfectly conserved. But the narrator's matter-of-factness about the situation ("Voylà que c'est!") makes us forget, momentarily, that nothing has been canceled out in this equation: with each lost hatchet leading to a lost head, waste—in a grossly material sense, rather than in a sense of exhilaratingly empty excess—has piled up on both sides.

## The Dregs: Laying Up Waste

To return to the pickle barrel whence we came, another way to understand Rabelais's textual production, besides in terms of subversive excess, anxious overcompensation, or grand design, is through his mundane concerns with the management of waste and the maintenance of bodily health—as endless as Bacchic barrel-rolling, but in a way more tedious than festive. Instead of solely associating Rabelais with wine, in other words, we might also pair him with vinegar.[42] Vinegar is a product of wine that has been further altered by dilution and exposure to the air, *vin* soured into *vinaigre*. A treatise by Giovanni Battista Cavigioli, one of several contributions to a vigorous mid-sixteenth-century debate about the health benefits and drawbacks of vinegar, cites the common complaint that because it is corrupted wine ("uin putrifié"), vinegar is "l'ennemy de nature," and announces his intent to convince his readers of the benefits of vinegar to human nature: the best thing for the "conseruation" of men's health and to "preseruer" them from illness, infection, and putrefaction, vinegar is the most effective way to prevent or reverse alteration, and precisely because it has itself been altered from its original state.[43] Cavigioli defines *vinaigre* as, ultimately, wine that has become something "other" than wine, in a perfectly balanced substitution of qualities: "Vinaigre est uin corrumpu, qui a perdu une chaleur, une humidité, une force, & une saueur: & a acquis une froideur, une siccité, & une aultre force, & une aultre saueur"; in exchange for losing heat, moisture, potency, and flavor, it has acquired a chillness, a dryness, and another potency, another flavor, "une force" met equally and equivalently by "une aultre force."[44]

Galen, far less of a vinegar sympathizer than Cavigioli, explains the humors with a metaphor of winemaking gone awry. He asks us to imagine what happens when "new wine which has been not long ago pressed from the grape, and which is fermenting and undergoing *alteration* through the agency of its contained heat," produces "residual substances," namely the lees, corresponding in the body to black bile. Potentially a benign substance, black bile can nonetheless become "sharp like vinegar," with an acidity that "corrodes the animal's body." Distempered bile "produces a kind of fermentation and seething, accompanied by bubbles—an abnormal putrefaction having become added to the natural condition of the black humour."[45] Bile, already a superfluous by-product of fermentation, can itself be refermented, to fetid ends.

Doubly processed, vinegar is over-altered wine, the corrosive counterpart to sweet wine's lubrication. Its sharpness is not, evidently, always salutary. And yet it can be used to preserve perishable foods, to prevent waste and forestall alteration. Charles Estienne wants to make absolutely clear that "vinaigre est un vice du vin" (vinegar is a corruption of wine), and yet because vinegar is so useful not only for condiments and sauces but also for numerous other essentials ("plusieurs autres necessitez"), he will of course offer his readers detailed instructions on how to make it.[46] As an anonymous early seventeenth-century recipe less ambivalently sums it up, even spoiled wines are good: "Toutes sortes de vins sont bons, encore qu'ils soient gastez."[47] For Rabelais, such food processing turns out to be a compelling synecdoche of civilization, in which textualization plays an important part. As in the domestic georgic impulse in humanism to restore and organize ancient knowledge in minor and not necessarily or immediately productive ways, in food processing what would otherwise be wasted or useless is made, by ingenious human manufacturing, valuable—though to what ends that value will be put remains an open question. Chronicling the accomplishments of Gaster, inventor of the agricultural arts, the narrator in the *Quart Livre* asserts that no matter how astonishing we may find a technology that turns enemy bullets back on their shooters, nature has been manipulated in more extraordinary ways: when the flesh of the naturally unalterable remora, a fish thought to delay voyages by stubbornly attaching to ships, is altered and preserved by the culturing of salt and time ("conservée en sel"), it becomes productive for rather than detrimental to humanity, capable of drawing gold when plunged deep into wells (734).

To most readers of Rabelais, Gaster is less notable for his scientific contributions than for his self-appointed position as a tyrannically stomach-centered cult leader, his insincere gestures at Lenten self-denial (his "jours maigres" menu compensates for meatlessness by including almost literally every other food), and the repressive desublimation of his subjects: "Et tout pour la trippe!" is their mandated motto. Excess, with negative connotations, seems to be the inescapable theme of the episode. Yet many of the daily operations in Gaster's regime are carried out in more temperate terms, as in the mundane odyssey of grain, a cornerstone of civilization for which Gaster is responsible. Grain begins its process of self-actualization at the mill (also Gaster's brainchild), where it is reduced (that is, refined) to flour ("reduire en farine"). The most important steps in grain's evolution come in the baking process:

> Le levain pour fermenter la paste; le sel pour luy donner saveur (car il eut ceste congnoissance que chose on monde plus les humains ne rendoit à maladies subjectz que de pain non fermenté, non salé user); le feu pour le cuire, les horloges et quadrans pour entendre le temps de la cuycte de pain, creature de Grain. (730)

> (Yeast to leaven the dough and salt to give it its savour—for he knew as a fact that nothing in this world would make human beings more subject to illness than unleavened and unsalted bread—fire to bake it; clocks and sundials to regulate the time of the baking of that which grain produces: bread. [848])

The process described here is one of leavening, of seasoning, of adding that which preserves the integrity of the material by slightly altering it (the preservative properties of these alterations—the warning that not adhering to this recipe threatens health—are noted in a qualifying parenthetical). Finally, the process is tempered by time, as temporal instruments are introduced to moderate the length of cooking. The necessity of undertaking this long and painstaking process is understood as a "benediction du ciel" (450): in the optimistic georgic spirit, the divine malediction to till the soil to make one's own bread is converted into blessing not by a miracle but by laborious tempering. As the title of chapter 61—"Comment Gaster inventa les moyens d'avoir et conserver grain"—makes clear, it is not enough to have ("avoir") our daily bread: it must also be preserved ("conserver"), an enterprise that requires even more infrastructure than the windmills and myriad other kinds of mills involved in grain production (730). Gaster's ancillary inventions—military arts and weapons, medicine, astrology—aim to "defendre" and "guarder" the crop, to keep it safe from intemperate weather, pests, and thieves (730). He even achieves the wildest georgic dream of controlling the weather by inventing means both to make it rain and to suspend ("suspendre") unwanted precipitation in the sky and redirect it elsewhere (731).

But such suspending interventions also run risks. Moderate and moderating fermenting, even if it sometimes appreciates the value of otherwise wasted or wasteful things, might also result in physical corruption, becoming corrosive black bile or turning lost hatchets into lost heads, creating waste on both sides without any authoritative hermeneutic that would recast the waste as productive. Cave's claim of Rabelais's books that "the contamination of a principle of abundance by a principle of *écoulement* or entropy remains central" can be modified to suggest that the real threat to the enjoyment of the Rabelaisian feast is "contamination" not by sterile emptiness but by potentially contagious waste.[48] Food in pickled form threatens to condense the metonymic transformation of food into excrement, the gradual process of digestion into a single unappetizing metaphor. Thus pickles, confits, conserves, mustards, and marinades in Rabelais always might produce rather than prevent waste, themselves being produced by—or uncomfortably closely compared to—waste matter. Florence Weinberg notes, for example, the connection in contemporary parlance between a "mustard barrel" and the "lower abdomen, bowels, and their contents" and concludes that the Andouilles, the sausage-people who attack Pantagruel and his crew and for whom mustard is a panacean "Sangreal," are healed and born again by virtue of fecal matter, which she sees as allegorical of Luther's teachings: a disturbingly uncontrolled blending of bodily waste with spiritual nourishment.[49]

The confusion of ridiculous waste with strategic wasting, of destructive reduction with (re)productive *reductio*, becomes more complicated in the case of immoderate textual traditions that may or may not have moderating effects. In the zeal for glossing classical texts Rabelais finds an unhealthy and impoverished model of linguistic production, recalling those identified by Cicero and Quintilian as abuses of *copia*: "empty prolixity," lack of *varietas*, or "Asiatic over-elaboration," as Cave describes their diagnoses.[50] Yet Rabelais nonetheless incorporates these negative examples, past the point of expository value, in his own text. The bloviating judge Bridoye would exemplify Erasmus's cautionary tale of those who "mix the sordid with the elegant, disfigure their purple with patches, thread together jewels and paste, and add garlic to Greek confections,"[51] who, in other words, poorly temper their rhetoric. Bridoye's lengthy explanation of his judicial process, which, in practice, amounts to the throwing of dice, is interlarded with gloss to the point that the seasoning begins to overtake the main ingredients:

Je consydère que le temps meurist toutes choses; par temps toutes choses viennent en évidence; le temps est père de verité, *gl. in l. j. C. de servit., Autent, de restit. et ea quae pa. et Spec. tit. de requis. cons.* C'est pourquoy, commes vous aultres, Messieurs, je sursoye, délaye et diffère le jugement afin que le procès, bien ventilé, grabelé et

débatu, vieigne par succession de temps à sa maturité, et, le sort par
après advenent soit plus doulcettement porté des parties condem-
nées, comme *no. glo. ff. excu. tut. l. Tria onera : Portatur leviter, quod
portat quisque libenter.* Le jugeant crud, verd et au commencement
dangier seroit de l'inconvénient que disent les médecins advenir
quand on perse un apostème avant qu'il soit meur, quand on purge
du corps humain quelque humeur nuysant avant sa concoction. Car,
comme est escript *in Autent. haec constit. in Inno. const. prin.* et le
répète *gl. in c. Caeterum. extra de jura. calum.* : *Quod medicamenta
morbis exhibent, hoc jura negotiis.* Nature dadventaige nous instruict
cueillir et manger les fruictz quand ilz sont meurs. (494–95)

(I consider that Time ripens all things; that Time brings all things
to light, that Time is the father of Truth *as in the gloss on Law 1 of the
Codex, "Of Servitudes"; Authentica, "Of Restitutions, and of the Woman
who gives birth"; and Speculator, title, "Of Requests for Advice."* That
explains why, just like you, my Lords, I prorogue, stay and postpone
my judgment in order that the suit, having been thoroughly venti-
lated, sifted through and disputed over, may come in due time to maturity, so that the decision thereafter reached by lots may be borne
more kindly by the losing parties, *as is noted by the gloss on Pandects,
"Of Excusing the Tutelage," the Law, "Three Burdens": Kindly is borne
what is willingly borne.* If you were to judge at the outset, when it is
unripe and green, there would be a danger of the mischief which
the physicians say occurs when one lances a boil before it is ripe or
purges the human body of some nocive humour before it has been
concocted, *for (as it is written in the Authentica: "This Constitution,"
Innocent IV, First constitution, and repeated in the gloss on the Canon
"But"; Extravagantes: "Of Sworn Calumnies"): "What Medicines Do
for Illnesses Justice Does for Difficulties."* Nature moreover teaches us:
to pick our fruits and eat them when they are ripe. [566–67])

Bridoye's audience, to say nothing of the reader, might demur that this
habit of postponing, deferring, and delaying with his banal and repetitive erudition does not macerate or ripen ("meurist") judgment so
much as waste time and dissolve meaning. It does not help Bridoye's
case that he compares the raw ("crud, verd") matter to be judged to
a harmful humor purged before its "concoction." An abscess, unlike a
fruit, gains no intrinsic value by being seasoned by time, and Bridoye's
unappetizing use of the language of healthy digestion to describe the
progression of disease smacks of garlicky Greek sweets. The addition of
a more palatable adage (that we are not to eat fruit before it ripens) as

an appendage—an appetizing image of food as a superfluous byprod-uct of the "concoction" of disease—confuses the order of eating and digestion. This, we might say, is poor menu planning on the part of the speaker.

Of course, the reader is unlikely to have come to Rabelais for legal clarification. And if the speech is nonsensical as an elucidation of the law, it is valuable as a careful laying-up of textual material. Like many of his contemporaries, Rabelais happily offers a scornful verdict on gloss-ing as a misguided attempt to add value to ancient texts and ideas. At the same time, Bridoye—and Pantagruel's ultimate approval of a legal approach that relies entirely on chance—make a serious appeal to read-ers to suspend not only our judgment but also our comprehension. As Greene says of the episode, "Nowhere else in the entire book must one remember so continuously not to be too quick to understand," a bold claim to make of a work that traffics so heavily in allusion, errancy, and nonsense.[52] Even if the young Pantagruel compares Accursius's noto-rious mangling of the *Pandectes* to embroidering a golden robe with "merde," the humanist contempt for the sloppy commentaries of the previous age masked a debt that often went unacknowledged: glossing, a "brodure" made of "ordure," could ensure the copying and preserva-tion, enrobed in a protective layer of waste, of texts that might other-wise have been lost (211). Rabelais is not the unequivocal celebrator of waste that some have made him out to be, nor is he a straightforward critic of the wasted words of schoolmen, Protestants, and his other ide-ological enemies.

The epistemological incoherence of the *Tiers* and *Quart Livre*, with knowledge represented as contained in individual episodes, might appear to be evidence that the pursuit of knowledge is utterly self-defeating. But the fact that we receive parts of the narrative like frag-ments of a shattered encyclopedia, as Jeanneret puts it, does not mean that the narrative lacks all principles of selection and organization.[53] Rather, the narrative has put these fragments into suspension, separat-ing them the better to preserve them. This is what Seneca, in a favor-ite humanist commonplace, claims bees do with pollen, and that good humanist readers do with knowledge—keeping their sources separate in order to incorporate them later into a proprietary recipe of original honey (i.e., style):

> We also, I say, ought to copy [*imitari*] these bees, and sift through whatever we have gathered from a varied course of reading, for such things are better preserved if kept separate [*melius enim distincta ser-vantur*]; then, by applying the supervising care [*cura*] with which

our nature has endowed us . . . we should so blend [*confundere*] those several flavours into one delicious compound.[54]

Rabelais's text freezes a moment in the Senecan composition process between gathering and synthesizing material in a way that also recalls the final book of Columella's *De re rustica*, an important ancient source for early modern georgic. Transitioning from the duties of the farmer to those of his wife, Columella devotes the bulk of book 12 to preservation: how to make brine, how to pickle herbs, how to dry fruit, what kind of vessels she should use to conserve different types of provisions. Like Nostradamus, the narrator of *Le Menagier*, and other purveyors of domestic preservation techniques who came after him, Columella insists that proper storing requires frequent check-ups:

> She ought not, however, to limit her care [*cura*] to the locking up and guarding [*custodiat*] the goods which have been brought into the house and which she has received [*receperit*], but she ought to inspect [*recognoscat*] them from time to time and take care that the furniture and clothing which have been stored away [*condita*] do not fall to pieces with decay [*dilabatur*] and that the fruits of the earth and other things in general use are not ruined [*corrumpatur*] through her neglect and laziness.[55]

The instruction to *recognoscere* household effects, like that for the *menagier's* wife to *gouverner* her confitures, effectively makes household management into an intellectual activity, requiring a similar "cura." But it also has the inverse effect of making intellectual activity something like household management. Without both, things would go to pieces, become *réduit à néant*. Rabelais's willingness to preserve huge swaths of wasted words—in cheerfully excessive dinner-party descriptions, discomfiting lists of ways to "se torcher le cul," or mind-numbingly dry accounts of scholastic speeches—means that it is not excess itself, but its careful management, that he finds worth taking seriously, and worth preserving.

## Frozen Food: Reproducing Metabolism

Voyaging far in the north near the end of the *Quart Livre*, Pantagruel and his crew encounter some frozen but rapidly thawing words floating in the sea. This was not an uncommon event in early modern literature. With an origin in Plutarch's *Moralia* (overlaid with back-references to Homer and Plato), the "frozen words" topos condensed and dramatized early modern debates over the substantiality of language.[56] And indeed, Pantagruel's initial response, before the pilot corrects him, is to suggest multiple possible philosophical significations of the verbal debris, which—even if discredited by the explanation that these are the remains of a cacophonous naval battle from the previous winter, a claim substantiated when the frozen flotsam begins to thaw into inarticulate sounds—have been taken by some critics as discarded possibilities worth dwelling on.[57]

Duval, however, counsels us to cast aside these false etiologies as swiftly as the reasonable Pantagruel, noting approvingly, "Faced with irrefutable evidence, Pantagruel of course immediately abandons his various idealizing hypotheses." Disabused of the notion that these are "priceless nuggets of *logos*," we should, Duval maintains, acknowledge the "plain truth" that these are common and therefore worthless words: talk is cheap.[58] Rabelais's narrator, however, fails to experience this enlightenment as quickly as his hero. When Pantagruel, grabbing a gratifyingly graspable handful of as-yet-unthawed words, tosses them on the deck, where shining like "dragée, perlée de diverses couleurs"—seeds candied in layers of colorful syrup[59]—they make a sound like whole chestnuts chucked on an open fire (714-15), the narrator, his appetite piqued, suggests that they preserve some of these "gullet-words" in oil and straw. Pantagruel summarily dismisses this plan:

> Je vouloys quelques motz de gueule mettre en réserve dedans de l'huille, comme l'on garde la neige et la glace, et entre du feurre bien nect. Mais Pantagruel ne le voulut, disant estre follie faire réserve de ce dont jamais l'on n'a faulte et que tous jours on a en main, comme sont motz de gueule entre tous bons et joyeulx Pantagruelistes. (715–16)

> (I had hoped to preserve a few gullet-words in oil, wrapping them up in very clean straw [as we do with snow and ice]; but Pantagruel would not allow it, saying that it was madness to pickle something which is never lacking and always to hand as are gullet-words amongst all good and merry Pantagruelists. [830])

If Duval attributes Pantagruel's frustration to the narrator's failure to understand "the plain truth" of how prosaic and unremarkable these "motz de gueule" are—they are just "motz," mere literal words, not divine "parolles"—others see the words as inherently mystical and poetic, feistily resisting the narrator's attempts to condemn them to the stasis of the literal. To Jeanneret, the narrator and the rest of the crew—

like most everyone else Pantagruel quarrels with—are hopeless liter-
alists: instead of respecting, like our hero, the "polyvalence" of words
and things, they fix them ("les figent"), like so many *pierres mortes*, to
restrictive meanings.[60] Pantagruel thus objects to what Jeanneret calls
a pernicious hardening ("durcissement maléfique") of the word, an
abomination by which words' free-flowing "mystère" is violently "do-
mestiqué."[61] This desire to domesticate, Jeanneret argues, denies the reality that language is not conserved but "se recrée constamment": it
constantly reproduces itself, with a Bakhtinian natural inevitability.[62]
If Jeanneret must admit that Rabelais, as a writer, wants to mummify
living language into an immortal work, wrenching from the natural life
cycle that which should naturally decay and get replaced, he finds this
writerly tendency overpowered by the irrepressible words themselves,
so that Rabelais's text resists its own freezing into print. Celebrating the
polysemy of the living word and resisting the ossifying effect of text, the
books' characters cheerfully destroy from within the coffin that would
contain them. Preservation, in this reading, is as good as death: Jeanneret's concept of putting words in reserve is confined to the image
of a book as an ultimately unsuccessful "tombeau pétrifié" (petrified
tomb).[63]

That Rabelais's language reflexively rejects all that is fossilized and
fixed has itself become a rigid critical commonplace.[64] By assuming that
language spontaneously re-creates itself, these arguments—like Pantagruel himself—fail to consider the necessity of the maintenance work
that must be performed on both language-producing bodies and the
cultural material they reproduce. The narrator's desire to pickle ("faire
réserve de") that which "tous jours on a en main" is not so patently
ridiculous when one considers that having words "always at hand" requires the labor of maintaining not only linguistic material but also our
bodies' ability to access it, of preserving both bodies and the enzymes
that allow them to digest the world, to make the world metabolically
available to them. The temporary suspension—in oil, brine, syrup, or
another kind of confiture—of organic material from the natural life cycle is necessary to sustain nature's ability to replenish its stores. The
health of living language requires repeated acts of domestication and
provisional conservation, acts that imitate the domestic and agricultural practices to which the narrator alludes with his hopeful comparison of frozen words to snow preserved in oil and straw. Language
does not reproduce itself automatically, and Pantagruel's followers, the
"bons et joyeulx Pantagruelistes" invoked as the natural producers of
such language, could, should they be so altered, slip into less "good"
and "joyous" states. Conversation must be fed ("alimentée") not only

by real-life events, but also by words strategically thawed from the reserves of them we keep in books.

The early modern discovery and cataloging of ancient textual material has often been understood—by both scholars of the time and scholars of those scholars—as either a supernatural calling (something *more*
than mere organizing) or a task better suited to support staff than authors, subordinate to the work of original creation. We have seen in this
book's introduction how Thomas Greene's "humanist necromancer-
scholar," for example, heroically rescued lost texts from oblivion and
miraculously resurrected them, and Timothy Hampton notes Guillaume Budé's comparison of ancient texts to sepulchers whose inhabitants can be brought back to life by talented imitators.[65] On the more
mundane end, Aaron Kunin describes "the humanist imperative to preserve cultural artifacts" as "a secondary form of culture-making" that
fell short of "creation" or "transformation."[66] But in the case of Rabelais's narrator, preservation is at once as ordinary as maintenance work
and as impressive as necromancy. This act is both reproductive and
transformative, and insofar as freezing words in print is (as Jeanneret's
"tombeau petrifié" suggests) precisely the process of writing, it is a primary form of culture-making, indistinguishable from the identification
and maintenance of what is valuable.[67] The narrator's impulse to preserve derives from the value placed on the activity of preservation itself.
"Mettre en réserve" is for him interchangeable with "faire réserve"; to
organize and to make are one and the same.

More than madly proliferating *copia* or just as anxiously rushing to
cover up its underlying emptiness, the author's task is to carefully arrange the vast linguistic and cultural store he has inherited. Another
name for this task is *oikonomia*, discussed by Kathy Eden as an important principle in Renaissance rhetoric: a commitment to *copia*, properly executed, may require some level of heroic ambition, but it also requires, tempering that ambition, a skill closely analogous to household
management.[68] Bridging the practical and the rhetorical more explicitly, Lorna Hutson explains how Xenophon's portrait of the good wife
as preservative agent prompted early modern writers to think of "the
figure of a woman as agent of rhetorical retrieval, or 'readiness for use,'"
helping to define *oikonomia* as an arrangement that frees men to turn
their sights to matters of public significance.[69] Yet in Rabelais it is difficult to separate such "readiness for use" from actual use. Hampton locates Rabelais's literary authority in an ability to manage the transition
from technical terms to colloquial ones, as in the toggling of the learned
medical jargon and popular midwives' slang generated in response to
Gargamelle's childbearing body.[70] If Rabelais's narrative and rhetorical

power resides, as Hampton puts it, not in simple mastery or persua-
sion but in the "manipulation and organization of linguistic resources,"
it may be that the not strictly productive and merely maintenance-
minded management skills more proper to housewives or midwives
and so scorned by learned men are in fact the very source and necessary condition of humanist authors' creative capabilities.[71]

Not all preservative management of language is necessarily productive or positive. Taking the time and having the patience needed for rev-
elations to thaw out means acknowledging the risk that not all sounds
will thaw out meaningfully. Some may grow rancid or rot. Rabelais's
suspension, rather than outright rejection, of a Platonic explanation for
the frozen words echoes the suspension M. A. Screech finds in the *Cratylus* itself, where "Plato leaves everything undecided"; even Socrates's
claim for the immutability of ideal forms "is put forward with striking
tentativeness."[72] Thus we might not be surprised at Socrates's warning
to the young not to try to resolve difficult problems too quickly, to take
a long time in the learning process and reach maturity, like Bridoye writ
large, before judging difficult matters. We might also think of how the
response of Rabelais (like that of Clément Marot, Marguerite de Na-
varre, and others) to the broadening religious schism was to bide time,
or temporize, while hoping some compromise could be reached.[73] Such
moderate, tempered approaches do not always lead to moderate and
temperate results, ending just as easily in violent conflict, in the case of
France, or the incoherent cries of violent conflict, as in the would-be
divine *parolles* thawing into disappointingly meaningless *motz*.

The operations of preservation, more than materials themselves, require the direct application of preservative intervention: the renewing
of the pickling solution that keeps unalterable Pantagruelism unaltered.
The absurdity, for Pantagruel, of preserving "motz de gueule" ("gullet-
words" that any good Pantagruelist's esophagus can, inverting consumption and production, produce at will) rests on the weak assumption that what can be constantly, locally provided by the body—and,
by implication, the body itself—is in no danger of running out. But
Rabelais does not take the body's ability to maintain itself for granted.
To have words "tous jours . . . en main" requires that the body will maintain its ability to grasp those words; linguistic production is a metabolic
function. Metabolism—which comes from the Greek for "change"—
has as its goal the preservation of the body, a preservation that occurs
only by the alteration of foreign material into the stuff of the self. By
putting words that suggest words' perishability in his narrator's mouth,
Rabelais highlights the precarious position of his own words, which
no one will be able single-handedly to preserve forever. But the textual

body, itself preserved by its own processing of waste and by its constant maintenance by a community of readers, can preserve words in a way the individual human body cannot.[74] It may be that certain words, "gullet-words" among them, are simply unfit for such preservation, needing to be produced spontaneously.[75] Yet it still remains true that the conditions for the production of those words must be preserved for any words to be produced at all. Ultimately, for Rabelais, the labor of maintaining the external world is a primarily interior process: the best way to keep words is not by preserving them in straw, but by preserving the mechanisms that produce them from within.

CHAPTER 2

# Spenser's Secret Recipes

LIFE SUPPORT IN *THE FAERIE QUEENE*

*In the same way as god created Eve to give pleasure to Adam, so did capital create the housewife to service the male worker physically, emotionally, and sexually, to raise his children, mend his socks, patch up his ego when it is crushed by the work and the social relations (which are relations of loneliness) that capital has reserved for him. It is precisely this peculiar combination of physical, emotional and sexual services that are involved in the role women must perform for capital that creates the specific character of that servant which is the housewife, that makes her work so burdensome and at the same time so invisible.*

    SILVIA FEDERICI, "Wages against Housework"

*Take weapon awaye, of what force is a man?*
*Take huswife from husband, & what is he than?*

    THOMAS TUSSER, *Fiue hundreth points of good husbandry vnited to as many of good huswiferie*

In book II, canto ix of *The Faerie Queene*, as their hostess Alma takes them on a guided tour of her castle, Arthur and Guyon are suddenly struck with amazement by something that would seem to be entirely unextraordinary: a group of cooks cooking food. Arrested in "gazing wonder," our heroes stare as different workers supervise the cooking, plate the dishes, and skim the scum from the boiling cauldron, "for neuer had they seene so straunge a sight" as the orderly operations of this kitchen.[1] What this scene at the heart (or rather, the stomach) of the House of Alma, a model of the human body, allegorically represents is even less striking: the normal digestion of food, a process that occurs on a near-continuous and usually unremarkable basis inside Arthur and

Guyon's own bodies. And yet it has apparently never occurred to these knights to consider how their bodies are re-created every day both from without, by laborers like these cooks, and metabolically from within.

Allegory's concretization and personification of abstractions, emotions, vices, virtues, and drives represent as external those forces that exist within individuals. But at moments like this, in Alma's kitchen, allegory exposes as already external the support systems that keep bodies and communities alive by performing the near-constant work of preservation, maintenance, and restoration that I have defined as domestic georgic. In the aristocratic and protobourgeois circles in which Spenser moved, this maintenance work was performed and managed by servants and their mistresses under the general rubric of "housewifery." It might seem incongruous to consider Spenser in the twentieth-century terms set forth by Silvia Federici and other modern theorists of housework as reproductive labor. But the broadly "capitalist society" that Federici takes as her context could also describe that of the "new men" and aspiring gentlemen of late sixteenth-century England, where what would later be called bourgeois values animated the entrepreneurial designs of families like the Sidneys and the colonial ambitions of parvenus like Spenser.[2] The three sites of maintenance work in *The Faerie Queene* that this chapter will focus on—the Castle of Alma, the House of Holiness, and the "stately mount" of the Garden of Adonis—are all overseen by women who concern themselves with the repetitive, ceaseless labors that maintain or restore the health of individual men, from feeding them to nursing them to remembering them to themselves. In *The Faerie Queene*, in other words, it takes a full-time staff of domestic laborers to fashion a gentleman. Or, to put it another way, Spenser's male characters are "unfashioned," stripped of autonomy not only as allegorical personifications—each of whom is arguably meant to represent only one of the ideal gentleman's virtues, not the complete gentleman himself—but also as characters, who are revealed to have no selves at all if not for the work of other characters.[3] If Guyon, Arthur, Redcrosse, and Adonis, like the impotent unarmed man conjured by the sixteenth-century self-help writer Thomas Tusser, lack "force" without their weapons and armor, they are also, like Tusser's "husband," nothing without a "huswife," without the domestic tasks performed by wives and their (male and female) servants.[4]

This is not to suggest that Spenser's hidden agenda was to declare cooks, porters, secretaries, and housewives, rather than aristocratic knights, as the world's real heroes (though it is also not to ignore that Spenser, in the days before he could call himself a gentleman, put himself through school as a sizar, waiting on his better-born peers as a domestic servant).⁵ As Jeff Dolven has persuasively shown, care work in *The Faerie Queene* consistently falls outside the poem's bipartite division of good and bad characters: for all the poem's ambiguity and parody, some characters are straightforwardly bad—like Duessa and Night—and yet the poem lingers on moments when they provide care to injured men, moments that derail not only the forward trajectory of epic but also the clear lessons of allegory.⁶ I am not proposing a valuation of domestic georgic as the poem's true ethical center. Rather, I argue that in sites of ceaseless and (in Adam Smith's terms) "unproductive" labor, the "endlesse worke" (IV.xii.1) of Spenser's own writerly travails becomes literalized as the unending labors of domestic staff: what Federici calls the "endless work" of in-home caregiving, or what Tusser calls the "huswiues affaires" that "hath neuer none ende."⁷ In these sites, the distinction between intellectual or poetic labor, on the one hand, and manual labor, on the other, breaks down. This breakdown comes about through the breaking down of allegory, when the personifications of certain internal principles are revealed, and to an extent treated, as actual persons, albeit minor characters who fail to meet the heroic threshold of the Knights of Holiness and Temperance: the cooks, secretaries, caregivers, and housewives that keep the bodies of middling, gentle, and noble men like Spenser and his heroes alive.

Spenser's "endlesse worke" has, in much scholarship, been understood in terms of genre or narrative, perhaps appropriately enough, as Spenser's narrator uses the phrase to lament the impossible poetic task of naming every nymph in the sea. Patricia Parker identifies romance in general, and Spenser's use of it in particular, with spatial and temporal dilation, a trial over time that resists a premature ending.⁸ Jonathan Goldberg sees in "the narrative principles that induce frustration, that deny closure," a failure to reach any meaningful ending at all.⁹ When *The Faerie Queene*'s preoccupation with endless work has been seen in more material terms, as an indication of its participation in a georgic mode, it has been with a triumphant air: William Sessions takes the Virgilian *labor omnia vicit*, and Spenser's influence by it, as a positive declaration—"labor is now the only heroic mode of the human condition"—rather than the resigned recognition that with the fall of the golden age, we are all slaves to all-conquering labor.¹⁰ Michael Schoenfeldt's humoral analysis similarly takes on the task of redefining nonteleological work—the somatic operations of the House of Temperance in particular—as heroic, arguing that temperance achieves in Spenser an "active, dynamic nature," made to conform with "a pattern of heroism based on strife and excess."¹¹ And yet, in the House of Temperance and elsewhere, Spenser portrays endless work as more domestic than heroically georgic, with the demands of feminized domestic labor as resistant to teleology as the dilation of the feminized genre of romance. In all three of this chapter's main examples, the cause of endless work is neither the limitlessness of interpretive desire nor the unquenchable spirit of the individual but rather the unremitting dependence of aristocratic masculinity on the support work of housewives and servants.

This dependence is both outlined and mystified in the domestic manuals that proliferated in sixteenth- and seventeenth-century England, many of them inspired by Xenophon's Socratic dialogue *Oeconomicus* and its popular English translation, first published in 1532. These manuals present the housewife's labor as in perfect symmetry to her husband's: the man's outdoor work is to get the goods; the woman's indoor work is to save and keep them. Though such schemas of the division of labor were simplistic, these manuals were, Lorna Hutson argues, serious economic treatises: scrupulous attention is paid to the managerial duties the wife is expected to perform, among them supervising her servants, while her husband goes out on heroic mercantile adventures.[12] In this way, the ideology of housewifery straddles aristocratic and bourgeois value systems, with the wife's anxious accounting and management—the role of the "mulier economica" that, arguably more than the merchant, exemplifies the early capitalist mindset—complementing the husband's risky enterprises in the commercial sphere.[13] As Louis Montrose puts it, despite Spenser's aim "to affirm his status as a gentleman rather than to assert his place in the vanguard of the bourgeoisie," his poetry betrays "adumbrations of those values and aspirations that came increasingly to characterize the lives of the middling sort and the culture of mercantile capitalism," specifically those values and aspirations having to do with the keeping of a home.[14] Even before the explicitly domestic poetry Montrose discusses, *Colin Clouts Come Home Again* and the *Epithalamion*, we can see in the 1590 *Faerie Queene* a fascination with the ordinary activities that constitute domestic order.

In *The Faerie Queene*, encounters with the labor that preserves domestic spaces, no matter how tedious or routine that labor may be, consistently evoke wonder. This awe at a well-run household also appears in the key source text for early modern domestic manuals. As Ischomachus, the titular "economist" or estate manager of Xenophon's dialogue, exclaims to his young wife in Gentian Hervet's translation, nothing is more aesthetically pleasing than an organized linen closet:

But howe goodly a thinge is it to se sewtes of all a mannes apparell, lyenge by it selfe, keverlettes, and counterpointes by them selfe,

shetes, towels, and all naprye ware by them selfes, pottes, pannes,
caudrons, and other garnitures of the ketchyn by them selfe, al that
longeth to the table by it selfe, and so lyke wyse all other thynges,
that long to an house, wher at he that is unwise, & knoweth not good
order, wyl laugh.[15]

In Ischomachus's breathless account, this inventory of clothing, linens,
and kitchenware, beautifully set apart from each other for easy retrieval,
is as "goodly a thinge" as there is. Guyon and Arthur, struck dumb by
the "goodly order" of the well-oiled operations of Alma's kitchen, take
"rare delight" in a spectacle similar to that invoked by Ischomachus:
the ability of Digestion to "order all th'Achates in seemely wise," the
efficient division of labor between the kitchen clerks, and the clean
separation of food from waste (II.ix.33, 32, 31). As Ischomachus acknowledges, the idea that a decluttered house or smoothly run kitchen
should spark joy and wonder has indeed caused some, then and now, to
"laugh." For Simone de Beauvoir, the modern housewife deludes herself if she thinks anyone will recognize such work at all; a job well done
necessarily escapes the notice of her husband, who brings a critical eye
to bear on domestic negligence but who "takes order and neatness for
granted," assuming that these things simply happen by themselves.[16]
But Ischomachus insists on his aesthetic idea of order, comparing himself to an appreciative audience of "plays and enterludes, where a great
company of men is assembled to plaie their partes": the effect is spoiled
when they ad lib and talk over each other, "but when they do and speak
every thynge in order, the audyence hath a very greate pleasure bothe
to beholde them, and also to here them."[17] What Guyon and Arthur find
so wondrous is perhaps not only the work ethic of the kitchen laborers
but how well, in what "goodly order," they stay on the allegorical script,
even though these men are only extras in the cast, not even speaking
parts. At the same time, the knights are forced to confront the fact that
these laborers are not only dramatizing how they are nourished internally. The well-arranged objects and subjects that keep the kitchen going have lives of their own, outside the cognitive reach of Guyon's and
Arthur's wondering eyes.

## Keeping It Together in the Legend of Temperance

Beginning with Kenelm Digby's 1643 Neoplatonic exegesis of canto
ix's description of the castle's architecture, the Castle of Alma has been
understood on a level that would seem to soar far above the garbage disposal of the Port Esquiline.[18] For Angus Fletcher, the House of Alma is a

domestic space only insofar as domesticity is built on the model of the sacred. Fletcher identifies Alma's castle as perhaps the most paradigmatic example in *The Faerie Queene* of what he calls a "temple," an "image of gratified desire" that provides relief from the "terror and panic" of the "labyrinth," where characters wander aimlessly in search of the consolidated meaning that only the temple can provide.[19] The temple is thus a domestic space by analogy alone: "Experientially the temple provides the perfect model for the creation of a home. . . . The temple is the house of life."[20]

Of course, the House of Alma, like the House of Holiness to be discussed in the following section, is also simply a house, and in addition to providing the spiritual sustenance of life, it relies on a domestic workforce, referred to by Fletcher as a mystical "ministry," that literally as well as spiritually sustains the lives of those within it.[21] Indeed, many of what Fletcher sees as the sacred qualities of the temple also define the sixteenth-century household as prescribed by domestic manuals, where an increasing insistence on the idea that the home should be a refuge from the market—so that, for example, the religiously sanctioned sexual labor of the unpaid Protestant "huswife" can be clearly differentiated from that of the paid "hussy"—is echoed in Fletcher's temple by a "removal from the ordinary world we live in, into a life beyond the clock and the marketplace."[22] The containment of the housewife to the interior space of the house is crucial to the ideological separation of the domestic from the commercial sphere, her circumscribed domain preserved from the corrupting influences of the profane world, with the sometimes explicit corollary that her will and voice should be likewise shut up. She is, the preacher Henry Smith pointedly reminds readers of his *A preparative to mariage*, sprinkling in biblical references, a "housewife, not a street wife like Thamar, nor a field wife like Dinah, but a housewife, to show that a good wife keeps her house: and therefore Paul biddeth Titus to exhort women that they be chaste and keeping at home."[23] Despite such insistence on the wife's properly Christian servitude, these manuals' directives slide from the spiritual into the practical, and many concern the housewife's active management of servants. If the sixteenth-century middling English housewife's role was, as Federici says of her more modern counterpart, of a "specific character" because of its mix of manual, emotional, and sexual labor, as well as the even more invisible work of making the house feel like a "home"—a combination of immaterial and material labor that condenses Fletcher's "temple" with the home for which it is only, for him, a figure—"that servant which is the housewife" might well have her own paid servants, whose lives and work were not necessarily confined to one household.[24]

Some of the middling and noble households that relied on the material and immaterial labors of a housewife and her team were like Spenser's own colonial Irish plantation. From Steven Shapin's bringing to light of the unnamed household servants who made experimental science possible to Ann Blair's recent work, building on that of Franz Bierlaire, on Erasmus's live-in coterie of double-duty domestic and secretarial laborers, historians have worked to demystify the persistent conception of the intellectual as the solitary genius.[25] For the most part, the necessary work of such support staff was indeed invisible, because it was inconvenient for the picture of autonomy sought by scholars, poets, and, to a certain extent, aristocrats.[26] Bierlaire, Shapin, and Blair have had to dig deep in some cases to uncover servants' hidden presence in the work of their better-known bosses. And yet, in *The Faerie Queene*, Spenser goes out of his way to highlight the manual labor that goes into maintaining both biological and intellectual life, lingering on the logistical details of how his heroes' bodies are maintained through domestic care. Though this labor is patently fictional, ostensibly the gauzy covering of Spenser's allegory, that makes it even stranger that he would emphasize its griminess. Spenser makes the unveiling of allegory—which he acknowledges in the Letter to Raleigh "will seeme displeasaunt" to many readers—perhaps less unpleasant than the veil itself. In the Castle of Alma, the kernel of "good discipline" seems less "clowdily enwrapped in Allegoricall deuises" than coated with dust, sweat, and kitchen grease.[27]

Guyon and Arthur are roving around in the "labyrinth" of book II when, in canto ix, they come upon a "temple": a castle under siege, or a human body bravely fending off its besiegement by insurrectionary passions. Guyon and Arthur, having done their part to keep the besiegers at bay, are warmly welcomed into the castle by Alma, the lady and soul of the house, who offers to show them around. The tour's highlights include the kitchen—corresponding, as we have seen, to the stomach and the rest of the digestive system—and the attic, corresponding to the brain. The didactic payoff of the visit to Alma's House of Temperance would seem to be the exemplary embodiment of the virtue of temperance, with all the individual body's parts working in harmony to preserve the bodily autonomy of the gentleman or noble person, Spenser's ideal reader, and to make him an even more ideal version of himself, through that famous "vertuous and gentle discipline."[28]

As Schoenfeldt notes, the idea of a house as an allegory of the body would have been quite conventional, and Renaissance readers were less squeamish about the body than later ones.[29] Indeed, in 1715 John Hughes took umbrage at Spenser's besmirching of the noble virtue of temperance with the dirty details of this allegory, his too-real discussion of physiological rather than purely spiritual interiority, protesting that the House of Alma is "debas'd by a Mixture of too many low Images, as *Diet, Concoction, Digestion*, and the like; which are presented as persons."[30] Hughes's complaint seems to be not only that Spenser is bringing gross bodily functions to the fore (as Schoenfeldt discusses) but also that, in so doing, he draws our attention to the real-life "persons" who performed such labors in Elizabethan England, thus exposing another kind of unseemly "interiority": the inner workings of the household were just as disgusting to some readers as those of the body, if not more. What is unusual about Spenser's House of Alma is not the frankness about bodily functions but how much explicitly menial labor is necessary to maintain what Jonathan Sawday memorably refers to as this "body-building," requiring a small army of household workers constantly tasked with smelly and annoying jobs, particularly in the stomach/kitchen and the brain/attic.[31] This body requires a lot of other bodies. Eager as Spenser apparently was to get past his youthful service work as a sizar and ascend to the gentlemanly class, to be served in his own home rather than to serve in others', he nonetheless offers us, in the House of Alma episode, ways of valuing the domestic labor and laborers that most aristocratic-adjacent, aspiring gentleman writers would find beneath contempt. Here there is no mystification, either through invisibility or through spectacle, of all the support work needed to produce the noble subject Spenser has in mind. This is in contrast to the seventeenth-century depictions of the operators of experimental machinery as cherubs, noted by Shapin, or aristocrats' flaunting of large retinues of servants as a display of wealth. Spenser's personifications of bodily and mental processes sweat right through the cloudy wrapping of allegory and confront us with a bare fact about Elizabethan aristocratic personhood: far from being fashioned autonomously, it relies on the labor of others—specifically, social inferiors.

In his description of "Concoction" in the House of Alma, a word used in the Renaissance to describe both cooking and digestion—and thus here the allegorical representation and its literal referent have already been blurred on a semantic level—Spenser spares no dirty detail. Having passed through the well-appointed "stately Hall" (II.ix.27), Guyon and Arthur end up in the kitchen:

> In the midst of all
> There placed was a caudron wide and tall,
> Vpon a mightie fornace, burning whott,
> More whott, than *Aetn'*, or flaming *Mongiball*:

For day and night it brent, ne ceased not,
So long as any thing it in the caudron gott.

But to delay the heat, least by mischaunce
    It might breake out, and set the whole on fyre,
    There added was by goodly ordinaunce,
    An huge great payre of bellowes, which did styre
    Continually, and cooling breath inspyre.
    About the Caudron many Cookes accoyld
    With hookes and ladles, as need did requyre;
    That whyles the viaundes in the vessell boyld,
They did about their businesse sweat, and sorely toyld.

The maister Cook was cald *Concoction*,
    A carefull man, and full of comely guyse:
    The kitchin clerke, that hight *Digestion*,
    Did order all th'Achates in seemely wise,
    And set them forth, as well he could deuise.
    The rest had seuerall offices assynd,
    Some to remoue the scum, as it did rise;
    Others to beare the same away did mynd;
And others it to vse according to his kynd. (II.ix.29–31)

The place is described as thoughtfully organized—the martial or legalistic connotations of "goodly ordinaunce" are domesticated into "goodly order" two stanzas later—but infernally hot (hotter than Aetna, site of Vulcan's workshop, that *locus classicus* of both extreme heat and extreme labor). It is also smoke filled and eternally boiling—the burning furnace "ceased not"—despite the mitigating cooling air of the bellows, themselves working "continually," which have been installed as a basic safety regulation ("to delay the heat, least by mischaunce / It might breake out, and set the whole on fyre") rather than for the comfort of the workers.

The perfect hostess Alma has been identified as the antitype to the miserly Mammon, whom Guyon encounters several cantos earlier lording over his money hoard. Harry Berger Jr. contrasts the life-leeching effects of Mammon's food desert—upon emerging from which Guyon faints, not having eaten for three days—with the life-giving effects of Alma's kitchen, whose "end product . . . is the living tissue of the moral and spiritual organism which itself contains the kitchen, which gives it its meaning, its clarity, its function, its proper end."[32] The contrast of fruitless coins to nourishing food is clear enough. But Berger insists not only on the superiority of Alma's product to Mammon's but also on the higher worker satisfaction levels of Alma's labor force. Comparing Mammon to Stalin, Berger asserts that "Mammon's government is totalitarian and his workers automatons," while "the workers in Alma's kitchen seem to be doing their jobs with some purpose," citing the more detailed descriptions of the workers' care.[33] From the perspective of the laborers, however, the mine is arguably less hellish than the kitchen:

> Therein an hundred raunges weren pight,
> And hundred fournaces all burning bright;
> By euery fournace many feendes did byde,
> Deformed creatures, horrible in sight,
> And euery feend his busie paines applyde,
> To melt the golden metall, ready to be tryde.

> One with great bellowes gathered filling ayre,
>     And with forst wind the fewell did inflame;
>     Another did the dying bronds repayre
>     With yron toungs, and sprinckled oft the same
>     With liquid waues, fiers *Vulcans* rage to tame,
>     Who maystring them, renewd his former heat;
>     Some scumd the drosse, that from the metall came;
>     Some stird the molten owre with ladles great;
> And euery one did swincke, and euery one did sweat. (II.vii.35–36)

Both work sites are compared to Vulcan's volcanic smithy; the work in both cases is sweaty toil, executed "sorely" in the kitchen's case; no one in either workforce seems to get any time off. But Mammon's workers are afforded more humanity than Alma's. Russ Leo has argued that if Mammon's fiends are (in Guyon's word) "worldlinges" (II.vii.39)— referring to those who "swink and sweat in an activity they perform unreflectively"—they also display a capacity for wonder.[34] This capacity is not afforded to Alma's workers, who are only wondered *at*. When the miners "wonder at the sight" of a mortal man, as Guyon later wonders at the cooks in Alma's kitchen, "their staring eyes sparckling with feruent fyre" (II.vii.37), it is unclear whether this fire is merely a reflection of the furnaces, or of some internal source; the latter possibility is certainly available. Given his identification of these subterranean creatures as "worldlinges"—whose labor is "legible in its relationship to the moral economy of the poem" as well as to him—Guyon is not dismissing them as subhuman.[35] Guyon's "dismay" might be not only at the "vgly shapes" of the demons' eyes but also at the uncomfortable realization that these infernal laborers are *not* simply automatons but may well have their own subjectivities that are not subjected to their overlord, a private interior space that might well reflect the commercial sphere but that is also preserved from it, a space in which their labors can be suspended.

The narrator's conclusion to the description of Alma's kitchen—with Guyon and Arthur fixed in "gazing wonder," "for neuer had they seene so straunge a sight" (II.ix.33)—is strange not only because Guyon had just seen something quite similar in the cave of Mammon, but also because, again, this is quite normal activity for a kitchen in an early modern noble estate. Nor does this wonder earn them a scolding from Alma, who a few stanzas later, when Guyon is staring agog at the blushing maiden Shamefastnes he meets in the part of the castle corresponding to the heart, clucks, "Why wonder yee / Faire Sir at that, which ye so much embrace? / She is the fountaine of your modestee" (II.ix.43). Here, Guyon is mocked for not recognizing the source of his virtuous self-construction, while his "wonder" at the basic functions of digestion passes without comment. Then again, like many lordly gentlemen, perhaps Guyon and Arthur had simply never stopped to consider just how much work it takes to keep aristocratic households running.

As Guyon and Arthur ascend through the house, they fail to transcend the menial messiness of the lower bodily stratum's functions. When they reach the turret that represents the brain, we learn that it is the residence of three wise men, who "counselled faire *Alma*, how to gouerne well" (II.ix.48). As is the case for other ideal housewives—like the one instructed by the *menagier de Paris* to "gouverner" her confiture, or the one who figures in John Dod and Robert Cleaver's influential prescriptions for a "godly form of household government"—Alma's governance of the house and its servants is itself subjected to male governance. And yet these men appear to need some help themselves. After viewing Phantastes's fly-filled chamber of fancy (II.ix.51), Alma's guests stop in briefly on the unnamed Reason or Diet, wordlessly digesting images of the "memorable gestes" of the past (II.ix.53–54), before coming upon the third room, whose occupant is as "ruinous and old" as his decrepit surroundings (II.ix.55), but possessed of a powerful mind:

> This man of infinite remembraunce was,
>> And things foregone through many ages held,
>> Which he recorded still, as they did pas,
>> Ne suffred them to perish through long eld,
>> As all things els, the which this world doth weld,

But laid them vp in his immortall scrine,
Where they for euer incorrupted dweld. (II.ix.56)

Eumnestes, this personification of memory, is first introduced to us
as a master of his art, capable of collecting "infinite" "things foregone"
and storing them neatly in his "immortall scrine," immaculately "incorrupted." Eumnestes would seem as creepily capable of automatic
caching as the internet, and his archive of secrets recalls Spenser's
own request to access the "antique rolles" from the Muses' "euerlasting scryne" in order to write his poem (I.proem.2). Richard Rambuss's
study of Spenser's secretarial career emphasizes the unique privilege
that comes with a secretary's role as a custodian of confidences, identifying Eumnestes as a "surrogate" for Spenser's authorial role and associating secretary status primarily with epistemological power.[36] By
the next stanza, though, for all this seamlessness of data transfer to an
"immortal scrine," this operating system seems to be rather buggy:

His chamber all was hangd about with rolls,
And old records from auncient times deriud,
Some made in books, some in long parchment scrolls,
That were all worm-eaten, and full of canker holes.

Amidst them all he in a chaire was sett,
Tossing and turning them withoutten end;
But for he was vnable them to fett,
A litle boy did on him still attend,
To reach, when euer he for ought did send;
And oft when thinges were lost, or laid amis,
The boy them sought, and vnto him did lend. (II.ix.57–58)

Eumnestes's study is full of "worm-eaten" books and scrolls, ridden
with "canker-holes" and in such disarray that he needs an assistant, a
boy named Anamnestes, to help him find misplaced volumes. Eumnestes is, in other words, buried under paperwork.[37] His labor in organizing the mess of documents is physically exhausting and literally
endless, calling to mind a sleepless night or an equally restless research
session: "Tossing and turning them withouten end."

Unlike Spenser's own "endlesse worke" according to Jonathan
Goldberg—defined, again, by "narrative principles that induce frustration, that deny closure," working to produce a poem that is "frus-
tratingly incomplete and inconclusive"—this perpetual all-nighter fails
to inspire a breathless appraisal of the unfathomable potential of lan-

guage.[38] Memory's frustration here stems, instead, from the annoying material conditions that would be familiar to any archivist, scribe, or secretary. Rather than sitting magisterially on his throne as the crown of the body, the personification of memory, introduced to us as a frictionless Google incarnate, is in fact as anxiously trying to keep it together as the rest of us, and he cannot do it alone. Like Erasmus, whose Herculean battle with similarly worm-eaten manuscripts discussed in the introduction was likely aided by numerous (unacknowledged) copyists and household servants who made up his *famuli*, Memory requires backup. In an early seventeenth-century school play by Thomas Tomkis parodying Spenser's Castle of Alma, and that Alan Stewart and Garrett Sullivan argue draws out some of its implications, that backup sounds fed up himself. The play casts Anamnestes more explicitly as Memory's unappreciated servant; he complains that he is always sent on errands to collect Memory's lost articles and must be at his boss's constant (and implicitly sexual) disposal.[39] If Tomkis's Memory, beset by both the increasing mnemonic demands of history's inexorable progress and needy antiquarians who "must know of me forsooth how euery idle word is written in all the mustie moath-eaten *Manuscripts*, kept in all the old Libraries in euery Cittie betwixt *England* and *Peru*," feels like he is singlehandedly keeping all of human history together, he needs Anamnestes to keep him together, to fetch him his glasses by day and "lie" with him "all night."[40]

Schoenfeldt's reading of canto ix seeks to show how Spenser is redefining the rather mundane operations of the brain, digestive tract, and other organs as heroic. But Spenser's attention to the constant tedium of the body's physical and mental upkeep makes temperance an active virtue while resisting any high notes of heroism, deflated by its dependence on the collective labor of housewives and servants. To return to Arendt's categories in *The Human Condition*, discussed in the introduction, the scummy and moldy jobs of figures like concoction's cooks and memory's paper pushers are firmly ensconced in the realm of "labor," incessant and fundamentally futile even if biologically necessary, as opposed to "work"—where individual artifacts achieve some kind of durability in the world—or, more to the point, "action," the only sphere of human activity, according to Arendt and the classical writers she draws from, where heroism is possible. Unlike Herculean labor as characterized by Arendt, and like "the daily fight in which the human body is engaged to keep the world clean and prevent its decay," the labor within the House of Alma is unheroic in Arendt's terms, defined by "endurance" rather than "courage," "relentless repetition" rather than "danger," condemned to the endless and degrading cycle of production and consumption.[41] The labors of Alma's upstairs and downstairs servants, with their swinking and sweating and paper pushing, can only barely stave off degeneration. "To keep the world clean and prevent its decay," constantly combating waste and worm holes, is the full-time job of both the digestive system and the memory, and it is too annoying to be heroic.[42]

Insistent as he is on Spenser's commitment to heroism, Schoenfeldt does point out that the self Spenser constructs throughout his poem through allegorical personifications of virtue is hardly invincible or impermeable. Guyon passes out after his underground sojourn with Mammon; Redcrosse, in book I, takes off his armor and is overwhelmed by how nice the wind feels; and the House of Alma is connected to the outside world both through its besiegement by the passions and its carefully constructed waste removal system, carried out by dedicated members of the kitchen staff. Yet such acknowledgments on Spenser's part of the interconnectedness of self and world are taken, by Schoenfeldt and others, to be in the service of a redefinition of heroism, or, alternatively, a romantic embrace of "vulnerability"—a radical dependency on God, nature, or vague abstract forces.[43] In arguing that Spenser's conception of masculine virtue is centered on vulnerability, Joseph Campana claims that "Spenser seems to have imagined a world in which instances of pain, pleasure, sensation, and affect might be experienced in a way that would be transformative rather than obliterating, that would suggest the importance of a concept of shared vulnerability." Campana marks out a crucial middle ground when he positions the version of masculinity he identifies in *The Faerie Queene* in between the "masterful 'self-fashioning'" theorized by Stephen Greenblatt and the "obliterated 'self-shattering'" explored by Cynthia Marshall.[44] But this vulnerability calls for transformation in the much more mundane, concrete, and immediate sense of the restoration of tired, injured, and hungry masculine bodies by other bodies—housewives, cooks, secretaries, and other surrogates for physical and mental labor—without whom they could not be themselves.

The House of Alma dramatizes how much work it takes—and how many people are involved in this work—to keep an individual body alive on a daily basis. This is how Alma's governance calls to mind not only the rule of the soul over the body, as the allegory has most straightforwardly been read, but also the management of a housewife over a household, where provisions must be made for the day-to-day needs of nourishment and household accounting. The arguments of Federici and other Marxist feminists that the work performed in the home by women—the reproduction and re-creation of the male workforce—is what makes capitalist production possible could thus be applied, in terms of class as well as gender exploitation, here. Campana's argument that "in the literature of epic and chivalric romance, heroic masculinity is that form of estranged labor by which the energies of the human body are deployed as virtue" overlooks the fact that when Spenser's male heroes achieve the relief they seek from this estranged labor, it is the labor of domestic workers that restores them to wholeness.[45] In book II, canto x, as Guyon and Arthur hungrily take in the chronicles of their respective homelands borrowed from Memory's "scrine," Alma needs to remind them to eat their dinner:

> So long they redd in those antiquities,
> That how the time was fled, they quite forgate,
> Till gentle *Alma* seeing it so late,
> Perforce their studies broke, and them besought
> To thinke, how supper did them long awaite.
> So halfe vnwilling from their bookes them brought,
> And fayrely feasted, as so noble knightes she ought. (II.x.77)

Alma's reminder of the necessity of food and her dutiful provision of an appropriate feast, filling her role toward the "noble knightes" exactly as "she ought," provide a model not only for what Stewart and Sullivan call the "interpenetration of bodily self-regulation and specific reading practices" but also for the dependence of some bodies upon others for their regulation.[46] Guyon and Arthur have so fully forgotten not only time but their own bodies that they are apparently unable even to summon themselves as grammatical subjects: it is Alma who "feasted" them, having "brought" them to the dining room, as if they were literally, on the level of language, incapable of feeding themselves.[47]

## Home Remedies in the Legend of Holiness

If Alma's calm and careful governance of the bodies and operations within her well-functioning temperate household makes her not only an abstract, personified soul of a tempered body but also an exemplary sixteenth-century Protestant housewife, such an analog may be less obvious in book I's House of Holiness, a more literal "temple" run by a suspiciously Catholic mother superior. The quality of "collapsed time" that Fletcher identifies in "temples" like the House of Alma—"emptied of business, it is full; quieted and stilled, it is a breathing, hovering kind of time, the hierophant of stillness in motion"—provides a hinge between sacred and domestic space, the latter of which is likewise cultivated to hold the material and psychic world in suspension, as in Tusser's association of a well-kept household with heaven on earth: "As order is heauenly where quiet is had, / so error is hell, or a mischiefe as bad."[48] In both houses, bodies need to be worked upon in order to become whole again, to be transformed in order to remain themselves, and both the mundane metabolic reconstitution of body and mind, on the one hand, and its miraculous recovery, on the other, are represented in the poem as worthy of wonder.

Book I, canto x opens in an emergency situation. Una has brought Redcrosse, "feeble, and too faint" from his long imprisonment by Orgoglio, to the House of Holiness; she is worried about "his late decayed plight" (I.x.2). And yet this decay, however severe, is understood by Una as reversible, through a regimen of "diets daint" (I.x.2), and the extraordinary measures brought to bear upon Redcrosse are not so different from the collective effort necessary to keep the "body-building" analogous to Guyon's body alive. In an early modern household, housewives often oversaw the production of medicines as well as foodstuffs, and the lack of sharp distinction between everyday nourishment and occasional treatments is reflected in the organization of recipe books like Thomas Dawson's *The good huswifes jewell*, where a recipe for "a Caudle to comfort the stomacke, good for an old man" is sandwiched between a recipe for manus Christi (a medicinal hard candy, but also a step in the general candy-making process) and a recipe for a trifle meant to be served on silver.[49] For Gervase Markham, whose popular handbook *The English house-wife* outlines both the "inward and outward vertues" that a housewife must command, "one of the most principal vertues which doth belong to our English Hous-wife" is "the preseruation and care of the family touching their health and soundnesse of body," a care that "consisteth most in the diligence."[50] Sustaining the life of the household requires medical intervention but also preventative care, guided by inward virtue, on a daily basis.

Like the House of Alma, the house headed by Cælia is famous for being well "gouerned" and is fully staffed: Una and Redcrosse are met by a porter and guided in by a franklin named Zele, and Redcrosse is assigned a personal groom named Obedience (I.x.6, 17). Cælia, her dutiful daughters Fidelia and Speranza, and her domestic servants are attuned to both the physical and spiritual needs of their guests, which are continuous: outward virtues slide into inward virtues. Acknowledging their weariness from their "toyle" and "labours long," Cælia makes sure that Redcrosse and Una's "wearie limbes with kindly rest, / And bodies were refresht with dew repast," after which Una asks if Redcrosse may "taste" of Fidelia's "heauenly learning"—spiritual sustenance for dessert (I.x.17–18).

Then begins Redcrosse's extended hospital stay, an allegory for his spiritual revival that goes into a level of detail unnecessary for us to get the point of the allegory—that Redcrosse is being remade, or being prepared to be remade, into Holiness—and that dwells in the drudgery of the labor that goes into care work, a remaking whose physical involvement takes over its ostensible status as spiritual grace. Miraculous as Redcrosse's recovery may be, it is the result of ongoing, intermittent labors. The surgeon Patience applies "salues and med'cines," a prescription fortified by comforting words ("thereto added words of wondrous might") and supplemented by "corrosiues" in an attempt, recalling Rabelais's doctor Rondibilis, to mortify or macerate the flesh (I.x.24–25). Still, though, Redcrosse's "inward corruption," unaffected by Patience's initial treatments, continues "festring sore," and Patience's assistant Amendment can only "pluck . . . out" the patient's infected tissue at increments: "And euer as superfluous flesh did rott / *Amendment* readie still at hand did wayt, / To pluck it out with pincers fyrie whott, / That soone in him was lefte no one corrupted iott" (I.x.25–26). After this gradual process of restoring Redcrosse to himself, the medical team of Patience and Repentance return the healed knight to Una's care. At this point Cælia's daughter Charissa emerges from her birthing chamber to meet Redcrosse: "By this *Charissa*, late in child-bed brought, / Was woxen strong, and left her fruitfull nest; / To her fayre *Vna* brought this vnaquainted guest" (I.x.29). In an editorial footnote to this stanza, A. C. Hamilton reads these lines as suggesting that the reborn Redcrosse is the one who has been birthed by Charissa, who initially is indisposed and unable to meet the travelers. Cælia had apologetically explained that Charissa could not receive visitors so soon after being in labor, only to quickly transition to the subject of Redcrosse and Una's "labours" ("I wote that of your toyle, / And labours long, through which ye hither came, / Ye both forwearied be"), blurring the difference between reproductive and heroic labor (I.x.15–16). She also conflates Redcrosse's chivalric efforts and Una's support work on the campaign trail: Cælia imagines that "both" must be exhausted from their "labours long."

Redcrosse's rebirth thus becomes a new way to understand Spenser's georgic, particularly insofar as this is not a rebirth but rather multiple rebirths, a new self fashioned through the daily labors of reforming his body. At the end of the canto, Contemplation reveals that Redcrosse was kidnapped as an infant and brought to "this Faerie lond," where he was discovered by a fairy plowman in a furrow, and must thus be reconceived as English by birth (I.x.66). Learning that his foster father named him "Georgos" after the Greek word for "farmer" (from which "georgic" gets its name), born anew from a "furrow," the future St. George is reintroduced to us as literally down to earth. As Linda Gregerson puts it, this is Spenser insisting "that the work of civility and redemption be performed by one with dirt on his hands."[51] But this return to georgic roots is less a redemptive triumph than an anticlimax, a footnote to the many iterative rebirthings of Redcrosse that Cælia, her daughters, and her medical staff have been laboring to deliver throughout the canto and that Redcrosse will endure more dramatically in the next canto. The Knight of Holiness was not born once and for all—instead requiring repeated rebirths both within the narrative and by report—just as, despite the "decay" he was undergoing when he arrived at the House of Holiness, he did not die once and for all, nor will he in the following canto. The rebirth of Redcrosse as St. George depends on the repetitive reproductive labors of care workers and of natural forces that echo the human labor we have just seen.

In canto xi, in his much-anticipated trial by fire, Redcrosse is repeatedly vanquished by the dragon, only to be brought back to life by miraculous substances: "the well of life" and "the tree of life," the waters and balm of which he marinates in overnight, waking up restored and reborn. These magical spa sessions seemingly belong to a different realm than the very effective but somewhat clinical procedures, however spiritual they may be allegorically, performed on Redcrosse in canto x. But they can also be understood as quotidian, the daily re-creation required of all bodies to remain themselves, as much like what recipe book author Hugh Plat calls the "sweetest grace" of confectionery as the divine grace of resurrection.[52] After getting scorched by the dragon, Redcrosse falls backward into the well of life, "From which fast trickled forth a siluer flood, / Full of great vertues, and for med'cine good" (I.xi.29). Our hero's virtue of holiness, recently shored up in the House of Holiness, has been upstaged by the "vertues" of this healing water:

> For vnto life the dead it could restore,
>     And guilt of sinfull crimes cleane wash away,
>     Those that with sicknesse were infected sore,
>     It could recure, and aged long decay
>     Renew, as one were borne that very day. (I.xi.30)

Here we see a slippage between the powers to resurrect, to remove sin, to cure sickness, and to reverse senescence. The capacities assigned in canto x to the housewife and her crew, who know how to apply their "salues and med'cines," are here displaced onto spontaneously generated medicines from the earth. What Campana sees in Spenser as

a rebranding of "virtue" as a vulnerable manliness could thus also be
the displacing of virtue from subjects to objects. The healing powers of
plants, external agents that act on vulnerable bodies, are what become
associated with "virtue" at times like this, as they are in medicinal recipes that advertise the "vertues" of specific ingredients and their combinations. One popular recipe book, for example, promises to teach its
readers how to make "sweet and pleasant Waters, of wonderfull Odors,
Operations & Vertues" and features chapters detailing "the sundry vertues of Roses, for divers medicins," "the sundry vertues of Lyllies," "the
sundry vertues of Milfoyle," and "the sundry vertues of Rosemarie" to
supplement its recipes.[53]

Redcrosse stays soaking in the pool till morning, when he emerges,
"drenched" from the thorough steeping, as a "new-borne knight"
(I.xi.34), like rehydrated fruit, or like the dried artichokes that one recipe promises "will come to themselves, and be as good . . . as if they
were fresh gathered" when soaked in warm water.[54] Having slept it off,
on the second day Redcrosse is again struck down by the dragon, and—
rinse and repeat—his second recovery is described in similar terms to
the first. Fortunately falling near the tree of life, he comes into contact
with its balm, which, like the trickle from the well of life, is described in
terms again borrowed from medicinal recipes:

> A trickling streame of Balme, most soueraine
> And daintie deare, which on the ground still fell,
> As it had deawed bene with timely raine:
> Life and long health that gracious ointment gaue,
> And deadly wounds could heale, and reare againe
> The senceless corse appointed for the graue. (I.xi.48)

Again, one night's marinade in this "soueraine" "ointment" is the recipe for restoration: the next morning, "Then freshly vp the doughty
knight, / All healed of his hurts and woundes wide" (I.xi.52). This description sounds like a satisfied customer review of a medicinal recipe
included in Dawson's *The good huswifes jewell*, a volume whose subtitle
advertises "sundry approued reseits for many soueraine oyles, and the
way to distill many precious waters, with diuers approued medicines
for many diseases." Although witnessed by Una, anxiously watching
over Redcrosse's battle with the dragon, this medical treatment is overseen by her only literally. The earth restores the hero's body with the
kinds of sovereign remedies that would have been applied by housewives or domestic servants, but here they are autonomous, the labor of

mixing and administering medicines—the labor of keeping bodies alive
that we saw in the Houses of Temperance and Holiness—replaced by a
fantasy of a natural world that generates restoratives without intervening human labor. It is as if the thoroughly described maintenance work
of canto x, conducted in the privacy of Cælia's house, has prepared for
the apparently purely natural spontaneous grace in the public spectacle
of canto xi—or perhaps we are being asked to reimagine events we take
as either natural or miraculous as in fact the results of housewifery.

## Conserving Men in the Legend of Chastity

Like the landscape that regenerates the mortally wounded Redcrosse,
the Garden of Adonis in book III seems to dispense its restorative materials completely on its own: a fully operational apothecary's garden,
sans apothecary. The garden is described as a completely self-sustaining
ecosystem, maintained by no gardener, pumping out unending itera-
tions of generation and decay:

> Ne needs there Gardiner to sett, or sow,
>> To plant or prune: for of their owne accord
>> All things, as they created were, doe grow,
>> And yet remember well the mighty word,
>> Which first was spoken by th'Almighty lord,
>> That bad them to increase and multiply:
>> Ne doe they need with water of the ford,
>> Or of the clouds to moysten their roots dry;
> For in themselues eternall moisture they imply. (III.vi.34)

Yet despite the marked absence of any "Gardiner" to provide order to
the garden, there is someone putting some work into this place, namely
the narrator himself: "Long worke it were, / Here to account the endlesse progeny / Of all the weeds, that bud and blossome there; / But
so much as doth need, must needs be counted here" (III.vi.30). Labor
may not be necessary to make the plants grow, but it is necessary that
they be "counted" and accounted for, which means "long worke" for
the accountant. The stocks of warehoused animals, waiting to be deployed into the world—a wide array of fish "in endlesse rancks along
enraunged were" (III.vi.35)—recall Bacon's description in this book's
introduction of the utopian Salomon's House, where animals are prop-
agated through breeding programs or lie preserved in "coagulations,
indurations, refrigerations, and conservations" for future experimen-

tal use.[55] Here, prepared materials sit passively but require the active taking of inventory, so that the revolving door of inputs and outputs is regulated at the proper pace:

> Daily they grow, and daily forth are sent
>   Into the world, it to replenish more,
>   Yet is the stocke not lessened, nor spent,
>   But still remaines in euerlasting store. (III.vi.36)

In addition to, or perhaps as a surrogate for, the narrator–stock manager, the poem dwells on the figure of Venus as a kind of housewife *manquée*, regretting her inability to arrest or at least slow the degeneration of organic matter of which she is the "mother." Venus, cognizant of that inevitable degeneration and of the fact that she is powerless to stop it, nonetheless wishes she could:

> And their great mother *Venus* did lament
> The losse of her deare brood, her deare delight . . .
> Yet no'te she find redresse for such despight.
> For all that liues, is subiect to that law:
> All things decay in time, and to their end doe draw. (III.vi.40)

As Campana has noted, Spenser identifies Venus not only with sexual pleasure but also with "parental care": the garden is where Venus takes the infant Amoret "to be vpbrought in goodly womanhed" (III.vi.28), to be raised like the flowers that constitute "her deare brood." But this care can also be defined as reproductive in a broader sense, as a form of domestic georgic, a desire to do to the garden's ecology what housework, in Wendy Wall's formulation, does to the home economy: suspend its flux through order, restoration, and preservation, "providing a limited exemption" from the natural degradation wrought by time.[56]

And Spenser's narrator does admit the possibility that Venus is more able to halt that decay than it might appear. The kind of preservative labor so central to early modern households is both at the heart of the garden and, like much domestic labor, occluded from outside gazes. The "stately Mount" at the garden's center can easily be understood in sexual terms, in the sense of *mons veneris*, but its features also call to mind the feminine arts of distillery and confectionery: "sweet gum," "pretious deaw" ("dew" in recipes could refer to distilled vapors), "dainty odours, and most sweet delight" (III.vi.43).[57] Gum tragacanth, or gum dragon, was used to make sugar paste and is similar to gum arabic, the binding agent in ink, also sometimes used in confectionery; these gums were used to enhance sugar's malleability and preservative quality.[58] The garden's temporal meantime, where both spring and fall exist at once—"There is continuall Spring, and haruest there / Continuall, both meeting at one tyme" (III.vi.42)—is effected through the same trick as that of culinary preservation: flattening time so that harvest is almost a literal repetition of spring, both "continuall," with fruits and flowers existing on the table as if they were on the tree. Ann Goodenough's eighteenth-century recipe book provides instructions for "how to Candy Violetts or any other Flowers and Keepe them that they will looke as Fresh as when they are first gathared"; Plat goes a step further, advising housewives on how to create "flowers candied as they grow": three hours after gum water is applied to flowers and topped with a sprinkling of sugar, "you may bid your friends after dinner to a growing banquet."[59] C. S. Lewis's dichotomous summation of the Bower of Bliss and the Garden of Adonis—"The one is artifice, sterility, death: the other nature, fecundity, life"—is complicated by Venus's role as the artificial manipulator of nature, sterilizing life only in order to forestall death.[60] Like the narrator, who lists the flowers named after ill-fated young lovers "to whom sweet Poets verse hath giuen endlesse date" (III.vi.45), Venus performs the poetic and housewifely role of keeping men alive:

> There wont fayre *Venus* often to enioy
> > Her deare *Adonis* ioyous company,
> > And reape sweet pleasure of the wanton boy:
> > There yet, some say, in secret he does ly,
> > Lapped in flowres and pretious spycery,
> > By her hid from the world, and from the skill
> > Of *Stygian* Gods, which doe her loue enuy;
> > But she her selfe, when euer that she will,
> Possesseth him, and of his sweetnesse takes her fill. (III.vi.46)

According to this unverified rumor, Venus partakes of Adonis like a confection she has prepared and hidden away in a cabinet, when she "of his sweetnesse takes her fill." Well preserved in "pretious spycery," Adonis is this sugar mama's arm candy, like the character in John Crowne's play *The Married Beau* who assures his would-be mistress that "conserve o' man is more luscious" than conserve of roses: "Wou'd you lock me up in your Closet," he asks rhetorically, "if you did not reckon me among your Sweet-meats?"[61] Crowne's cad presumes to know exactly what goes on in ladies' closets—namely, the illicit conservation of men—in a way Spenser's narrator does not: this is only what "some say."

Spenser thus gives us a picture of female domestic preservative labor, the gums and dews and sweets and spices that preserve both the botanical world and the bodies of the men whom housewives and other domestic workers are tasked to care for, but without claiming epistemological power over it. In a slight correction of his making visible of Cælia's medical staff and Alma's cooks and secretaries, the poet here both identifies with Venus as the preserver of men—through poetry and other forms of preservation—and confesses the limits of his knowledge of her arts. Unlike the recipe books that proudly claim special access to women's secrets and bodies—like the anonymous, triumphantly titled *The Ladies cabinet opened* or Plat's audacious request to his female readers to "let my wearied muse / Repose her selfe in Ladies laps a while"—Spenser keeps his distance.[62] This is not to commend Spenser on his chivalry. Rather, it is to suggest that *The Faerie Queene*'s insistence on how the reproductive labor of a household eludes epistemological capture—how it stuns heroes into wonder, how its workings could be confused for miracles, how it claims a space that cannot be penetrated by outside eyes, how it is as eternal (though its eternity is a threat more than a promise) as the Muses' "euerlasting scryne"— identifies domestic georgic as the source, and the secret, of both heroic virtue and poetic production.

# CHAPTER 3

# Correcting Montaigne

## AGITATION AND CARE IN THE *ESSAIS*

*J'ay assez affaire à disposer et ranger la presse domestique que j'ay dans mes entrailles, et dans mes veines, sans y loger, et me fouler d'une presse estrangere. (I have enough to do to order and arrange the domestic pressures that oppress my entrails and veins, without giving myself the trouble of adding extraneous pressures to them.)*

MICHEL DE MONTAIGNE, "De mesnager sa volonté"

*Car, & les Vins s'esventent, & se poussent, par faute d'en estre leurs tonneaux tenus curieusement nets & fermés; & trop tost defaillent ils, par les avoir prodigalisés sans penser à l'avenir. Les tonneaux se perdent de moisisseure, chansisseure, puanteur, par faute de les fermer, ouvrir, hausser, baisser, ... & autrement les conduire selon la nécessité de ce mesnage: qui aussi requiert un soin continuel. (For the wines oxidize and go off if their barrels are not kept carefully clean and secured, and they lose their taste too soon if dispensed without thought for the future. The barrels are lost to mold, mustiness, and odor for failure to close, open, lift, or lower them, ... or otherwise handle them according to the necessity of this household business, which also requires a continuous care.)*

OLIVIER DE SERRES, *Le théâtre d'agriculture*

*Vaines pointures, vaines par fois, mais tousjours pointures. (Trivial pinpricks: sometimes trivial, but always pinpricks.)*

MICHEL DE MONTAIGNE, "De la vanité"

Like Spenser's Eumnestes, and without any acknowledged Anamnestes to serve as undersecretary, Montaigne approaches the management of both his writing and his estate as unenviably endless work. In "De l'oisiveté" (Of idleness), a kind of belated preface to the first book of the

*Essais,* Montaigne explains how his planned peaceful retirement to his home has mutated into never-ending drudgery. His hopes of pasturing himself in his tower, resting in solitude, and never getting mixed up in anything else for the rest of his life—"ne me mesler d'autre chose que de passer en repos, et à part, ce peu qui me reste de vie"—has horribly, depressingly backfired.[1] His mind, instead of mildly maturing unto death, has become perversely productive, bearing him so many random and malformed monsters ("m'enfante tant de chimeres et monstres fantasques, les uns sur les autres, sans ordre, et sans propos" [33]) that he has no choice but to devote himself full-time to organizing and managing them all. Adopting practices of household accounting, he has taken on the role of what Virginia Krause calls "contemplative as bookkeeper":[2] he has begun to set them down in writing, "les mettre en rolle" (33).

But if the proclaimed goal of this accounting is, eventually, to make his mind ashamed of itself ("avec le temps, luy en faire honte à luy mesmes" [33]) by exposing its formless excretions for what they are, it seems as Sisyphean a task as Erasmus's slog through the "monstrous scribal errors" of the textual laborers who came before him.[3] By the beginning of "De la vanité" (Of vanity)—deep in the third book of the *Essais,* after hundreds of pages of this *mise en rolle*—Montaigne is at the point of asking, in vain, "Quand seray-je à bout de representer une continuelle agitation et mutation de mes pensées?" (579) (When shall I make an end of describing the continual agitation and changes of my thoughts?).[4] The answer, we may guess at this point, is never: endless work indeed. It is a defining feature of the *Essais* that Montaigne continually rewrote them, working on the first edition from 1572 to 1580, revising and expanding it into the 1588 edition, and revising and expanding even more until his death in 1592, at which point the work was carried on by his editor, Marie de Gournay; modern editors embed the letters A, B, and C to indicate which text comes from which edition (1580, 1588, and 1595, respectively; I have included these letters in quotations when directly relevant). But revision is also a more local feature of Montaigne's writing. Even in the space of his rhetorical question in "De la vanité," the idea of describing his disordered mental activity as "agitation" seems to require immediate rethinking, demanding a mollifying—or is it exacerbating?—modification into "mutation."

The uncertainty on both Montaigne's part and our own about whether this management of local mental and textual agitation produces calming effects or only further agitation is central to my account of Montaigne's domestic georgic ethos, his attempt to manage his body, his household, and his writing in slight, local, and temporary ways. His interest in the domestic differed from that of Rabelais and Spenser, and from that of some of his contemporaries, who embraced concrete domestic practices as offering clear strategies for addressing literary, intellectual, and political problems. Montaigne's best friend, Étienne de la Boétie, translated Xenophon's *Oeconomicus* as *La Mesnagerie* in 1571, discovering in the ancient writer's conception of a well-ordered household a set of instructions for the proper governance of the state. In 1601 Pierre Charron, picking up on Xenophon's preoccupation with beauty as well as utility, declared that household management ("la mesnagerie") is a beautiful, just, and useful business ("une belle, juste, et utile occupation"); there is in fact nothing so beautiful to Charron as a well-run, peaceful household ("Il n'y a rien si beau qu'un ménage bien reglé, bien paisable").⁵ Olivier de Serres, reflecting incidentally on the wars of religion in a Xenophonic treatise published in 1600, claims to have found a refuge from that violence in estate management; his own preference as well as the exigencies of civil war kept him at home in the country ("m'ont retenu aux champs en ma maison"), where he was proud to report that he had kept both himself and his neighbors safe, attending simply to his own domestic business ("en me conservant avec eux, je me suis principalement addonné chés moi, à faire mon mesnage").⁶

Unlike these contemporaries, Montaigne found nothing of much aesthetic or political interest in the organization of utensils or in a husband's education of his young wife in how to keep the cellar stocked and the servants in line. Nor did his *mesnage* successfully distract him from the decades-long wars of religion, which continually preoccupied and sometimes interrupted him while writing the *Essais*. He professed ignorance of and indifference to the day-to-day affairs of running his estate, which could involve, as Serres describes in the epigraph above, tedious vigilance on the part of the master and mistress (if supervision of wine fermentation is left to servants, Serres insists, "tout va mal").⁷ But what he did dwell on, and what he shared with the other authors discussed in this book who saw both literary production and self-reproduction as acts of domestic drudgery, was the frequent futility, or even apparent counterproductiveness, of the daily operations we perform to keep ourselves and our writing going. "Nous nous corrigeons aussi sottement souvent comme nous corrigeons les autres" (964) (We often correct ourselves as stupidly as we correct others [736]), Montaigne complains, with a typical minor qualification: often, but not always. He is less categorically excluding self-correction than correcting any expectation that it will always be salutary.⁸ Like the modern housewife conjured by Simone de Beauvoir, Montaigne is painfully aware that no matter how boring keeping a household running may be, "even in this area, things are capricious": even in the most tedious domestic operations, predictable results are not guaranteed.[9] He is also aware, like Beauvoir, that the minor catastrophes of the household—the moth-eaten clothes, the burned meat, the broken china—are constituent parts of a domestic ecosystem that could itself easily be destroyed by forces without: "Wars with their looting and bombs threaten wardrobes and the home," Beauvoir writes, shortly after the end of World War II.[10] This casual acknowledgment of the effects of total war, like Montaigne's frequent passing references to the wars of religion in the essays I will discuss, elicits no further comment from Beauvoir, metabolized into the text's more mundane body as she proceeds with her long list of the housewife's ridiculously pointless activities.

Montaigne's ambivalent mania for the most minor acts of *mesnage*, coupled with his lack of faith or interest in self-improvement and even in the future itself, locates his life's work in the management (or rather, the indefinite forestalling of management) of caprice and contingency. Montaigne's attitude toward contingency has usually been understood as either a disciplined ethical outlook or a quirky aesthetic.[11] His commitment to the endless description (and redescription) of his unpredictable agitations is often seen as an ethically exemplary practice of calm introspection even in the face of uncertainty. His constant vigilance over his body and mind is taken as a philosophically sophisticated technology of the self, a *mise en rolle*, that, whatever its practical failures, fulfills a moral imperative to tell the truth about oneself.[12] At the same time, this open-ended self-examination is often celebrated as one of our essayist's purely literary, or even decadent, charms: his frequent close-ups on his idiosyncrasies have been likened to shameless selfies, a harmless narcissism that makes us feel better about our own self-involvement by being so completely autotelic, too absorbed in its own process to make any ethical claims at all.[13] Montaigne's tendency to diverge from such important topics as theology, education, cruelty, judgment, and honorable death to devote the same attention to salad, thumbs, cats, and laziness is part of his ecumenical appeal. But looking to Montaigne as either an ethical exemplar or a blogger avant la lettre, lofty and laudable or comfortingly close to home, prevents us from seeing the profound—or rather, profoundly superficial—agitation and irritation pulsing awkwardly and irregularly on the surfaces of both the *Essais* and the human body with which Montaigne claimed his book was "consubstantial."[14] The annoyances of domestic life and the pain of his kidney stones, like the agitation of his thoughts, can be quieted only (and temporarily) by constant adjustments. The resulting smoothing out of irritation, only ever partially and provisionally successful—in a kind of incomplete exfoliation—is the stylistic form of Montaigne's domestic georgic: the constant, iterative, small-scale labor that works, however irritatingly, to maintain his text, body, and community.

This chapter will take Montaigne's complaint of "continual agitation" seriously, if not quite to heart, as a manifestation of his domestic georgic spirit, bringing to the fore the affective dimension of both domestic and intellectual labor. Elizabeth Guild's recent effort to "unsettle Montaigne" poses an important challenge to self-help-friendly readings of his tolerance and equanimity: the goal of Montaigne's writing, she states at the outset of her book, is "not tranquillity, but a more provisional containment of anxiety."[15] When she addresses Montaigne's thinking through and performance of unsettling affects like agitation, however, Guild concludes with a serene assurance that ethical ends are always clearly in Montaigne's sights: "For the soul to be moved to act well, it must be shaken out of tranquillity."[16] The implied causal connection here between being shaken and acting well suggests that the point of being agitated out of tranquility is then to recollect oneself *in* tranquility, an end that, if ever temporarily achieved in the *Essais*, is continually shaken off. When Guild goes on to focus on intense, operatic feelings of fear and grief and attributes to Montaigne's unsettlement a therapeutic function, it can sound like Montaignean peace of mind may have to be worked for, but it can be heroically achieved nonetheless. I will suggest, by contrast, that both the apparent capacious calm and the apparent benign playfulness of the *Essais* are unsettled not by surges of emotion that can then be cleanly assimilated into an ethical program but rather by what Sianne Ngai calls, in her diagnosis of textual irritation, "a minor but continuous state of inflammation or discomfort."[17] This state is caused by an affect that is "explicitly *a*moral and *non*cathartic, offering no satisfactions of virtue, however oblique, nor any therapeutic or purifying release."[18] Ngai explains that irritation, like each of the apparently trivial affects she documents in *Ugly Feelings*, functions as "a mediation between the aesthetic and the political." She attributes the etiolated state of contemporary emotional life to the fact we no longer live in a time when emotions translate as smoothly into political terms as they did for thinkers like Aristotle or Hobbes, who understood the affective dimension of politics under the sign of "relatively unambiguous emotions like anger or fear."[19] But affective responses to politics could be ambiguous even before late capitalism, and for Montaigne, agitated both in sympathy with the corrupted social and political body and by the incongruity of that sympathy, ambiguous emotions may have been all that was available.

Montaigne responds to his "siecle desbordé"—an age so disordered, the adjective implies, that it is overwhelming its bounds—with the merely skin-deep and noncathartic affect of irritation (946). His excruciatingly local discomforts, deeply but only literally internal to his house and body, complicate our impulse to identify with the essayist either ethically or aesthetically. They also complicate our understanding of the relationship Montaigne models between the private, domestic self and the public, political world, while refiguring the material conditions of Montaigne's production—likely interrupted, as George Hoffmann details, by the frequent impositions that came with running an estate—as literary ones.[20] Montaigne's repeated failure to accommodate himself to household management—his taste "ne s'accommode aucunement au ménage" (244)—is legible in the form as well as the content of the *Essais*.

## Irritating Humors: Montaigne in Trouble

Disproportionately discomfited by his kidney stones and household chores (incongruously paired, in my analysis and in the *Essais* themselves, under the same affective rubric), Montaigne experiences irritation as something like how Ngai defines it: an affect associated with semipermeable boundaries between self and world—like the skin, or the urethra, or the walls of a constantly encroached-upon domestic space—and incommensurable with its object, if it has an object at all. Defining irritation as "a mood" as opposed to an emotion, Ngai draws on Annette Baier's distinction: while emotions are "about something," "moods, if they are about anything, seem to be about nearly everything"; they are "either objectless, or have near all-inclusive and undifferentiated objects. They sometimes involve emotions searching for appropriate objects."[21]

Part of what makes Montaigne's irritation so irritating to himself and to readers is that, at some moments and under certain light, it does not *quite* seem to qualify as irritation, chafing against the category discordantly, if only slightly so. Montaignean irritation is a kind of mildly frustrated expression, the low-level but unshakeable sense that some kind of vague blockage is disrupting the normal commerce between internal and external spaces, or between signifier and signified. In this, it sits most comfortably with Ngai's definition of irritation as "offishness," "incongruity," "disproportionality," or "a strangely aggressive kind of weakness"[22]—the experience of a perpetual microaggression. Ngai derives her understanding of this feeling in part from Aristotle, who diagnoses the irritable man as one who is affected too much or for too long (we are "irritated *by the wrong things, more severely and for longer than is right*"),[23] and adds a corollary: we are irritated by people who do not feel outraged *enough*, who feel merely irritated at what should be really upsetting.[24] In Ngai's case study, Nella Larsen's 1928 novel *Quicksand*, when the biracial protagonist displays the same psychosomatic annoyance when confronted with unattractive teacups as she does with assertions of racial inferiority, readers often balk. They accuse her not exactly of feeling the wrong thing but of feeling it incorrectly and in the wrong proportion, or of confusing bad aesthetics—which should merely irritate us—with bad politics or ethics, which should enrage us.[25]

Some theorists of the passions have, however, seen irritation as salutary, or at least as preservative of virtue. The Renaissance humanist Juan Luis Vives saw irritation (*offensio*) as less an improper than a preliminary response, the early stirrings of what may ripen into the full-fledged feeling of hatred, anger, or envy: an "initial brush" or "first contact with something discordant or harmful," a small shock to warn us that we have crossed, if only infinitesimally, an invisible moral boundary, checking evil's seductions and teaching us what our body and soul ought to want.[26] In eighteenth-century German philosophy, irritation (*Reiz*) can be found working at the heart of life itself, or, in Johann Gottfried Herder's account, at the heart of the heart. "Has anything more wonderful ever been seen than a beating heart with its inexhaustible irritation?" Herder asks, noting how such irritation "spreads out from this inexhaustible fount and abyss through our whole *I*, enlivens each little playing fiber."[27] In this sense of small-scale energetic animation, irritation rubs up against what is elsewhere referred to as "agitation." Steven Goldsmith's *Blake's Agitation* takes as its point of departure the convergence—in Blake, in Enlightenment and Romantic thought, and in our own contemporary critical practice—of agitation's two senses: affective and political. Agitation is at once "an interior, *affective* state" of unsettled emotion, what Jean-François Lyotard calls a "visceral vibrato, an excitation of the life force," and a form of public activism that aims to unsettle a political state.[28]

For Montaigne, however, agitation's continual excitation is not exactly exciting, and the interior commotion of his irritation never seems to produce any discernible echo in the political world. If agitation, in Goldsmith's account, articulates a bridge between private and public, making internal feelings "legible on the body's surface,"[29] the effects of Montaigne's "continual agitation" are often invisible; sometimes, the invisibility of effects is precisely the cause of irritation. That his household affairs are materially limited and particular to his estate literalizes the "domestique" use and "commodité particuliere" Montaigne circumscribes in "Au Lecteur" as his book's only scope (3), and his failure to discharge his kidney stones means not only that his pain continues but also that he lacks an external referent to express that pain. Both his bodily and his linguistic products are—as he complains when calling his writing the "excremens" of an old brain, barely more presentable than the contents of a chamber pot—always undigested (946).

The somewhat illegible and somehow incomplete character of irritation makes it like those minor, microscopic movements of and between bodies identified by affect theory as worthy of consideration not despite but because of how they elude our detection, wafting somewhere under the threshold of the bigger, bolder emotions. In Melissa Gregg and Gregory J. Seigworth's introduction to *The Affect Theory Reader*, evocatively titled "An Inventory of Shimmers," the sifting out of these ineffable phenomena can sound like a foraging expedition in an enchanted forest, the specimens collected in (and gently released from) the "sieves of sensation and sensibility" with an awe at their "vaporous evanescence," their "intracellular divulgences."[30] In theoretical approaches like this, affect, even or especially in its most ephemeral appearances, is always extremely seductive, always teasingly escaping the bounds of our reason. But for all such romanticizing of the "mere" and the "slight," irritation—while just as minor as any fleeting flight of fancy—is far less charming. What Montaigne offers us is an inventory not of shimmers, but of pinpricks. Somehow flat even in their sharpness, recurrent enough to feel constant but never regular enough to be predictable, what Montaigne calls, describing his household cares in "De la vanité," "vaines pointures" (950) (trivial pinpricks [725]) suspend themselves on the surface of the skin, never quite reaching the intensity of passion—or any significance beyond the immediate and domestic—despite their occasional half-hearted gestures in that direction.

Montaigne's general lack of intensity is sometimes taken as a robust political and moral philosophy in itself. In his book on Montaigne's ethical and political commitments, David Quint argues that Montaigne provides a more than adequate response to his political situation with the *Essais*, taking us into an enlightened ethical age with his forward-thinking attempts to reform the French nobility out of the pettiness and cruelty that had led to civil war. Montaigne, for Quint, "offers a pliant goodness that is the product not of heroic effort and philosophical discipline, not even of Christian charity or meekness, but rather of ordinary fellow feeling," an ethos that can be summarized as "accommodating to other human beings."[31] By absorbing, and by reading Montaigne as absorbing, all potential conflict into a flexible and forgiving moral program, Quint overlooks some of the weaker, messier moments in the

*Essais.* These moments, like those occasional "vaines pointures," do not quite muster any real resistance to assimilation into tolerance and tranquility. They provide only, as Guild puts it, a "precarious suspension of excessive 'trouble,'" with that word carrying both affective and political weight.[32]

I aim to trouble as well as be troubled by Montaigne not only by taking his negativity seriously, as Guild does, but also by not seeking to recuperate negative moments as part of a healthy moral system and by instead preserving them in suspension. In this I take a cue from Ngai, whose stated goal in *Ugly Feelings* is to "dwell on affective gaps and illegibilities, dysphoric feelings, and other sites of emotional negativity" in order to explore "ambivalent situations of suspended agency."[33] The chapters of her book, Ngai explains,

> draw together two seemingly disparate philosophical definitions—Hannah Arendt's claim that "what makes man a political being is his faculty of action" and Baruch Spinoza's description of emotions as "waverings of the mind" that can either increase or diminish one's power to act—and attend to the aesthetics of the ugly feelings that index these suspensions.[34]

My aim, then, is to exfoliate how the private, trivial, and futile preoccupations of Montaigne's *Essais*, especially in "De la vanité" and "De la ressemblance des enfans aux peres" (Of the resemblance of children to their fathers), constitute a prepolitical dimension, barely dimensional though it may be, that complicates not only the (early) modern conceptual separation of action and passion but also Arendt's particular distinction between the *oikos* and the *polis*, or between the nonpolitical (labor and work, the distinction between which Montaigne also troubles) and the political (action). The merely skin-deep, shaky, and noncathartic affect of irritation is Montaigne's response not only to his medical condition and his housekeeping responsibilities but also to what he views as a badly "disordered" historical moment: a "siecle desbordé" of which endless, aimless scribbling ("escrivaillerie") is both a symptom ("simptome") and a management strategy (946).

The demotion from the vehement passions that are the focus of Guild's study to the more minor and mundane affect of irritation and its management is part of what makes Montaigne's *Essais* an example of domestic georgic. Ugly feelings, characterized by a "flatness or ongoingness" rather than the dramatic entrances of emotions like anger or fear, require a management analogous to that of an estate or household.[35] The management of and between domestic and moral economies is attempted, in part, through the management of text. Pointing to the characteristic instance of textual adjustment in the opening sentence of "De mesnager sa volonté" (Of husbanding your will), the essay that treats Montaigne's mayoralty at greatest length—"peu de choses me touchent, ou, pour mieux dire, me tiennent" (1003) (few things touch me, or, to put it better, hold me [766])—Timothy Hampton finds in "the halting *correctio*, 'pour mieux dire,'" that the problem of describing an "engaging but not entangling" public service "is both a problem of ethical action and a problem of writing."[36] Retouching his sentence to insist on his indifference to what touches him superficially is one iteration of how Montaigne's smoothing out of, or glossing over, the effects of his irritation can bear an uncanny resemblance to irritation itself. When he goes on to elaborate on the difference between what touches him and what holds him, what engages him and what entangles him, Montaigne agitates to and fro through repeated examples, as if entangled in his own refusal of entanglement. Of "affaires estrangeres," he says he has agreed

> de les prendre en main, non pas au poulmon et au foye; de m'en charger, non de les incorporer; de m'en soigner ouy, de m'en passionner nullement: j'y regarde, mais je ne les couve point. J'ay assez affaire à disposer et ranger la presse domestique que j'ay dans mes entrailles et dans mes veines, sans y loger, et me fouler d'une presse estrangere. (1004)

> (to take them in hand, not in lungs and liver; to take them on my shoulders, not incorporate them into me; to be concerned over them, yes; to be impassioned over them, never. I look to them, but I do not brood over them. I have enough to do to order and arrange the domestic pressures that oppress my entrails and veins, without giving myself the trouble of adding extraneous pressures to them. [767])

Montaigne's obsessively rehearsed policing of the borders of his body, patrolling back and forth between what he will and will not do, suggests that even his refusals to manage external pressures require syntactical management on the page.

In "De la vanité," Montaigne's irritation comes from both the obvious incommensurability of his own trivial occupations and the national crisis of civil war, on the one hand, and, on the other, his suspicion that talking about his own stupid life really is an appropriate way to respond to the degraded political climate—even more appropriate, somehow,

than either his actual engagement as Mayor of Bordeaux and peace ne-
gotiator or any ideal, philosophical retirement from public concerns altogether. The *Essais* are peppered with expressions that express so little that readers might be left unsure whether to be pleased with their
aphoristic pith or irritated by their self-negating glibness, recalling the
self-purging rhubarb that figures the skeptic's proposition in the "Apo-
logie de Raimond Sebond."[37] "De la vanité" opens with a self-reflexivity
so annoyingly satisfying it seems to settle the subject as soon as it is
posed. Here what irritates is not "offishness" but a too-perfect coincidence of content and form, as involuted as an ingrown hair: "Il n'en est
à l'avanture aucune plus expresse que d'en escrire si vainement" (945)
(There is perhaps no more obvious vanity than to write of it so vainly
[721]), which is exactly what this sentence does.

At once an index and an exhaustion of Montaigne's limited resources,
this opening does not prevent the chapter from going on for fifty-five
pages, in which vanity begins to take on, and periodically shake off, political dimensions. After suggesting that his idle cataloging of agitations
ought to be illegal, Montaigne backtracks: in such ignoble times, doing nothing is "comme louable" (946)—something *like* "praiseworthy,"
but not quite. A page later he adjusts himself again; far from a check
on the national trend of corruption, his personal "desolation" in fact
perfectly coincides with that of his age, "se rencontre à la desolation de
mon aage" (947). If the personal is political for Montaigne, it is only insofar as both are completely hopeless, and yet both are in constant need
of comment, and those comments in constant need of revision, like the
vessels of wine Serres insists must be adjusted with constant care ("un
soin continuel"). If the situation is hopeless, however, it is not serious,
or at least not spectacular, not dramatic, and not transformative.

## Vain Things: Montaigne at Home

That both the personal and the political could be understood in terms
of constant and incorrigible agitation is thus a sign less of a satisfyingly
necessary homology of private and public states than of their unhappy
coincidence. In Montaigne's toggling in "De la vanité" between his worries about the *police* (political state) and "cette police d'affaires domestiques" (951), we might expect to find an instructive analogy between
estate management and civil government, as La Boétie and others saw
in Xenophon. But Montaigne is quick to preempt any suggestion that
his private experience might have some significance for public life,
much less that the former maps neatly onto the latter. He claims that

his domestic activities are so politically meaningless that he would be among the last to be held to account—which would give him, luckily, ample time to reform his ways. Yet his professed lack of interest in being of public use is not, as we have already seen, because of any preference for home economics. Even when he admits the pleasure he derives from running his household, that pleasure is "trop uniforme et languissant" (too monotonous and languid), and what's more, it is "par necessité meslé de plusieurs pensemens fascheux" (necessarily mingled with many bothersome thoughts), to the point that it hardly seems a pleasure at all: at the end of the day, this occupation is "plus empeschante que difficile" (949) (more bothersome than difficult [723]).[38]

As if to prove this, Montaigne has a hard time getting away from this topic he has so little interest in, constantly impeded by his compulsion to narrate yet another chore that irks him. "Je ne suis pas philosophe," he finally says in exasperation, insisting that the inconveniences of estate management simply are what they are and oppress him in exact accordance with their weight: "les maux me foullent selon qu'ils poisent" (950). But just as he seems about to close the issue with a summarizing "En fin," his irritation subsumes his entire being, becoming at once verb, subject, and object: "pour sotte cause qui m'y aye porté, j'irrite mon humeur de ce costé là, qui se nourrit après et s'exaspere de son propre branle; attirant et emmoncellant une matiere sur autre, de quoy se paistre" (950) (however stupid the cause that so impelled me, I irritate my humor in that direction, and then it feeds and exasperates itself by its own movement, attracting and accumulating matter to feed on [725]). Montaigne's "humor" is motored by irritation, until the humor seems to become irritation itself, chafing against itself ("s'exaspere") as it sustains itself ("se nourrit"), or even sustaining itself *by* chafing against itself. (Randle Cotgrave's 1611 French-English dictionary defines "exasperer" as "to make sharpe, harsh, rough, or angrie; to aggravate, provoke, vex; incite unto crueltie, urge unto curstnesse, whet unto choller"[39]—or, we might say, to irritate both physically and spiritually, without a sharp distinction made between the two.)

The close proximity of self-nourishing to self-exasperation informs Montaigne's approach to managing not only his household but also his writing. In the midst of explaining—and, with his constant additions and recapitulations, performing—how something always goes wrong ("Il y a tousjours quelque piece qui va de travers"), Montaigne once again seems on the point of pithily summing it all up: "Vaines pointures," the 1588 version (the B-text) runs, "mais toujours pointures." But a few years later, in his final revision (the C-text), he adds, for some reason, a qualifier: "BVaines pointures, Cvaines par fois, Bmais toujours pointures" (950) (BTrivial pinpricks: Csometimes trivial, Bbut always pinpricks [725]). This point—emphasizing the sometime triviality, which has already been established, without elaborating on what, if not trivial, these *pointures* might be—adds nothing, except another syntactical tic, extending our experience of pinpricks without clarifying anything. Even if they are not always *vaines,* no other word seems to be available to describe them, and so here we are again, redoubling the prick of triviality even if the point was to temper it.

Throughout the *Essais,* Montaigne associates his innovative literary form with unremarkable, housebound activity, identifying writing as a cyclical compositional and recompositional labor more evocative of the daily interruptions and necessary corrections of domestic life than of the singular act of literary publication, much less the invention of a modern genre. Montaigne's constant references to his own triviality or marginality are in keeping with his conceit of confinement to a domestic space whose activities, he suggests in the opening "Au Lecteur," ought to be irrelevant to anyone outside it, even if necessary to those within it: his only purpose, famously, is one that is "domestique et privée," his only material "frivole" and "vain" (3). His deeply personal style makes his writing unfit for public consumption, being too "particulier," too "privé" (252). He claims his book is completely built ("massonné purement") out of the recycled spoils ("despouïlles") of Seneca and Plutarch (721); he describes his reading process as unceasingly filling up and pouring out ("remplissant et versant sans cesse") like the mythical Danaïdes, so that while something evidently adheres to the page on which he writes, little or nothing does to himself: "J'en attache quelque chose à ce papier, à moy, si peu que rien" (146). If the first metaphor of gathering scraps to make an original recipe recalls the resourcefulness of an economical housewife, the second, with words rolling like water through a sieve, offers a more pessimistic image of cyclical labor: here, insofar as Montaigne's work is housework, it is in the dead-end production that, in Arendt's schema or in Beauvoir's portrait of the housewife, leads only to its products' depressingly immediate consumption and the incessant demand for further production, a *mise en rolle* whose enrollment will always have an interminable backlog.

Montaigne thus complements his commitment to irrelevance by insisting, repeatedly, on his impermanence, falling short not only of the heroic immortality of Arendtian action but also of the more modest longevity of work. In "De la vanité," after pages of complaining about the never-ending demands of his household staff and ever-renewed necessities of building maintenance, he explains his decision to write in the flimsy, contemporary (and, he surmises, temporary) domestic vernacular rather than in the eternal, universal language of Latin:

> $^B$J'escris mon livre à peu d'hommes et à peu d'années. Si ç'eust esté une matiere de durée, il l'eust fallu commettre à un langage plus ferme. Selon la variation continuelle qui a suivy le nostre jusques à cette heure, qui peut esperer que sa forme presente soit en usage, d'icy à cinquante ans? $^C$Il escoule tous les jours de nos mains et depuis que je vis s'est alteré de moitié. (982)

> ($^B$I write my book for few men and for few years. If it had been durable matter, it would have had to be committed to a more stable language. In view of the continual variation that has prevailed in ours up to now, who can hope that its present form will be in use fifty years from now? $^C$It slips out of our hands every day, and has halfway changed since I have been alive. [751])

If we are to take Montaigne at his word, his essay writing, far from fashioning a monumental and unique product, would be categorized, in Adam Smith's terms, as "unproductive labour," its imminently obsolete language making it liable to be replaced with new material within a few years—an amount of time described as so trivial as to be almost immediate—which strikes our author more as a relief than as cause for concern. The French language "escoule tous les jours de nos mains," trickling away like the Danaïdes' water supply, and has not even been able to keep up its form for the brief span of Montaigne's life, having been in that time "alteré de moitié"; the fluidity of Montaigne's text itself is evidenced by that later C-text addition. Like the menial services that Adam Smith says "generally perish in the very instant of their performance, and seldom leave any trace or value behind them," and unlike the nonperishable traces left in the collective memory by Arendt's archetypal public man, Montaigne's activity, at least as his deflationary description has it, leaves nothing, or infinitesimally little, behind: "quelque chose à ce papier; à moy, si peu que rien."[40] But if the Danaïdes' constant filling up and pouring out added up to nothing, Montaigne, who puts his reading in parallel to their incessant labor, ends up with "quelque chose." And if "si peu que rien" is less than something, it is not exactly nothing, either.

In these throwaway, microscopic, apparent self-cancellations and self-corrections, something—"quelque chose"—accrues, although what that something is, beyond words on the page, can be difficult to

say. Terence Cave's influential reading of *copia* in the *Essais* alerts us to
the "risk" that, "in the cornucopian text, empty repetition is always the
alternative face of productive proliferation."[41] But what looks in Montaigne like empty repetition or futility is more properly considered a
form of iterative, reproductive activity whose results are not fully dis-
tinguishable from those of either what Arendt calls productive "work"
or, in their fundamental unpredictability, "action." Pretending at something like—but not quite achieving—the immediate loop between
production and consumption that for both Smith and Arendt defines
all menial labor, Montaigne deliberately confuses stasis and change,
moving us infinitesimally and unexpectedly while claiming to get us
nowhere. When he qualifies a statement about his gleaner-like reading
practices by saying he keeps ("garder") none of the sentences that he
reads, because he has no place ("gardoires") to put them—"non pour
les garder, car je n'ay point de gardoires" (136)—the aside reads like a
tic of an inveterate but ineffectual textual housekeeper who can't help
but put away words he sees lying around in the makeshift storehouses
of subordinate clauses.

Asides, self-corrections, suspensions, and their relatives are the
mechanisms by which Montaigne's metabolic machine reproduces itself, repeating with a minor or unquantifiable difference, preserving
meaning by slightly altering it.[42] Unsatisfied by conventional modes
of transmission, Montaigne avails himself of more provisional and
less predictable reproductive technologies. That his micromovements
lead us forward would be an overstatement, but they do not lead us
in circles, either. As he puts it in "De la vanité," reflecting on his life
and work:

> [B]Nous nous corrigeons aussi sottement souvent comme nous cor-
> rigeons les autres. [C]Mes premieres publications furent l'an mille
> cinq cens quatre vingts. Depuis d'un long traict de temps je suis en-
> vieilli, mais assagi je ne le suis certes pas d'un pouce. Moy à cette
> heure et moy tantost sommes bien deux; mais, quand meilleur, je
> n'en puis rien dire. Il feroit beau estre vieil si nous ne marchions que
> vers l'amendement. C'est un mouvement d'yvroigne titubant, ver-
> tigineux, informe, ou des joncs que l'air manie casuellement selon
> soy. (964)

> ([B]We often correct ourselves as stupidly as we correct others. [C]My
> first edition was in the year 1580. Since then I have grown older by
> a long stretch of time; but certainly I have not grown an inch wiser.
> Myself now and myself a while ago are indeed two; but when bet-

ter, I simply cannot say. It would be fine to be old if we traveled only toward improvement. It is a drunkard's motion, staggering, dizzy, wobbling, or that of reeds that the wind stirs haphazardly as it pleases. [736])

In the last sentence, his form taking a cue from his content, Montaigne declines even to follow through with the image of the staggering drunk ("yvroigne titubant"), shifting midsentence to some randomly blowing reeds.

Putting this disavowal of linear progress in parentheses, the next section of this chapter will experiment in moving mostly incrementally, but not without inconsequent leaps, through an essay that takes a continuity through ancestral lines as its ostensible subject but which ultimately does not itself progress in a continuous manner. In "De la ressemblance des enfans aux peres," the aim of life's "drunkard's motion" is maintenance: a movement that is paradoxically sustained by its constant, minor, unexpected alterations. That these alterations sometimes take the form of irritation alerts us to how stuttering, oblique movement is not necessarily beneficial to the health of the body or the soul. But the maintenance work performed by that movement is a necessary precondition for anything else to happen, or, for that matter, not happen.

## Living Stones: Montaigne in His Kidneys

The constant "vaines pointures" of household cares, which Montaigne later renames "espines domestiques" (950), or domestic thorns—these compulsive, miniscule self-corrections that are both exasperating and sustaining to whatever animates the text—intrude everywhere in the *Essais*. In "De la ressemblance des enfans aux peres," we find these thorns further domesticated into Montaigne's body, in the form of his extremely irritating kidney stones.

In the chapter of the *Essais* most explicitly, at least nominally, concerned with the progressive transmission of individual qualities through generational lines, Montaigne focuses on the stone, a recurrent metabolic formation of his own body that arrives with all the irregularity and sharp annoyance of the "vaines pointures" of household management. His stony condition ("qualité pierreuse") is his body's capacity to petrify biological material into crystalline formations that, though they thankfully do not endure forever, last longer than their sufferer might hope (763). Arriving intermittently, with neither predictable punctuality nor the habituating permanence of other innate qualities, Montaigne's kidney stones preserve a family legacy in private, comic, and temporary ways. For Montaigne owes this "qualité pierreuse," like the estate that so vexes him, to his father, Pierre.

What irritates him about these recently inherited internal pinpricks, like the "vaines pointures" of estate-management woes that always arrive at inopportune times, is their instability. The pain he feels is excruciating, but it arrives in unpredictable intervals; "even in this area," as Beauvoir says of the household, "things are capricious." His condition persists as a constant "qualité," but its existence is proven only when it (temporarily) no longer exists, and even when the stone passes, the puny physical evidence is in comic disproportion to the intensity of the pain it caused. Though Montaigne makes gestures in the direction of ennobling his long struggle with kidney stones, and though the condition causes severe pain, there is something irrevocably comical about the stubborn interiority, smallness, and ordinariness of the "stone," in spite or even because of the inordinate suffering it causes and its frustration of the body's most basic natural functioning. This condition is entirely unheroic for Montaigne. Alison Calhoun notes that, as deaths from illness began to overtake military deaths in the late sixteenth century, men of the noble classes had to think of more creative ways to stage heroic deaths—even the notion of dying while defending one's religious beliefs during the civil wars fell short of the epic ideal, which required spilling blood on foreign soil. From Montaigne's account, the courageous performance of La Boétie on his deathbed would seem to elevate an ignoble death from the plague into a valiant act on par with a battleground fatality.[43] Montaigne himself, meanwhile, refigures the source of his physical pain not as something like a weapon of war but rather as something like a bean ("comme une fève").[44] In "De la ressemblance," rather than preparing for a singular, monumental act of death—*la belle mort* carefully planned by any *gentilhomme* deserving of the name—Montaigne treats the formation of his legacy as metabolic labor, to be constantly altered, adjusted, and corrected, with expectations that are both modest and never guaranteed.

Montaigne's chapter titles notoriously have little to do with their content, but the opening to "De la ressemblance des enfans aux peres" does address the theme of fathers and children directly, if figuratively and imprecisely. Montaigne begins by telling the origin story of the body that is consubstantial with his own, his *Essais*: "Ce fagotage de tant de diverses pieces se faict en cette condition, que je n'y mets la main que lors qu'une trop lasche oisiveté me presse, et non ailleurs que chez moy" (758) (This bundle of so many disparate pieces is being composed in this manner: I set my hand to it only when pressed

by too unnerving an idleness, and nowhere but at home [574]). It is
perhaps not flattering to the *Essais* to say that they were conceived for
lack of anything else to do, under extreme conditions of housebound
boredom. It is important, though, that the book has been composed
piecemeal, a "fagotage" gathered up like sticks to feed the stove and that
"s'est basty à diverses poses et intervalles, comme les occasions me de-
tiennent ailleurs par fois plusieurs moys" (758) (has built itself up with
diverse interruptions and intervals, as occasions sometimes detain me
elsewhere for several months [574]). Unlike a child, whose conception
is discrete and whose growth can be understood as continuous, the *Essais* are built in fits and starts, without a satisfying linear narrative of development. The closest they come to a final form is as a bunch of sticks
whose implied ultimate purpose is their own destruction, flimsy twigs
fit for kindling.

But for all Montaigne's implied willingness to throw his pages to the
flames, he announces his commitment to preserving the potential of
his book to grow, if not as his child, then as a representation of his interior state over time. Like the other authors discussed in this book,
Montaigne approaches reproduction less by analogy to childbirth, or
the creation of something new, than as the metabolic reconstitution
of already-existing bodies and texts. Still, in the opening paragraph of
"De la ressemblance," he assures us, "Je ne corrige point mes premieres
imaginations par les secondes" (I do not correct my first imaginings by
my second) a claim immediately (or, rather, several years later) tempered by the C-text correction that follows: "ouy à l'aventure quelque
mot, mais pour diversifier, non pour oter" (758) (—well, yes, perhaps a
word or so, but only to vary, not to delete [574]). Correcting his claim
that he never corrects himself by adding that he does sometimes add
things, Montaigne gives credence to the claim that follows (which, as
part of the A-text, chronologically precedes the first): "Je veux representer le progrez de mes humeurs, et qu'on voye chaque piece en sa
naissance" (758) (I want to represent the course of my humors, and
I want people to see each part at its birth [574]). The "naissance" that
matters to Montaigne is not the monumental publication of the book itself, but the emergence of each "piece"—it is unclear whether he means
pieces of his moods or, more logically, of the *Essais*-cum-"fagotage." Either way, the *Essais* record their author's presence in a way that is both
continuous and fragmentary, pieced together over time.

That the *Essais* are in a way the faithful reproduction of Montaigne's
basic personal information and at the same time disposable pieces of a
languorously gathered bunch of sticks makes Montaigne's relation to
his text both proprietary and casual, as if they were less his child than

his hair, or dead skin.[45] A valet who served as his amanuensis for a time and thought he had made off well in stealing several pieces of his writing ("m'en desrober plusieurs pieces choisies") has in fact, Montaigne assures us, robbed his employer of very little: "Cela me console, qu'il n'y fera pas plus de gain, que j'y ay fait de perte" (758) (It consoles me that he will gain no more by it than I have lost [574]).[46] Someone robbed of a very large sum could say the same—the thief of a bag of gold might gain no more than a bag of gold, and still be quite satisfied—but the statement of equality here has the effect of reduction: what has been gained and lost is effectively nothing. The pilfered pages of writing—an irreplaceable record of the movements of their author's interiority on the one hand and a commodity more or less worthless on the market on the other—are both priceless and quite literally unable to fetch a price outside the domestic sphere to which they are appropriate. For Montaigne, this pricelessness and worthlessness are ultimately more or less the same.

This indifference to divergent quantitative values—"ça m'est égal" would work as a paraphrase for many of Montaigne's declarations—applies to time as well as to material wealth. "Je me suis envielly de sept ou huict ans depuis je commençay" (759), Montaigne informs us, the microcorrective "ou" converting certainty to ambiguity and reducing accounting to approximation, as if whether he has aged by "seven or eight years" since beginning his project were not significant enough to warrant precision but significant enough that the field of possibilities should be narrowed to two years. His indifference extends even to indifference: as explained in a parenthesis, the afflictions most people find "horribles" are—in a disproportionate affective response—"à peu près indifferentes" to Montaigne, who with his approximating "à peu près" declines to specify the exact relationship of this feeling to true indifference (760). If the steady and, in theory, exactly quantifiable progress of chronological time is not the most important metric for Montaigne, it is because he has another system of measurement available, both more immediate and, paradoxically, less knowable (*contra* Elaine Scarry's well-known claim, Montaigne's great pain gives him little certainty): the development of his kidney stones.[47]

The stones provide one answer to the question of what actually accrues in the *Essais*. Their acquisition is a direct result of time, and, as he puts it, a gift afforded him directly by the "liberalité" of the years themselves, the "commerce" and "longue conversation" of which have not passed "sans quelque tel fruit" (759). The fruit of his temporal commerce is not, Montaigne is at pains to make clear, the one he would have preferred. The stones themselves might come and go with infuriating

unpredictability, but Montaigne's fear of them goes back to his childhood ("dès mon enfance"), a continuous strain of anxiety imparted
from the child to the man (759). Montaigne is quick to let his readers
know, though, that over the course of the eighteen months of his afflic-
tion, he has managed to make it consubstantial with his writing project. Montaigne describes his "five or six" previous episodes with the
stone as essayistic affairs: "J'en ay desjà essayé," implicitly comparing
his *Essais*, as he does explicitly in the reference to his writing as mental "excremens" in "De la vanité," to metabolic byproducts. But these
experiences have not gone to waste, for there is in them "dequoy se
soustenir"; something about them has been sustaining, and even profitable, though this profit is described as coming out even, and coming out
even means coming to nothing: "J'ay aumoins ce profit de la cholique,
que ce que je n'avoy encore peu sur moy, pour me concilier du tout et
m'accointer à la mort, elle le parfera; car d'autant plus elle me pressera
et importunera, d'autant moins me sera la mort à craindre" (760) (I
have at least this profit from the stone, that it will complete what I have
still not been able to accomplish in myself and reconcile and familiarize
me completely with death: for the more my illness oppresses and both-
ers me, the less will death be something for me to fear [576]). This creative if not exactly smooth way of domesticating his own death is one
place where Montaigne, as he puts it, enters into composition with his
rocky condition, with "composition" as at once essayistic invention and
experiential equanimity: "J'entre des-jà en composition" (I am already
growing reconciled [575]) to this colicky life, he says, finding in it consolation and hope ("de quoy me consoler et dequoy esperer" [759]). Irritation is woven into the structure of his text, just as when he irritates
his humor he metabolically becomes one with irritation, exasperating
himself both into and out of being.

Later in the essay, Montaigne's domesticating process of composition leads him back, circuitously, to his title. Awestruck at how a single drop of sperm could contain a panoply of characteristics passed on
from father to son, Montaigne deflates his admiration for the miracle
of sexual reproduction in a B-text addition that emphasizes how erratic
this transmission of physical and mental qualities can be. The "impressions" passed through family lines follow "un progrez si temeraire et si
desreglé que l'arriere fils respondra à son bisayeul, le neveu à son oncle"
(763) (so heedless and irregular a course that the great-grandson will
correspond to his great-grandfather, the nephew to the uncle [578]),
discontinuous and avuncular lines as well as straight and paternal ones.
(In the following chapter on Andrew Marvell, who like Montaigne was

writing in the context of civil war, we will see a similar concern with the uncertainty of political and genealogical continuity spark a retreat to the domestic sphere and a suspension of productive ends—at least for a few years.) As an example of this heedless and irregular "progrez," Montaigne cites the recurrence of cartilage-covered eyes in one famous ancient family, where those cases, he clarifies in an aside, appeared not in successive generations but intermittently: "non de suitte, mais par intervalles" (763).

That sons are seldom carbon copies of their fathers would seem obvious, and was a common humanist topos: Petrarch famously insisted that humanist *imitatio* should strive for the slightly divergent similarity of son to father rather than the mechanically imitative replication a portrait makes of its sitter. Humanists following Petrarch generally embraced the fact that family resemblance necessarily involves difference, seeing in the accrual of difference a model of the progress of knowledge and culture: the Renaissance's improvement on the past went beyond mere reproduction. As Petrarch puts it, taking up his classical ancestors and doing them one better, "This is the substance of Seneca's counsel, and Horace's before him, that we should write as the bees make sweetness, not storing up the flowers but turning them into honey, thus making one thing of many various ones, but different and better."[48] For Montaigne, by contrast, making new material out of the old does not imply improvement. Progress, in his example, is both heedless and irregular and exactly, repetitively reproductive of a specific genetic trait.

David Simon's definition of Montaignean "progrez" as "simply a temporal trajectory or mutation," without any implications of teleology—a definition Simon associates as well with Marvell—is one way of understanding Montaigne's attitude toward the future as domestic georgic.[49] Rather than associating progress with the building of the modern nation-state, in the Baconian georgic sense, Montaigne understood it as the constant derailing and temporary correction of forward movement, as small-scale, as constant, and as provisional as domestic labor. This complication of the idea of progress as teleological can also be seen in Montaigne's superlative praise of Virgil's *Georgics*—that middle ground that Renaissance imitators so often leaped over on their way from pastoral to epic—as the most accomplished poetic work ("la plus accomply ouvrage de la Poësie"). The *Aeneid*, Montaigne complains, is diminished by the noticeable spots where the author could have combed things out a bit more ("donné encore quelque tour de pigne") had he had sufficient leisure (410).[50] Disregarding the hierarchy of the Virgilian literary career—if the *Aeneid* was understood to be unfinished, it was still generally thought to supersede the *Georgics*—Montaigne finds the pinnacle of style stuck precisely in the middle, while what is usually regarded as its height remains in need of additional adjustment.

Sidesteps, tangents, and disappointing repetition with only trivial differences define Montaigne's engagement with the past, whether textual, ancestral, or having to do with the very recent history of the latest incremental developments in the maintenance of his estate. Like the constant mollification of recurring irritation, history repeats itself without necessarily passing down any coherent lessons. When we learn, a bit belatedly, the provenance of "cette qualité pierreuse" in Pierre Eyquem, this is only a probability ("Il est à croire"), not a certainty (763). And it is not quite the "pierres" themselves that Montaigne has inherited from his father, but the potential—"qualité"—they qualify. The stubborn propensity to produce stones ad infinitum—if, that is, it could continue to be passed on—could outlast any stone monument that endures into the future, though its sometime products are both unpredictable and undesirable. Montaigne himself, who later in the chapter claims to have devoted himself to creating his life rather than his book, has infinitesimally self-monumentalized in a manner akin to that of his self-forming kidney stones. Having spent a lifetime building himself up but, frequently stalled by contradictions and aporia, not quite getting anywhere, Montaigne finds an equivalence between the body of medical knowledge—riddled with inconsistencies but still apparently holding strong—and his own opinion, which are both formed by examples and experience ("par exemples et experience" [764]). By this account, the microtradition of an individual life—which again, for Montaigne, does not progress forward so much as move in small lateral ways, like the "titubant, vertigineux, informe" movement of a drunkard—is as legitimate as tradition passed down cumulatively, with the illusion of knowledge accumulating over time, through generations. Citing the long, medicine-free lives of his father, grandfather, and great-grandfather, Montaigne deems these self-contained, local "exemples domestiques" sufficient. And yet, Montaigne avers, his "antipathie" for the medical art is "hereditaire" (764), or, as he reiterates later, "derivée en moy par mes ancestres" (785). His distrust for tradition has itself been passed down through generations, its origins superfluous to the bounds of the individual body, making his examples "domestiques" in a broader or deeper sense than he lets on.

Thus hereditary history structures Montaigne's understanding of how transmission works, but his conception of the family—as suggested by his opening the chapter on fathers and sons with a meditation on his literary creations—is expansive. At a later point in the essay,

Montaigne tells two stories. In the second, only loosely related to the first (both feature mutilated goats and medical cons), we move in a flashback to a pre–stone age, "avant ma subjection graveleuse," when Montaigne decides to follow the dubious health trend of raising a goat on a special diet and drinking its blood, which was purported to be a panacea for the "conservation de la vie humaine" (779). Upon the goat's slaughter, though, despite having fed and cared for it exactly according to the recipe ("selon la recepte"), Montaigne's cook finds three stones, evidence of some "qualité petrifiante" (780)—a forerunner of Montaigne's own "qualité pierreuse"—in its intestines. Montaigne orders the entrails to be brought into his presence so he can examine and interpret them. Of the three stones, one is perfectly round, and the others "un peu moindres, ausquels l'arrondissement imperfect, et semble qu'il s'y acheminat" (a little smaller, imperfect in roundness but seeming to be progressing toward it [593]), which he discovers, upon inquiry, is an anomaly: "un accident rare et inusité" (779). The goat's stones, unevenly progressing toward roundness, follow a development more akin to Montaigne's haphazardly collected pile of sticks than to the more clearly progressive development of other entities that we might expect to find gestating in a creature's midsection.

Positioning this anecdote in arbitrary juxtaposition to another story, and in a patently absurd but strongly suggestive relation to his own condition, Montaigne implies a causality between the goat's stones and his own while almost mocking us for believing such a relation to be worth considering. It is, he suggests, plausible that these stones are "cousins" to "ours"—"Il est vray-semblable que ce sont des pierres cousines des nostres" (779–80)—and that their relation to human kidney stones is thus lateral and indirect but still familial. This alternative line of transmission works by contingency, not necessity. More than that, the existence of the goat's stones in the first place was "un accident rare." Coming after Montaigne's reflections on the imperfect and irregular inheritance of familial traits, the insinuation that these stones are his own stones' "cousins" extends that logic of accidental kinship to outside the human family.

Nearing the end of the essay and feeling near the end of his life, Montaigne reiterates his conviction that progress is no more than "un mouvement d'yvroigne," or the more literal residue of wine: "Je suis sur le fond du vaisseau," he says, not exactly melancholically, "qui sent tantost le bas et la lye" (784) (I am at the bottom of the barrel, which begins to taste of the lees [784]). The lees, a form of waste necessary for preservation (and that Galen compares to the form black bile takes in a healthy, functioning body), are the defining feature of Montaigne's

environment. The idea that a certain amount of waste would be necessary to preserve healthy material calls back to earlier in the essay, when
Montaigne, in the midst of assaying the medical community's infinite
contradictions, provisionally reduces the entirety of medical knowledge and practice to the sole end of voiding the bowels (which, he
adds, could easily be accomplished by any number of home remedies,
or "simples domestiques") but then inserts a B-text emendation: "Et si
ne scay si c'est si utillement qu'ils disent, et si nostre nature n'a point
besoing de la residence de ses excremens jusques à certaine mesure,
comme le vin a de sa lie pour sa conservation" (767) (And yet I do not
know whether this is as useful as they say, and whether our constitution
does not, to a certain extent, need the presence of excrements, just as
wine needs its lees for its preservation [581]), the uncomfortable necessity of containing our own waste itself neatly contained in a distancing
formula of uncertainty.

Emerging from these cloudy vinicultural depths near the end of the
chapter, Montaigne suggests that these preservative lees are indeed effi-
cacious. As he embarks on a long, isolated aside to Madame de Duras,[51]
expressing his hope that Madame will remember the qualities of his
that she has so graciously overestimated, Montaigne describes his *Essais* as, ideally, providing a secure container for those qualities:

> Je les veux loger (mais sans alteration et changement) en un corps
> solide qui puisse durer quelques années ou quelques jours après
> moy, où vous les retrouverez quand il vous plaira vous en refreschir
> la memoire, sans prendre autrement la peine de vous en souvenir;
> aussi ne le valent elles pas. (783)

> (I want to lodge them [but without alteration or change] in a solid
> body that may last a few years, or a few days, after me, in which you
> will find them when you are pleased to refresh your memory of
> them. [595])

Montaigne makes no explicit mention of waste in this outline of a preservation plan, but his suspension of superfluous possibilities in textual
asides performs a similar function. Having carefully packaged his virtues in the "corps solide" of the present book, to stave off (he clarifies
parenthetically) any "alteration et changement," he appends a strange
subordinate clause that effectively limits the duration of that container
to "quelques années ou quelques jours" after his death. To circumscribe
his legacy to "a few years"—which could simply be an understatement

for "many years"—would be strange enough, but to correct that to "a few days" is even stranger, as if years and days were interchangeable, or to abruptly disallow the reader's natural inclination to interpret "a few years" as perhaps a few hundred years. Madame, he continues, should limit herself to remembering his qualities only when it pleases her, and no more often than that: "aussi ne le valent elles pas."

This performed indifference to the difference between the products of labor—which last, at best, a few days—and the products of work, which endure significantly (at least for a few years) into the future, appears more explicitly in Montaigne's further claim that he does not intend his *Essais* as any kind of stockpile or hoard for his heirs: he is writing "non pour en faire magasin et reserve à mes heritiers" (784). He does, however, acknowledge that "faire magasin et reserve" is an important measure to take on his own behalf, though his reserve is as much of abstract possibility as of books and quotations. Jean Starobinski emphasizes that the goal of Montaigne's so-called retirement to his estate was not to avoid his public responsibilities but rather "to have secured the *possibility* of occupying his own private territory," and of "withdrawing at any moment into absolute solitude":[52] of reserving, in other words, an "arriereboutique" (241) preserved from—but, as a "back shop," physically contiguous to—the commercial concerns of the public realm. If, as Montaigne claims near the end of "De la ressemblance," home economics ("oeconomie de sa maison") is a more meaningful activity for a man to embark on than quests for literary glory (784), the only estate management he himself regards as anything other than irritating inconveniences is that of books and papers. Having carefully edited the works of La Boétie, a man he considered his brother, and taken pains to preserve and disseminate all he could of his friend's life and work after his untimely death—not to mention his absorption of La Boétie's library into his own—he entrusted his own literary estate to Marie de Gournay, his quasi-adopted *fille d'alliance,* sometime secretary, and posthumous editor.[53]

The annoying labors of "mesnage" or "oeconomie"—the careful arrangement and managed transmission of what the domestic sphere contains—preoccupy Montaigne far more than either the grand fantasy of progress or improvement over generations or the enjoyment of life in the present moment. The very triviality of domestic economy—the set of tasks he describes in "De la vanité" as "plus empeschante que difficile," the "vaines pointures" that are, despite what appears at first to be a mollifying qualifier, "tousjours pointures"—is what accounts for its persistence. Those little pinpricks are by no means lessened by the later tempering addition of "par fois," which, even in obliquely suggesting that the pricks are sometimes more than "vaines," still does nothing either to give them any gravity or to make them go away.

The mere reproduction of the same, no matter how trivial, requires a work of maintenance and, in its transmission, a domesticating transformation. As Montaigne explains near the end of "De la ressemblance," summing up his polemic against medicine:

> J'ay pris la peine de plaider cette cause, que j'entens assez mal, pour appuyer un peu et conforter la propension naturelle contre les drogues et pratique de nostre medecine, qui s'est derivée en moy par mes ancestres, afin que ce ne fust pas seulement une inclination stupide et temeraire, et qu'elle eust un peu plus de forme. (785)

> (I have taken the trouble to plead this cause, which I understand rather poorly, to support a little and strengthen the natural aversion to medicine which I have derived from my ancestors, so that it should not be merely a stupid and thoughtless inclination and should have a little more form. [597])

Montaigne understands his task as not simply defending what is "derivée" from his ancestors, but actively maintaining it: supporting and reinforcing it in order to give it form. The distaste for blindly following tradition may be inherited, but to inherit this distaste automatically would be a contradiction in terms.

Citing Montaigne's complaint that commentators have run amok, so that there are more books about books than about any other subject, Starobinski still believes that the *Essais* were meant to inspire a form of reproduction: "Montaigne hoped to find an *adequate* reader, one who could imagine the *infinite essays* for which his book might serve as a pretext."[54] I would temper Starobinski's enthusiasm by suggesting that if Montaigne hoped for a reader who would have the capacity to preserve his *Essais* by using them to infinite transformative ends, the ends he imagined are as minor as his own: the conversion of material at one's disposal from "une inclination stupide et temeraire" into something with "un peu plus de forme."

# CHAPTER 4

# Marvell in the Meantime

PRESERVING PATRIARCHY IN
*UPON APPLETON HOUSE*

*Meantime, whilst every verdant thing*
*Itself does at thy beauty charm,*
*Reform the errors of the spring.*

ANDREW MARVELL, "The Picture of
Little T. C. in a Prospect of Flowers"

*Meantime ye fields, springs, bushes, flowers,*
*Where yet she leads her studious hours,*
*(Till Fate her worthily translates,*
*And find a Fairfax for our Thwaites)*
*Employ the means you have by her.*

ANDREW MARVELL, *Upon Appleton House*

*When you perceive your Apples clear, and Syrup thick, then take them*
*up, and set them into a warm Oven from the Syrup, all night, the next*
*morning turn them, and put them in again, so do till they are dry; if you*
*please to glister some of them, put them into your Candy-Pot but one*
*night, and lay them to dry the next day, and they will look like Christal.*

HANNAH WOOLLEY, *The queen-like closet*

In Marvell's "The Picture of Little T. C. in a Prospect of Flowers," an
adult speaker observes a young girl with an attention so rapt as to inspire critics to level charges of pedophilia.[1] At the same time, this
nymph enjoying a rural retreat might play a role far exceeding both the
garden's prospect and the speaker's erotic imagination. She is, as John
Rogers puts it, "a potential agent of an unknown revolution": "Who can
foretell for what high cause / This Darling of the gods was born!"[2] That

Marvell's speaker would express such excitement at the uncertainty of little T. C.'s future, such wonder at "what high cause" she may be destined for, is especially surprising given how much the poem seems to be a straightforward prehistory of the child's eventual, inevitable marriage. If the predicted details of her courtship take on a violent, militaristic tone, with "conq'ring eyes" (18) that "wound" (19) suitors and "glancing wheels" that "drive / In triumph over hearts that strive" (20–21), this bluster is destined to settle eventually. The conjuring of these "glories" is preceded by the confident prophecy of one who will make them irrelevant: "Happy, who can / Appease this virtuous enemy of man!" (15–16).

The arrival of this happy husband is, however, indefinitely forestalled. The poem takes place in the "meantime" (25), in what might seem to be a lingering pastoral prelude before the outbreak of battle, "whilst every verdant thing / Itself does at thy beauty charm" (25–26), the reflexive "itself" after the enjambment stalling forward motion by referring back to the last line. This interjection of a "meantime" also recalls Virgil's famous *recusatio* at the beginning of his third georgic, where he announces the magnificent temple he will erect in Augustus's honor and spends forty lines detailing its features only to interrupt himself and suddenly downshift to the humbler theme he will arduously take on in the meantime ("interea"): cattle farming. The praise of Caesar and the poet's own glory will come soon ("mox"), but not yet.[3] T. C., like the georgic poet, is given a task to keep her occupied until her official business begins. She is set to work, though not to perform any traditionally muscular or straightforwardly productive georgic feats. She is not asked to plow, plant, or harvest in an open field but simply to make some temporary adjustments, like those that would have been applied in any middling or aristocratic garden or kitchen.

Indeed, the instructions to little T. C. read like a domestic georgic primer on how to "reform the errors of the spring." Step one: sweeten the tulips ("Make that the tulips may have share / Of sweetness," 28–29); step two: remove thorns from the roses ("And roses of their thorns disarm," 30); step three: extend the lifespan of the violets ("But most procure / That violets may a longer age endure," 31–32). If this last directive might sound like a fantasy of Edenic recovery, or even, according to Joseph Summers, an "impossible" task, the extension of botanical life is the advertised and to an extent attainable result of numerous techniques found in gardening guides and recipe books.[4] Hugh Plat's *Garden of Eden*, subtitled *An accurate description of all flowers and fruits now growing in England*, takes as its premise that the unerring spring of paradise can be, and is already, reproduced in a home garden. Plat's readers learn how "to have Carnations all the winter"; how to make roses bloom early, late, or twice; how to "preserve the life of a Carnation or Gilliflower . . . that is almost dead and withered"; and how to prevent flowers from surrendering to what may seem the inevitable effects of frost.[5] Granted a second life in the soil, a flower may cheat death yet again through the innovations of the kitchen. As attested by recipe books marketed to housewives, the violets whose longevity Summers so doubts could be preserved in myriad ways—as conserves, as oil, as syrup, in cakes, distilled, candied—to last at least a year, at which point a new crop could replace them, effectively erasing seasonal dearth. "To procure that violets may a longer age endure" was not considered an impossibility. It was a recipe: "Set the Violets in sallet Oyl, and strain them, then put in other fresh Violets, and let them lye twenty days, then strain them again, and put in other fresh Violets, and let them stand all the year."[6]

Gesturing toward an indeterminate, medium-term future of the "meantime," Marvell's poetry takes up the provisional ethos of domestic georgic: the constant, microfocused labor of tempering the furnishings and provisions of the world in order to keep them. This moderation or organization of nature, like Montaigne's attempted management of his "espines domestiques," can be on a scale so small as to approach irrelevance, especially given the charged political context of civil war.[7] Indeed, Marvell's preoccupation with young girls in, or as, flowers— also seen in "Young Love," "The Nymph Complaining for the Death of Her Fawn," "The Garden," and *Upon Appleton House*, which will be my focus here—has been understood as a refusal to engage with that context, "a retreat" to a world "that is private, enclosed, retired, safe from the public world of war and politics and the state."[8] But this green world is bounded temporally as well as spatially. The "meantime" of the garden state is temporary—the "longer age" that any given violet may endure is still not forever—and in need of constant maintenance or "reform," like the oil of violets that, in Hannah Woolley's recipe above, requires steeping violets, straining them, adding more violets, waiting twenty days, straining again, adding still more violets, and only then "let[ting] them stand all the year."

Sweetening, dethorning, and putting flowers on life support belong in the category of domestic georgic because these activities may not be the public affairs of the state, but they are also not a complete withdrawal from either work or the "hopes" (40) of the community, and in this the green scenes of Marvell's female-populated gardens are much like the early modern English households that were overseen by housewives. Both of these kinds of spaces—holding areas for public action

and poetic production, where the materials for biological and intellectual life are maintained in suspension—are governed by the domestic
georgic labor of adjusting, tempering, organizing, and preserving, always to only provisional ends. Rather than locating Marvell in the dramatic end times imagined by Margarita Stocker, who has argued that
"the whole range of his works should be seen as a coherent and inte-
grated expression of his apocalyptic preoccupations," I find him in the
"meantime," stuck in a state of suspended poetic and political futures.[9]

As we have seen, early modern housewives were charged with preserving both perishable organic material and, in an oft-cited concentric-
ity, the health of its eaters. People consumed preserves to help preserve
themselves and, by extension, larger cultural narratives in which the
woman-run household played an increasingly central part. Housekeeping was about "keeping" in a very broad sense that covered, in Wendy
Wall's survey of the word's semantic range, being "productive, chaste,
organized, silent, insulated, modest, and gifted at recycling, classify-
ing, and preserving."[10] The invisible female power to "keep" domestic
spaces and the materials within them—to maintain both the inventory
and the reputation of an estate, to make sure preserves are prepared so
as "to keep all the year," to manage servants, or even to run the household in the husband's absence—was understood as both practical and
aesthetic, even sublime. For Dod and Cleaver, the duty of the wife was
"to ouersee and giue order for all things within the house"; Woolley
claimed that "there is nothing more beautiful than an Houshold well
and peacably governed," which involves "an especial care that the goods
in the house be not spoiled by negligence."[11] When the estate manager
in Xenophon's *Oeconomicus*, the ancient inspiration for many early
modern domestic manuals first translated into English in 1532, exclaims
to his young wife in an effort to motivate her housewifely inclinations
"howe goodly a thinge it is" to witness clothes, linens, and kitchen
utensils arranged in "good order" and neatly separated from each other,
he conjures a perfectly disposed home as the pinnacle of life: "There is
nothynge, good swete wife, so profitable and so goodlye amonge men,
as is an order in euery thynge."[12]

This delight in the order orchestrated by the housewife, which we
have seen in Guyon and Arthur's open-mouthed admiration of Alma's
kitchen in Spenser's *Faerie Queene*, is also the organizing principle of
the most well-known country house poems of the seventeenth century. These poems, celebrating the ready fertility, hospitality, charity,
and beauty of an estate, did not usually center on the lady of the house,
but even passing acknowledgments of her role reveal that her virtue is
a necessary supplement to those of the estate. Aemilia Lanyer laments

that, for lack of Margaret Clifford's ordering presence at Cookeham, "The house cast off each garment that might grace it, / Putting on Dust and Cobwebs to deface it." In "To Penshurst," Ben Jonson attributes to Lady Barbara Sidney a household management style bordering on telekenesis, with her "high huswifery" allowing for her guests to "have her linnen, plate, and all things nigh, / When shee was farr," and closes the poem with a summation that requires an immediate appendix: "These, Penshurst, are thy praise, and yet not all. / Thy lady's noble, fruitfull, chaste withall."[13] Marvell's take on the genre in *Upon Appleton House* closes with a prolonged encomium not to the house's current mistress, whose failure to stay physically and figuratively in her wifely place had become a domestic and political problem for her husband, but rather to her barely marriageable daughter, a potential housewife whose role is analogous to the domestic georgic poet himself.[14] Both the poet and the housewife-to-be task themselves with a work of creation indistinguishable from the labor of preservation—or, at times, from leisure. Their power is not in their fail-proof fecundity but in their ability to keep things temporarily separated and organized—preserving that aesthetic middle space (*to meson*) that Xenophon's Ischomachus so admires between well-arranged household objects—and to do so in a temporal middle, in between immediate effectiveness and certainty about future results.[15] The vague hope, but not guarantee, of productive future use is maintained by keeping, or putting, things up.

Marvell's attachment to the meantime, his resistance to—or suspension of—predictable outcomes, in some ways would seem rather to challenge the heteronormative ideology that housewifery upholds, as would tendencies found elsewhere in his poetry and biography. Although a preoccupation with girls' future marriages to men, even when those marriages are indefinitely suspended, might be disqualifying for queer theorists whose motto is, as Valerie Traub puts it, "'just say no' to futurity" of any kind, the attractions for queer theory of Marvell—lifelong bachelor, gleeful transgressor of generic boundaries, romancer of plants—are many.[16] His polymorphously perverse interests in trees, solitude, and poetry itself could be called "queer" insofar as they demonstrate a reluctance to circulate sexual and economic assets through socially acceptable channels. Derek Hirst and Steven Zwicker claim that Marvell's famous reference to "vegetable love," like many other "all-but-neutered reproductive dreams" in his poetry, "is to confront, to challenge, the entire frame of heterosexuality"; a "subversion of patriarchy" extends across his oeuvre.[17] Insofar as "queer" could describe a refusal to yield to traditional literary and historical understandings, even to understandings of queerness itself, Marvell's indefinite and vaguely antiheterosexual ideas and lifestyle would seem to comport with queer early modern approaches like Jonathan Goldberg and Madhavi Menon's queer "unhistoricism," or with Carla Freccero's open-ended invitation to allow the word "queer" to continue "to exploit its productive indeterminacy as a word used to designate that which is odd, strange, aslant" and to resist the word's "hypostatization, reification into nominal status as designating an entity, an identity, a thing, and to allow it to continue its outlaw work."[18] That Marvell is participating in such "outlaw work" has been indirectly suggested in less explicitly queer framings. Andrew McRae is typical in pronouncing the man "elusive"; Rosalie Colie refers to him as "this poet-without-persona, or this poet-with-too-many-personas"; and Nigel Smith uses the subtitle of his biography, *Andrew Marvell: The Chameleon*, to put Marvell's undecidability in no uncertain terms.[19] Attitudes like these may help produce the inclination to associate Marvell with "queerness" in as imprecise a sense as possible, where imprecision on the part of critic and poet alike is often lauded as a virtue.[20]

The pleasure with which we locate queerness in early modern literature, however, can obscure how content or form that is "odd, strange," or "aslant" often helps reproduce the very normative structures it ostensibly undermines, "outlaw work" that only further entrenches the law. Marvell's ardent attention to the sexual possibilities of plants in "The Garden," for example, has been celebrated as offering alternatives to heteronormative structures of desire. Writing of that poem's solitary speaker, who luxuriates in flowers and melons and prefers a life "without a mate," Marjorie Swann has claimed that Marvell's erotic tree hugging can be understood as a version of Timothy Morton's concept of "queer ecology," because, as she quotes Morton, "to contemplate ecology's unfathomable intimacies is to imagine pleasures that are not heteronormative, not genital, not geared to ideologies about where the body stops and starts."[21] And yet, as this chapter will show, pleasures and practices can be polymorphous, "not genital," and not explicitly heteronormative themselves and still work, as they do in Marvell's poetry, in the service of heteronormative ideology. The very traits we may be tempted to identify with subversion, up to and including forays with flora, can also be understood as preservative, even conservative.

*Upon Appleton House* is perhaps the poem that most seductively puts forward the invitation to read a liberating queerness into Marvell's poetry, earning such blurbs as "unsettling" and "bafflingly private," "one of the most eclectic poems of the seventeenth century," a work of "dazzling subversion," "slipperiness," and "scandal."[22] The poem's indeterminate modes and resistance to linear temporality can easily be read as

subversive of poetic convention, aristocratic values, and general heterosexuality. Paying lip service to but straying alarmingly from the county
house poem formula of civic-minded aristocratic patriarch, chaste and
organized wife, magnificent (but tasteful) estate in perfect harmony
with nature, and assured looks backward to forefathers and forward to
heirs, *Upon Appleton House*'s main attractions include sybaritic nuns,
pastoral self-pleasuring, and the complication of dynastic lines.[23] But
the network of normative ideologies behind the country house genre's
conservative, deeply heteronormative conventions thrives on just such
safe "subversion" of chronology and genealogy. The poem dramatizes,
particularly through figures of aristocratic housewives and their analogs, how heterosexuality—in order to fill in its own gaps, gloss over its
own contradictions, and maintain its position of natural inevitability—
relies on that which seems to subvert it. This "paradoxical life support
system," as Lee Edelman describes queerness's relation to heterosexuality in another context, diverges from the New Historicist concept
of "subversion and containment," summarized by Louis Montrose as
the "capacity of the dominant order to generate subversion so as to use
it to its own ends."[24] The dominant order in Marvell's case was, after
all, in utter upheaval and did not have a clear enough view of its own
"ends" to generate anything that could be guaranteed to last longer
than a year's supply of oil of violets. The continuous, minor subversion Marvell generates in *Upon Appleton House* is less a rejection or
confirmation of teleology than a suspension of it, preserving the tools
of heterosexual ideology—as housewives preserved fruit, flowers, and
household order—for possible later, or indirect, use. Like Virgil with
his *recusatio* in *Georgics* 3, Marvell's valorization of the domestic practice of medium-term preservation situates his poem squarely "interea,"
in the meantime.

Understanding *Upon Appleton House* through a lens of teleological
suspension offers an alternative way of explaining Marvell's "queerness"
or ideological illegibility. By celebrating the kind of activity that appears at odds with futurity but that contributes to reproducing dominant social and cultural values, the poem demonstrates how freezing
forward movement can be crucial in keeping progress-oriented sexual
and economic ideologies going, even or especially when, as in the case
of Marvell's patron Thomas Lord Fairfax, who lacked a male heir, those
ideologies are facing real-world complications. The cloistered stanzas of
Marvell's epyllion stage as domestic drama the struggle between what
R. Howard Bloch calls "the genealogical discourse of the epic" and "the
lyric disruption" that threatens it.[25] The upshot of this struggle in *Upon
Appleton House* is that lyric disruption can *yield* epic continuity; even

"queer" interventions can serve the continuation of genealogical discourse.[26] More than simply exploring the tension between what David Quint usefully calls, in a variation on Bloch's formulation, the "linear teleology" of epic and the "random or circular wandering" of romance—the end-oriented narrative of history's victors on the one hand and the dilatory, interior exploration of losers on the other—Marvell suggests that the latter can provide the tools to effect the former.[27]

Thus the domestic georgic mode, where preservative labor could work to protect possibilities for futures that are different from the present, here appears as a more straightforward agent of conservatism. To acknowledge how Marvell works to (temporarily) keep gender- and class-based constraints in place might, as Stephen Best and Sharon Marcus anticipate of critiques of "surface reading," "be dismissed as politically quietist, too willing to accept things as they are," a silencing of queer potential or a reactionary resignation to the inevitability of heteronormativity.[28] But "things as they are," for Marvell as for the "nymphs" on which he fixates, are far less certain than our hindsight can lead us to believe. The constant precariousness that characterizes domestic georgic infuses both the most basic and the most grandiose of Marvell's visions of personal and political futures. "Who can foretell," as Marvell asks of little T. C., whether the expectations of heterosexual life—that virgins will marry, that houses will be kept, that lineages will be maintained—will really come to pass in the ways some authors or readers hope for, and others dread?

## Conserves at the Convent

The genealogical narrative of *Upon Appleton House* begins with an abbey acquired by the Fairfax family shortly after the dissolution of the monasteries a century before, giving the current Fairfax estate of Nun Appleton its name. An early invitation to read something like queerness in the poem comes with Marvell's imaginative conception of aristocratic lineage as something other than biological reproduction, with the Fairfax house as the legitimate if miraculous child of the now-ruined abbey: "A nunnery first gave it birth / (For virgin buildings oft brought forth)."[29] This revelation of the parthenogenetic abbey's intimate role in the family's history, even with its jocular parenthetical pseudoexplanation, does nothing to soften the poem's suspicion of the place as a den of luxury, idolatry, and lesbianism, a manifold threat to the continuation of aristocratic bloodlines and to what Edelman calls "reproductive futurism" more generally.[30]

And these nuns, even more than most nuns, are the avowed enemies of reproductive futurism: we learn they are trying to confine a young, rich, perfectly marriageable girl to a life of cloistered jouissance among women. "The blooming virgin [Isabel] Thwaites" (90), young girl in flower and future wife of Marvell's patron's ancestor William Fairfax, is a ward of the abbess, and the nuns are waging a campaign to keep her in their custody and off the marriage market. When the nuns' spokeswoman launches her lengthy recruiting pitch, giving Isabel a taste of life in the abbey, one perk in particular would seem to confirm the worst fears of a hopeful husband like William: every night Isabel will get a new "virgin bride" to sleep with her, lying "As pearls together billeted. / All night embracing arm in arm, / Like crystal pure with cotton warm" (186, 190–92). After going through a sample daily schedule of candle trimming, needlepoint, prayer, fruit candying, weeping, and air freshening—rituals and chores that are, the nun clarifies, just as pleasurable as they are pious—the nun concludes her speech by inviting Isabel to join the sorority on a trial basis, and Isabel seems to be seduced: "The nun's smooth tongue has sucked her in" (200). The abbey's self-indulgent, homoerotic way of life would tempt Isabel away from her feminine duty of reproducing an aristocratic family line.

But billeting with virgin brides aside, most of what the nun describes as the literal or figurative activities of the nuns are identical to those of the ideal aristocratic housewife that Isabel will eventually become: embroidery, perfumery, candying, and the preparation of skincare treatments and medicinal balms. Despite the Protestant superstition that monastic lands were cursed by God with decay, infertility, and a lack of productivity, these nuns' packed schedules make them sound quite industrious, for all the appearance of idleness.[31] Marvell prefaces the nun's speech by saying she "weaved, / (As 'twere by chance) thoughts long conceived" (95–96), where careful craft is dissimulated as aimless "chance" chatter, and "long conceived" conceits are passed off as extemporaneous emissions. The nuns' breath produces perfume, and their tears are a renewable source of a facial serum that rivals the homemade "beauty water" that Woolley claims can "clear the face and skin":[32]

Our orient breaths perfumèd are
With incense of incessant prayer.
And holy-water of our tears
Most strangely our complexion clears. (109–12)

Leisure blurs with industry, as if in a rendition of the title of John Murrell's popular recipe collection *A delightfull daily exercise for ladies and gentlewomen*, with the "delightfull" part tempering the "exercise":[33]

Nor is our order yet so nice,
Delight to banish as a vice.
Here pleasure piety doth meet;
One perfecting the other sweet.
So through the mortal fruit we boil
The sugar's uncorrupting oil:
And that which perished while we pull,
Is thus preserved clear and full. (169–76)

In all the activities of the nuns' "order," pleasure sweetly "perfect[s]" piety rather than posing a threat to it, just as during one of those activities, in the convent kitchen, fruit is preserved with sugar. With the "mortal fruit" suggesting not only the natural process of decay but also the fatal forbidden fruit itself, Eve's apple is confected into a sinful dessert. This procedure, after all, promises not only to preserve organic matter, but actually, unnaturally, to bring the "perished" fruit back to life, its corruption reversed by "uncorrupting" sugar. And yet this is not so different from the resurrective power claimed of Woolley's "water of life," a housewife's secret weapon to preserve that which has perished: "If you have any Wine that is turned," Woolley advises, "put in a little Viol or Glass full of it, and keep it close stopped, and within four days it will come to it self again."[34]

Preservative culinary labor might seem too boring to be damning. Noting the recipe-like instructions in Shakespeare's procreation sonnets, Richard Halpern quips that these poems' heavy family-planning emphasis "makes sex seem as exciting as putting up preserves."[35] The presumed unsexiness of putting up preserves in early modern kitchens has been convincingly contested by Wendy Wall, and recipe books played up the entertainment value of certain confections, but preserving's primary focus was generally function rather than fun.[36] While sugar could be synecdochal for the profligate expenditure of aristocratic banquets, using sugar to preserve food was a foundational practice of parsimonious housewives and central to a lived philosophy of frugality.[37] Both of these uses of sugar are suggested by the lavish preparation of whole fruit, which requires, in one recipe, "the best double refined sugar" and fruits that are pitted "curiously," drawing attention to the necessary expenditure of both money and care. The result of following this recipe "To preserve Abricots whole in syrup to keep all the year" is a beautiful delicacy that also performs the basic function of preservation: to keep decay at bay.[38]

Even the same-sex sleepover the nun alludes to is strangely tinted with productivity, conjuring up a commercial economy of luxury goods: "As pearls together billeted. / All night embracing arm in arm, / Like crystal pure with cotton warm" (190–92), with minerals and textiles replacing the bodies of the young women. The nunnery is a household that seems to consist of commodities, not bodies, or bodies that somehow spontaneously produce commodities like perfume or facial toner. For all the insistence on the cloister's exemption from commerce with men, literal and figurative commodities circulate freely in the nun's language. Labor here is visible, shamelessly advertised rather than obliquely lyricized, and it gestures to possibilities outside of home use. Thus it chafes against the idea of domestic space that, as Natasha Korda argues, had begun to be strategically preserved, at least in the rhetoric of prescriptive domestic literature, from the world outside: the beginning of an ideological separation of gendered spheres of labor in the late sixteenth century was meant to guard against the threat of "the market's infiltration of the household through the commodity."[39] Despite their apparently sequestered status, these nuns, like other enterprising medieval and early modern nuns, seem to be running a veritable convent industry.[40] They are trying to sell Isabel on a life not of sinful loafing but of productive labor—or rather labor that, with its pleasurable pursuit of possible profit, blurs the line between labor and leisure.

Performing the same tasks as those assigned to aristocratic women and their maidservants to keep a great house running, but without any male governance at all and without a clear sense that the products of their labor will remain within the abbey walls, the nuns highlight the ambiguous status of aristocratic women's labor as at once productive and unproductive, focused on the "keeping" of a house and the production of goods made to be consumed in either the short or medium term. The nun's catalog of tasks like perfuming cloths with ambergris, concocting medicinal balms, and molding pastes of sugar and marzipan—

Flowers dress the altars; for the clothes,
The sea-born amber we compose;
Balms for the grieved we draw; and pastes
We mould, as baits for curious tastes (179–82)

—reads like a recipe book's table of contents: entries in William Salmon's *Family dictionary, or, Houshold companion*, a compendium of "choice physical receipts for the preservation of health" that also explains "the mystery of pickling and keeping of all sorts of pickles," include *Ambergrease*, the Tincture" ("one drop of it is an excellent Perfume"); balms like marigold water, "very available and beneficial to the Party grieved"; and a mixture of rosewater and aromatics that resolves

into "a curious perfumed Past."[41] The nuns also move smoothly between the material and immaterial reproduction of needlepoints and
of saintly living, or as the domesticity guru Gervase Markham would
put it, of outward and inward "vertues," stitching saintliness into both
fabric and everyday life: "But what the linen can't receive / They in their
lives do interweave" (125–26). Lena Orlin argues that calling the manu-
factured "busy-ness of fancy stitchery" by the name of "needlework"
(or simply "work") was a "cultural myth" intended to make high-status
women feel that they were doing productive work and thus keep them
in their place. Embroidery that was valued as a product, not a time- and
soul-killing process, was generally done by professional men.[42] Here,
though, it is the women's product that is highly valued. As the nun flat-
ters Isabel that her face, as beautiful as the Virgin Mary's, would make
a perfect model for future needlepoints, she forecasts a sharp uptick in
the nuns' production, yielding more than the abbey could reasonably
use to decorate its own altars:

> Some of your features, as we sewed,
> Through every shrine should be bestowed.
> And in one beauty we would take
> Enough a thousand saints to make. (133–36)

Hirst and Zwicker find in such mimetic embroidery "a veritable reproductive technology, other ways of sowing, multiplying, disseminating"
than biological reproduction, an assertion of "female autonomy" that
"question[s] and counterpoint[s] masculine prerogative."[43] But the
threat here is less the power of art to immortalize than the earnings potential of a thousand beautiful altar hangings, only the latter of which
is actually incompatible with an ideology of domesticity that cleanly
divides male "getting" of resources from female "keeping." These nuns
present themselves as spinsters in both senses of the word: unmarried
women who both occupy themselves and potentially support themselves with textile work.[44]

What is so insidious, then, about the living arrangements of these
nuns and their bid to thwart Isabel's prospects of aristocratic housewifery is not only their seductive stance against reproduction but also the
asexual productivity that both echoes and exceeds the nominal productivity of aristocratic women, whose labor of perfuming and confecting
was often immaterial or ephemeral—like elaborate sugar works created
for the express purpose of being shattered at the end of a banquet—and
whose needlework was only called "work" as a euphemism.[45] What's
more, the nuns perform all their tricks of beautifying and preserving of

nature without male supervision.[46] As the nun asks rhetorically, after explaining the procedures for fruit candying, floral arrangement, perfuming, and confectionery, the production and perhaps sale of which the nuns oversee quite well on their own, "What need is here of man" (183)? The nuns' unhusbanded housewifery thus does not participate in the narrative of genealogical continuity that Isabel, by leaving the nunnery and marrying William, will soon buy into. The cloister keeps out *all* men, and not, as housewives were repeatedly and anxiously reminded in domestic manuals, all men except the master of the house:

> These bars inclose that wider den
> Of those wild creatures, callèd men.
> The cloister outward shuts its gates,
> And, from us, locks on them the grates. (101–4)

The nun articulates the idea of what the poem's speaker will later call, with reference to Thomas Fairfax's household, a "domestic heaven" (722) as a fortified refuge from chaotic forces without, the kind of home idealized by the jurist (and great-grandfather of "little T. C.") Edward Coke in 1605, sanctifying into law a sentiment that had long been proverbial: "The house of every one is to him his castle and fortress, as well for defense against injury and violence, as for his repose."[47] Except, of course, this fortress has been put up for the defense of women against the injury and violence caused by the very man, William Fairfax, who lays claim to it as his castle. The fact that many of the nuns' activities would be entirely ordinary if practiced by the mistress of an aristocratic household hits home how aristocratic womanhood could be so contingent and yet so persistent, and how desperately aristocratic men—as evidenced by the violence with which William attacks and destroys the nunnery and its "hypocrite witches" (205)—hoped to sustain the fiction that "high huswifery" depended on heterosexuality.

## Preservation Restored

The abbey's preservative labor, then, is too at odds with the ideology of aristocratic domesticity to be absorbed by it. It is, however, translated. If *Upon Appleton House* spends what seems an inordinate amount of time on the question of the virgin Thwaites's fate, any anxiety over her assimilation into ascendant Protestant family values is assuaged when William Fairfax extricates Isabel, the happy couple goes on its procreative way, and the ambiguously profitable, morally questionable preservation of mortal fruit gives way to the domestically oriented, morally sanctioned preservation of the Fairfax patriarchy. Isabel Fairfax claims her role as housewife as the domestic realm, appropriated from the nuns, is refashioned into a new and improved "cloister": "For if the virgin proved not their's, / The cloister yet remainèd her's" (278–79). Along with Isabel, the poem introduces a new cloistered entity: the poet-speaker himself, who recedes into his own mind as he wanders the estate's gardens, hallucinates a pastoral reenactment of the Civil War, and then retires to the woods in a way reminiscent of the current Lord Fairfax's recent, possibly ignoble retirement from public life.

Unlike the productive nuns, the speaker in these middle sections of *Upon Appleton House* seems defined by his idle errancy. The long middle section of the poem would seem to offer, even more than the extended dallying in the abbey, evidence for an "odd, strange, aslant" Marvell, a renegade, self-sabotaging poet doing what Freccero calls the "outlaw work" of queerness. But as the speaker retires to his "sanctuary in the wood" (482), he retains an interest in the structuring principles and practices of the domestic cloister: echoes of household activities are all around him. If his world descends into disorder, it also sets itself up, by maintaining the appropriate instruments, to be more perfectly reordered when the time comes. Diane Purkiss contrasts the speaker-poet's "pastoral" and "natural" reveries with the dreamy scenes evoked by the nun, which "are the result of and metaphorized through craft and artisanal labour," but the "pastoral" and the "natural" are always, and here in quite explicit ways, constructed by and described in terms of labor and domestic craft, much as the nun stitches literal and metaphorical labor together even while selling self-indulgence.[48]

No sooner has the poet entered the "abyss" (369) in the meadows than he encounters a scene of culinary labor. After a worker in the field mistakenly mows down a young bird hidden in the grass, the mood shifts from elegiac to practical as Thestylis, the camp cook reprising her role from Virgil's *Eclogues*, decides to make the best of the situation by preparing the rail for lunch:

> But bloody Thestylis, that waits
> To bring the mowing camp their cates,
> Greedy as kites has trussed it up,
> And forthwith means on it to sup:
> When on another quick she lights,
> And cries, "He called us Israelites;
> But now, to make his saying true,
> Rails rain for quails, for manna, dew." (401–8)

Supplying the mowers with their provisions ("cates"), she labors to sustain the labors of others. Available for the male mowers when they need her, Thestylis "waits" both in the sense of deferring action and in the sense of serving as an attendant at table. Her trussing of the rail begins the compost-like work that converts death into life. "Bloody" as she may be, her "quick" work is economical rather than excessive— mirrored in the economy of the poet's "on another quick she lights," where "quick" could describe both Thestylis's pace and the second bird's status as alive, which will quickly become obsolete as its life is subsumed into the ongoing project of sustaining the mowers' lives. Thestylis's dramatic breaking of the poem's frame—"He called us Isra-elites," she objects, somehow aware of the poet's comparison from two stanzas earlier—is also an evacuation of drama; the fulfillment of the prophecy ("to make his saying true") is also a deflation of it. This is just a meadow, mowed by laborers who have to eat: the heaven-sent quails and manna of Exodus are revealed to be simply rails and dew.

In other apparently destabilizing moments as well, a familiarly feminine world interrupts the poet's fantasies by domesticating them. Like the nun, the wandering poet "weaves" prophecies from leaves (578); he then finds himself "embroider[ed]" by oak leaves (587). Following the flooding of the fields, he observes "the meadow's fresher dyed" like "green silks but newly washed" (626, 628), recasting as a new, freshly laundered textile the space previously described as "quilted" with mown hay (422).[49] When he settles down to "securely play" (607), he adds to his inventory of household stuff by asking the woodbines to "bind" him in a "silken bondage," an echo of the warm cotton embraces suggested by the nun (609, 614). Though he describes himself as an "easy philos-opher," "careless" and "languishing with ease" (561, 529, 593), the poet languishes like an aristocratic housewife, whose idleness could often not be easily distinguished from productivity and whose production was not always clearly separated from consumption.[50] David Simon makes much of these phrases, inviting us to read them as transparent expressions of the poet's mood during what is "almost literally a walk in the park."[51] But for housewives as for poets, proclaiming something easy that is actually tedious is not necessarily an attempt at artlessness. It could also indicate a genuine confusion as to whether these activities are really "work." Needles and other sewing implements could be as easily understood as "idle utensils" as the poet's "quills" (649)—his fishing gear, but also implicitly the tools of writing, his other form of unproductive recreation. While Orlin, as mentioned above, claims that the very word "needlework" was a mystification of women's enforced idleness, Dympna Callaghan writes from the opposite side of the cross-stitching sampler, arguing that despite the clear value of embroidery as "an implement of women's cultural and material production," the work was devalued as feminine and thus "ceased to be defined as work at all."[52] Both these accounts seek to prove that the evaluation of embroidery was a symptom of patriarchal ideological control. But that control would seem to be based on a fundamental undecidability about whether what women did with needles was "work" or "not work," the same ambiguity about productivity in idleness that plagued the status of poetry.

Like the nuns, the poet experiences the world in terms of conventional housewifely activities, made unconventional only by the lack of the correct symbolic structures. But the symbolically unorganized housework of the embroidering, preserving nuns and the fantasy-weaving poet are both corrected with the entrance of Lord Fairfax's young daughter and Marvell's tutee, Mary Fairfax, whose power to domesticate the landscape prompts her tutor to abandon his "idle utensils" in embarrassment:

> The young Maria walks tonight:
> Hide trifling youth thy pleasures slight.
> 'Twere shame that such judicious eyes
> Should with such toys a man surprise;
> She that already is the law
> Of all her sex, her age's awe. (649–56)

As Hirst and Zwicker point out, the speaker's first reaction to Maria is erotic and antidomestic: a young woman walking outside at night would more likely be a hussy than a huswife.[53] But Maria goes on to manifest herself as the organized and organizing Xenophonic housekeeper, "the law / Of all her sex," in the following stanza, with her mere presence spurring the sun, like the poet, to pull itself together in shame ("The sun himself, of her aware, / Seems to descend with greater care," 661–62). If the nuns had promised Isabel that she had the power to restructure Cistercian discipline—"the rule itself to you shall bend" (156)—here Maria holds a power at once astronomical and modest: she can affect the movements of the sun but only to the point that it "seems" to set "with greater care."

What Maria is doing—or not doing—is a form of symbolic labor that reverses, or forestalls, the decomposition of her surroundings. Simply by providing herself as an organizational principle, she restores disintegrating material, as the nuns preserved fruit that had perished: "See how loose Nature," Marvell entreats us, "in respect / To her, itself doth recollect" (657–58). The "respect" nature affords Maria could be understood as both an affective and a formal relation: she inspires both spiritual awe and a physical reconfiguration of a degenerate scene, such that to "recollect" is both an ethical and a practical act by which the environment becomes more properly itself.

Maria's feminine power to organize the landscape, to provide the "good order" that Xenophon's Ischomachus rhapsodizes over, provides a composite image of overlapping class-based ideals of the early modern housewife. Korda explains how the valorization of the housewife's domestic leisure that Thorstein Veblen locates at the end of the nineteenth century was beginning to appear in England as early as the late sixteenth. Relieved of her duties to brew, bake, wash, spin, and card, which were outsourced to lower classes, a woman of a certain status could devote herself to what Veblen calls the "performance of leisure," in the sense that "little or no productive work is performed"—and yet, Veblen emphasizes, this makes her no less her husband's "drudge."[54] Her primary function as a housekeeper required labor whose products were either immaterial or immediately consumed, rather than "productive" activity, with both her semiotic and her manual labor understood as "unproductive" in Adam Smith's sense.[55] The middling housewife's task was thus not only to keep house but also to keep a cultural network of signs together, with an implicit mandate tying her to the larger social order in which aristocratic wives, praised for their hospitality and charity in poems like Jonson's "To Penshurst," had always been understood to play a public-facing part, though from within the physical confines of the estate.[56] Unlike Marvell's nuns, whose economy is oriented only toward the preservation of the convent itself, the housewife's aim was to preserve her household in order to help keep that larger system of signs intact. Throughout the seventeenth century, that preservation was understood to be itself in need of preservation: James I and Charles I felt the need to issue multiple proclamations commanding gentry to stop loitering in London and "keep hospitality" in their country houses; in 1660 the former cook Robert May looked back with nostalgia on the good housekeeping of his youth, since deteriorated: "Such Noble Houses were then kept, the glory of that, and the shame of this present Age; then were those Golden Days wherein were practised the *Triumphs and Trophies of Cookery*; then was Hospitality esteemed."[57]

The good housewife's arranging of signs and keeping of hospitality are continuous with physically keeping up material spaces. "'Tis she

that to these gardens gave / That wondrous beauty which they have"
(689–90) is a fitting tribute to an aesthetically minded gardener who
stakes trees to give them "straightness" and sows wildflowers to give
the meadow "sweetness" (691, 692); what can be read as hyperbolic
assertions of immaterial powers can also be read, as in the case of the
sweetening, dethorning little T. C., as complimentary descriptions of
garden maintenance. The manual aspect of housekeeping blurs with its
function as symbolic organization when Maria "vitrifie[s]" the world,
making it congeal like glass, or crystallized sugar (688). Like the "modest halcyon" who, in accordance with its fabled calming abilities, solidifies the river into a "jellying stream" and makes "stupid fishes hang, as
plain / As flies in crystal overta'en" (675, 677–78), the housewife uses
vinegar and isinglass to suspend tench, turbot, bream, perch, "or any
other fish that you have a desire to serve up in jelly," as one recipe book
puts it.[58]

For all the resonance with Revelation, this is what vitrification looks
like. Maria oversees the sort of divinely sourced and approved kitchen
experiments that reduce the world, or a discrete part of the world, to
an exquisite stillness. The claim that "by her flames, in heaven tried, /
Nature is wholly vitrified" (687–88) may be extreme, but it differs only
in degree from praise that might be earned by a housewife or other
domestic worker renowned for sugar work: using sugar to make dried
apples "look like Christal," as in this chapter's epigraph, or clarifying
it with egg whites until it is "as clear as Crystal," or applying it to preserved grapes with just the right timing so that they "begin to sparkle,"
or knowing how to boil it until the exact point when "it will snap be-
twen your fingers like glass."[59] In the cases of both Maria and the profi-
cient root- or fruit-candier, nature is not quite "wholly vitrified"—only
partly. As Marvell concludes in the poem's penultimate stanza, the difference between "Paradise's only map" (768)—Nun Appleton—and
the rest of the world—"a rude heap together hurled" (762)—is due
not to topographical accident but to the housewife's provision of order
over her domain. The "lesser world" is almost "the same," only quite
a bit tidier: a better home and garden, but only comparatively so, and
only because of Maria's capacity to make her corner of the world "in
more decent order tame" than the chaos that reigns outside. Like Mary
Astell's claim that without women's caretaking houses would be "meer
*Bedlams,*" culinary confections "but a rude Confusion of ill digested,
ill mix'd, Scents and Relishes," and costly household effects "but an
expensive Heap of glittering *Rubbish,*" Marvell's poem counterposes
a well-ordered domestic space to the confused heaps of rubbish into
which all human dwellings threaten to disintegrate.[60]

That this extended encomium climaxes with a would-be housewife's limited but impressive power to civilize a portion of the world's "rude heap" makes clear, as did the nuns' housewifely activities, that not all the workings of heteronormativity are directly related to sexual reproduction, even if they are related indirectly. In the case of the mythical "modest halcyon," biological reproduction plays an implicit role in the effecting of quiescence; the bird is able to charm stormy seas into stillness only when it is breeding.[61] The kingfisher that swoops into Marvell's poem takes on, with its poetic moniker, these ancient associations with both reproduction and environmental calming without needing to actually be the fabulous halcyon, or even needing to be fertile. Marvell performs a similar operation of association by calling to mind the presiding woman of the house whose domestic management in other country house poems goes hand in hand with motherhood, casting Maria, thirteen years old and at the cusp of menarche and marriageability, as a potential head housekeeper; the poem takes place in the "meantime" before her marriage, a meantime that will continue "(Till Fate her worthily translates, / And find a Fairfax for our Thwaites)" (745, 747–48)—in other words, when Mary Fairfax reincarnates Isabel Thwaites and is matched with a man similarly translated into "a Fairfax." This kind of willful translation on Marvell's part is necessary for the line to continue at all: Mary, Fairfax's only child, cannot carry on the family name the way a son could, no matter how good a household manager she proves to be. Summoning the phantom, indefinite male "Fairfax" who would somehow carry on the family name despite coming from outside the family papers over that problem. Setting the scene in the "meantime," with this impossible translation safely shelved in parentheses, conveniently keeps any such future in suspension.

This situation in the mundane meantime, rather than in the dramatic end times imagined by Stocker in her influential reading of the poem, suggests that the calm wrought by vitrification is, like the halcyon's hibernal nesting, a regular, secular phenomenon.[62] The apocalyptic overtones Stocker sees in Maria's vitrification of nature could also describe everyday conditions in an early modern kitchen; eschatological events can be thus recast as ordinary culinary routines, or perhaps ordinary culinary routines—like Thestylis's substitution of roasted rails for biblical quails—constitute the fulfillment of prophecy. As Rosalie Colie puts it, "This eschatology is entirely calm. The world turns to crystal, becomes clear, pure, transparent, translucent, without the dust-up and untidiness of the scarifying final fire."[63] The vivid present in which the poem's closing stanzas are, as Hirst and Zwicker have it, "brilliantly fixed" was also the tense that, in recipes for preserves, governed the brilliant fixation of fruit in sugar.[64] Instructions on how "To keepe Barberyes" note the desired fixity of the syrup ("lyke Birdlyme") and end, like many recipes of the kind, by projecting that present fixity into the future, with an entreaty to "kepe" things that way:

> Take claryfied Suger, & boyle it tyll it be thick, which you shal perceve yf you take a little betweene your fingers, it wyl rope lyke Birdlyme: Then put in your Barberyes, and let them boyle with a soft fyre, untyll you perceave thei be tender, then put them in a Glasse and cover them: and so kepe them.[65]

Hirst and Zwicker conclude of Marvell's treatment of Maria that "the child frozen in time, withheld from futurity," amounts to "a denial of name, lineage, and inheritance" that "question[s] the very ideology of dynastic continuity."[66] If Marvell is questioning that ideology, however, he is also gesturing to responses to such questioning, showing just how resilient the patriarchal model is: its logic is carried out in the nongenital reproductive labor performed by good housewives and perverse poets alike.

Even in its avoidance of the future, then, Marvell's poetry participates in the ideology of reproductive futurism as defined by Edelman, who equates that ideology with politics itself. "For politics," Edelman writes, "however radical the means by which specific constituencies attempt to produce a more desirable social order, remains, at its core, conservative insofar as it works to *affirm* a structure, to *authenticate* a social order, which it then intends to transmit to the future in the form of its inner Child."[67] This conservative core can hold even when the social order is not functioning as seamlessly as its most privileged participants would like. Hirst and Zwicker declare that English political patriarchy in the mid-seventeenth century had "exploded" and that marriage within Marvell's demographic was on the decline. They conclude, "It is of course in the nature of ideology not to be wholly coincident with social reality, and the greater the distance between them, the greater the violence ideology performs on social reality."[68] Yet something other than "violence" may be at play when social reality fails to follow the pattern of ideology: namely, the more aesthetically appealing but no less effective avenues of legerdemain, suspension, and distraction. Marvell's "subversive" machinations effect a suspension of Fairfax's particular patrilineal continuity that will prove necessary to the preservation of patriarchy as ideology.

## The Green World

If aristocratic reproduction relies on its strategic disruption at a narrative level, it also relies on such disruption at a practical level. In a different context, Barry McCrea explains the supposedly insular French aristocracy's counterintuitive dependence on outside interference with a reading of the opening of Marcel Proust's *Sodom and Gomorrah*, when the narrator waxes botanical while idly lying in wait for the arrival home of his aristocratic landlords. After implying that flowers, sessile though they may be, act coquettish with pollinating insects and do not await an apian "ambassador" any more passively than a writer in training awaits his experiences, the narrator continues to think about which modes of reproduction produce sweet flowers and which offspring are more likely to meet with base infection:

> If the visit of an insect, that it is to say the transportation of the seed from another flower, is generally necessary for the fertilisation of the flower, this is because self-fertilisation, the insemination of a flower by itself, would lead, like a succession of intermarriages in the same family, to degeneracy and sterility, whereas the crossing effected by insects gives to the subsequent generations of the same species a vigour unknown to their forebears.[69]

In McCrea's reading of what follows, the narrator—as he watches unfold before his eyes not the awaited homecoming of a heterosexual aristocratic couple but, instead, a scene of cruising between a middle-aged baron and a younger man of a lower class—comes to identify queerness with exogamous fertility, and aristocratic heterosexual reproduction with inbred sterility. Queerness, the narrator realizes in his idle repose, is not simply an aesthetically refreshing or ideologically destabilizing alternative to the dull linearity of hereditary lines. Rather, the continued dull linearity of a hereditary line depends on its habitual commerce with queerness.

This hypothesis can help explain how Marvell's antisocial quirks could strengthen Fairfax's sense of security in his precarious social role. Hirst and Zwicker carefully tease out how Marvell's slightly off-kilter mirroring of Fairfax's flaws—the poet both demonstrating the virtues of his patron's new apolitical lifestyle and displacing its more uncomfortable aspects from his patron to himself—allows Fairfax to "have it both ways."[70] Marvell's goal, though, is not only to absolve Fairfax for his choice of retirement; he must also recast Fairfax's failure to issue an heir as, effectively, a nonissue. In other words, Marvell serves as a "surrogate," as Hirst and Zwicker put it,[71] but in a sense beyond acting as a repository for potential accusations against Fairfax; he must also perform a task on par with producing a child. Outsider that he is, it is precisely Marvell's strangeness that makes him a fit for the role of perpetuating the family name. As McCrea reminds us, defining the "queer secret" at the heart of heterosexuality as the simple fact of exogamy, family names are always carried on by strangers:

> Queerness already has a structural role in the genealogical narrative template, and it is not so hidden and subversive. . . . Because genealogical continuity relies on the destruction of the nuclear family unit and the incorporation of an outsider into the line, an element of queerness, in the sense of a rival to the family, is an inherent part of the process.[72]

Thus the challenge the dysfunctional Fairfaxes pose to their encomiast is met by Marvell's insistence on an extrabiological continuation of the family name. In this case, destabilizing convention is the best way of ensuring its survival. If there will be no entailment, in the legal sense, of Fairfax's property to a son, then "goodness doth itself entail / On females, if there want a male" (727–28), where immaterial goodness "itself" stands as the more ideal form of mere material goods. After deriding vain women who place all their "useless study" on their faces instead of working on their souls, Marvell implies that Maria is a much more effective cultivator: "Hence she with graces more divine / Supplies beyond her sex the line" (730, 737–38). This praise for the "divine" graces Maria enlists in order to surpass what is expected of women places her virtues squarely in a world "beyond" one governed by male primogeniture, where they will keep well into the future.

Bequeathing a legacy of "goodness" and "graces" rather than of little Fairfaxes, performing "beyond" (while also, crucially, less than) the normal duties required of her sex, Maria would supply a line that was not patrilineal. But that does not mean her role is not wholly compatible with heteronormative ideology; rather, it is necessary to that ideology's maintenance. An occasional reprieve from understanding things in straightforwardly patrilineal terms may be necessary for the reproduction of the heterosexual couple as an institution. In McCrea's rendition of the structure of the marriage plot, the child's transition from his parental home to his own new household is interrupted by a foray into what Northrop Frye calls a "green world," a narrative middle space "free of parental supervision and social constraint, and it is characterized by unchecked erotic impulses, gender bending, and altered or mistaken identities," as in the comic confusion that makes up much of the action of *A Midsummer Night's Dream*.[73] With these "queernesses" safely out of the child's system, the comic plot resolves with weddings and foretellings of procreative futures. Patricia Parker, also in reference to *Dream*, argues by contrast that the reestablishment of an aristocratic heterosexual order in act 5 highlights how that order is just as constructed as the laborious, manual "joining" performed daily by "rude mechanicals."[74] Parker asserts that revealing the "Elizabethan World Picture" as artificially constructed would shake its very core, but a well-constructed plot proves the opposite to be true: more than affording "aery nothing / A local habitation and name," as Theseus scoffs before the workmen-players take the stage, the story maintained by poetic labor "grows," as Hippolyta gently corrects her husband, "to something of great constancy."[75] Calling attention to the growth potential of constructed forms—to how a well-sustained human artifact "grows" as if in nature—allows for the power of poetic labor to fix meaning even in the absence of a solid foundation in the physical world.

In *Upon Appleton House*, any dalliance in a green world, or in "queerness" more generally, more successfully serves as preparatory work for heterosexual coupling than offers any real alternatives to it. The "green world," moreover, provides models for passing off artificial connections as natural ones. Taking stock of the wood he has stumbled into in stanza 62, the speaker marvels at how the planted grove resembles a joint family tree as much as a series of independent biological organisms:

> The double wood of ancient stocks
> Linked in so thick, an union locks,
> It like two pedigrees appears,
> On one hand Fairfax, th'other Vere's. (489–92)

That cultural artifacts could be indistinguishable from natural formations is a convenient truth for a poet seeking to use his poem as cover for the lack of a dynastic heir.

Botanical language smooths over the progeniture problem most directly in stanza 93, where Mary, who "like a sprig of mistletoe / On the Fairfacian oak does grow" (739–40), is compared to what is botanically a parasite. But despite its leeching of nutrients from its host tree, mistletoe becomes, when processed by culture, a fruitful bearer of meaning: Druid mythology assigns the vine, in conjunction with the oak, the symbology of fertility.[76] In reference to Marvell's announcement that

"Whence, for some universal good, / The priest shall cut the sacred bud" (741–42), Hirst and Zwicker gloss, "when Marvell contemplates Mary Fairfax's entry into that frame [of heterosexuality], he does so not in terms of marital and sexual union but in a language of grafting—neutered, violent, and programmatically deployed," with "implications of dismemberment and displacement."[77] But gardening books, not to mention any number of poems, describe grafting as evolving organically from natural processes and, often, in the terms of romantic love. Gentlemen gardeners were advised that a rootstock must not simply tolerate the foreign scion joined to it but positively rejoice in its company. The author of *The Country-mans Recreation* explains the seriousness of the commitment by reminding readers "How Graffes never lightly take": the saps of stock and scion "must be set in just one with another: for ye shall understand, if they doe not joyn, and the one delight with the other, being even set, they shall never take together."[78] Or, as the disguised Polixenes explains to Perdita in *The Winter's Tale*:

> You see, sweet maid, we marry
> A gentler scion to the wildest stock,
> And make conceive a bark of baser kind
> By bud of nobler race. This is an art
> Which does mend Nature—change it rather; but
> The art itself is Nature.[79]

The archaic meaning of scion as "branch" or "shoot"—the natural outgrowth of a tree—later came to mean a cutting taken from one tree and grafted onto another, as if natural operations were etymologically evolving into (horti)cultural ones.[80] If grafting is, as Hirst and Zwicker suggest, "neutered, violent, and programmatically deployed," it is not any more so than the marriages of heterogeneous parts at the center of dramatic plots and the dominant sexual ideology.

To return to how my interpretation differs from one of "subversion and containment," I want to emphasize that the "ends" of the dominant order are, both in Fairfax's case and on a national level, frayed; the best thing to do for the moment is not to further them, but to suspend them in a poetic fabric. And to return to Quint's distinction between epic's victors and romance's losers, Lord Fairfax lives uneasily between the two: powerful enough to hold on to the trappings of aristocratic power and keep a personal poet in his employ, he is still not enough of a clear winner to let history, or genealogy, speak for itself.

*Upon Appleton House* is an encomium to the kind of symbolic domestic labor that preserves the fiction of aristocratic lineage in particular and of the linear narrative of history more generally *as a fiction* in a way that, following Parker, we might think would threaten the naturalized institution by outing it as "both constructed and manipulable."[81] But Marvell, for all his rhetorical self-positioning as a "trifling youth," is no rude mechanical, and he uses the power of poetry, like agricultural grafting, horticultural bloom-extending tricks, or preservative culinary techniques, as an artificial mode of giving artificial constructions all the legitimacy of, and more longevity than, the natural. *Upon Appleton House* presents literary production as the preservative and conservative domestic labor of putting futurity itself into suspension. This constant labor of maintaining the fiction of the family is performed both by those outside the dominant order—poets, idlers, nuns—and by the real and hopeful housewives within it.

# CHAPTER 5

# Milton's Storehouses

## TEMPERING FUTURES IN *AREOPAGITICA*, *PARADISE LOST*, AND *PARADISE REGAIN'D*

*In his Georgikes, lorde what pleasaunt varietie there is, the dyuers graynes, herbes, and flowres, that be there described, that redynge therin, it semeth to a man to be in a delectable gardeyne or paradyse.*

THOMAS ELYOT, *The Boke named the Governour*

*We purposely, and in transitu only, take notice here of the Pickl'd, Muriated, or otherwise prepared Herbs; excepting some such Plants, and Proportions of them, as are of hard digestion, and not fit to be eaten altogether Crude, . . . among which I reckon Ash-keys, Broom-buds and Pods, Haricos, Gurkems, Olives, Capers, the Buds and Seeds of Nasturtia, Young Wall-nuts, Pineapples, Eringo, Cherries, Cornelians, Berberries, &c. together with several Stalks, Roots, and Fruits; Ordinary Potherbs, Anis, Cistus, Hortorum, Horminun, Pulegium, Satureia, Thyme; the intire Family of Pulse and Legumena; other Sauces, Pies, Tarts, Omlets, Tansie, Farces, &c. Condites and Preserves with Sugar by the Hand of Ladies; tho' they are all of them the genuine Production of the Garden.*

JOHN EVELYN, *Acetaria: A discourse of sallets*

*What are sheaves bound up in a Barn to the Phalanx that hem'd Satan?*

RICHARD BENTLEY ON *PARADISE LOST* 4.977–85

Thomas Elyot finds in the variety of Virgil's *Georgics* a map of paradise: his pleasure in the variety of the poem's plant specimens echoes his contemporaries' delight in the mixing of styles and topics that came to be considered characteristic of the georgic mode, so that some readers find Marvell's eclectic *Upon Appleton House* to be as much a textbook georgic as an unusual country house poem.[1] But English georgic's very variety, its tendency to insinuate itself into other genres and to ground lofty epic flights, could cause consternation. Richard Bentley was neither the first nor the last reader of *Paradise Lost* to complain that moments of epic intensity—as when, at the end of book 4, the fiery angelic phalanx closes in on Satan in an attempt to prevent the Fall—can rapidly deflate into something more modestly georgic, in this case a literal description of farming practices: the combatant angels are compared to ears of wheat swaying in the field, which "the careful Plowman" hopes to harvest and painstakingly prepare for storage.[2] So widely noted are Milton's georgic downgrades that even the author of a book entitled *Milton's Grand Style* could conclude that the poet's greatness lies, counterintuitively, in the careful moderation of minutiae. Christopher Ricks closes his influential study by defining Milton's grandness as "balance": "A balance that is not precarious and is the result of a strength manifesting itself in innumerable tiny, significant, internal movements—this is the balance of Milton's Grand Style."[3] In these "innumerable tiny, significant, internal movements," the grandness of Milton's style is not a groaning contradiction held together with a singular Herculean effort but a constant and nearly imperceptible process of tempering diverse materials. Such tempering, I argue, reflects Milton's inclination not only to the temperate tones of georgic but also to a further tempering, in his modification of that mode to reflect a form of labor more like household chores than the farmer's furrowing in the open field: more cyclical domestic georgic than the future-oriented, imperial georgic of progress and profit. Faced throughout his literary career with uncertain political futures, Milton adopted the spirit of a kind of labor more domestic, more feminized, and less heroic than the optimistically Baconian mode with which he is often associated, turning to the rhetoric and practices of medicinal and culinary tempering that maintain local life in the face of collective future uncertainty. These tactics of tempering, unlike the balance posited by Ricks, *are* precarious, in the sense that any stability relies on a constant recommitment of minor acts of labor, visible in Milton's prose and poetry on the local level of the line.

As many readers of Milton have noted, "temperance"—usually associated with such puritanical prohibitions as not drinking and not eating too much—becomes, along with the more prosaic "tempering," a positive and dynamic virtue in Milton's poetry and prose.[4] Tempering, defined as the mixing of promiscuously gathered impressions, ideas, affects, and materials, is, Milton announces in his 1644 tract *Areopagitica*, the recipe for virtue: "Wherefore did [God] creat passions within us, pleasures round about us, but that these rightly temper'd

are the very ingredients of vertu?"[5] By considering Milton's participation in the georgic mode through the lens of domestic tempering in
*Areopagitica*, *Paradise Lost*, and *Paradise Regain'd*, I mean both to call
attention to Milton's georgic commitment to tempering as craft—his
conception of his writing as the measured and laborious gathering,
combining, and adjusting of textual ingredients[6]—and to emphasize
the radical uncertainty, subject to infelicities of time and season, of
that tempering. Domestic georgic thus offers a new avenue for thinking about the relationship between craft and contingency in Milton's
poetry and thought.

An uncertainty as to outcomes, as we have seen, is integral to Virgil's
*Georgics*, as it is to agricultural labor itself, though it is often overlooked
in the classical poem's early modern reception, where both the heroic
struggle to conquer nature—what Joshua Scodel calls the "hard" strain
of georgic—and the quasi-pastoral collaboration with the landscape, or
"soft" georgic, are more apparent and more appealing.[7] Citing Bentley's
scoffing remark about Milton comparing the army of angels surrounding Satan to something as pedestrian as "sheaves bound up in a Barn,"
Kevis Goodman points out that the swaying ears of wheat standing in
for Adam and Eve's heavenly would-be protectors are not yet, in Milton's simile, safely bound in the barn, and their undetermined status in
the field is the source of all the dramatic tension: if the sheaves "prove
chaff," they will be worthless to the plowman, and our hopes for the first
couple will be dashed.[8] This simile emblematizes both the unpredictable upshots of georgic labor and Milton's approach to Virgil's *Georgics*,
where hopeful possibility and fragile precarity grow up side by side,
and where the famous line sometimes taken to celebrate all-conquering
labor—"Labor omnia vicit"—is tempered, after an enjambment, with
a clarification that this conquest did not take place once and for all and
will always be accompanied by the necessity that first occasioned it: the
labor is unrelenting, "improbus," so that it is humanity, rather than nature, that has effectively been conquered.[9] If the necessity of labor is all
too certain, its results—so often thrown off by bad weather, bad seed,
or bad luck—are not.

Goodman's study of Miltonic georgic, focusing on the Orphic
"wasted labor" of *Georgics* 4 and Eve's affective labor in *Paradise Lost*,
aims to "testify to the challenge of imagining sympathetic and erotic
passion as productive action."[10] But her emphasis on georgic precariousness, on the short shelf life and indeterminate ends of any act of
labor, also has implications for Milton's preoccupation with the mundane and minor maintenance work that is a necessary, though not suf-

ficient, precondition for any productive action in the future. This work
has an affective dimension, but it fails to arouse the interest of "passion," more often inciting mere annoyance. Maintenance work tends
to be undervalued at the best of times, when things seem to be sustaining themselves just fine, and at the worst of times, when more press-
ing crises take priority. But in the optimism of the 1644 prose no less
than in the postrevolutionary defeat of the late poetry, Milton sees local maintenance work as vital to the reformation, in the sense of continual forming again, of biological and intellectual life, whether that life
is under the immediate threat of violence or the eventual threat of negligence. Like the "*Condites* and Preserves with *Sugar* by the Hand of
Ladies" that John Evelyn lists as pantry staples in his "discourse on salads," the products of georgic labor, "tho' they are all of them the genuine Production of the *Garden*," need to be re-produced and preserved
through domestic georgic.[11]

Like Marvell's *Upon Appleton House*, which assimilates a deviant
nunnery and an apocalyptic scene to the workspace of a Protestant
housewife, Milton's poetry and prose illuminate the mundane under-
pinnings of grand divine and human plans. Milton's domestic georgic
mode, like Marvell's, operates on a more modest scale than many other
projects associated with georgic in the seventeenth century—sweeping
agricultural programs; nascent imperialism; the muscular, masculine
enterprise of literally and figuratively breaking new ground—and often in much closer, even cloistered, quarters.[12] As Adam and Eve labor to maintain the garden in *Paradise Lost*, the poem's minor linguistic operations of repetition, rephrasing, and correction temper the text
into being. Milton's paradise, and our own work of reading Milton, often understood in terms of progress and self-improvement, can also be
understood as the more modest, and less assured, work of incremental maintenance. In this way, Milton's intellectual labors and our own
model the rhythms of domestic labor: of carefully preserving and combining ingredients in hopes of preserving ourselves and our communities, as a necessary but not sufficient precondition for any future transformative change on a larger scale.

## Subliming for Survival: *Areopagitica*

*Areopagitica*, written in response to a 1643 act authorizing prepublica-
tion censorship, has been read as such an unqualified endorsement of
the virtues of books that quotations from it have been emblazoned on
the walls of libraries.[13] In a famous passage that has furnished some of

those quotations, Milton conjures up a space, often understood as a kind of mausoleum, that also evokes the image of a virtual home apothecary. Books are imagined as immortal essences housed, strangely, in what sound like commonplace medicine vials:

> For Books are not absolutely dead things, but doe contain a potencie of life in them to be as active as that soule was whose progeny they are; nay they do preserve as in a violl the purest efficacie and extraction of that living intellect that bred them. . . . A good Booke is the pretious life-blood of a master spirit, imbalm'd and treasur'd up on purpose to a life beyond life. . . . We should be wary therefore what persecution we raise against the living labours of publick men, how we spill that season'd life of man preserv'd and stor'd up in Books; since we see a kinde of homicide may be thus committed, sometimes a martyrdome, and if it extend to the whole impression, a kinde of massacre, whereof the execution ends not in the slaying of an elementall life, but strikes at that ethereall and fift essence, the breath of reason it selfe, slaies an immortality rather then a life. (999)

Stanley Fish has observed that this ode to preserved relics has a decidedly un-Miltonic ring: the veneration of sacred treasures is for papists, not the friends of truth who scorn idol worship and are tasked with constantly and internally forming and re-forming themselves in virtue. For Fish, these attractive artifacts ultimately constitute nothing more than a temptation we are to overcome, idols fit only to be smashed by the heroic, iconoclastic reader.[14] Any potential hero might take pause, however, when confronted with the somewhat oppressive ordinariness of Milton's stock of images: "not absolutely dead things" are "preserve[d] as in a violl"; "life-blood" is "imbalm'd and treasur'd up," "season'd," "preserv'd and stor'd up." The parade of hyperbolic images of divine power and mass violence is punctually deflated by a repeated emphasis on small-scale storage that makes the exemplary "good Booke" less tantalizingly magical and more coldly clinical, and as the references to embalmed preserves pile up, the forbidden trove of treasures takes the increasingly prosaic shape of a supply of fluids sitting in containers, or, as in a typical description from a 1631 play, a woman's medicine cabinet: "With limbecks, viols, pots, her Closet's fill'd / Full of strange liquors by rare art distilled," where what may be "strange" or "rare" to an outside observer is perfectly expected for anyone who knows her way around such a "closet."[15] As Thomas Tusser reminds his readers, every housewife should make sure she is fully stocked with medicinal liquids:

Good huswiues provide, ere an sicknes do come,
of sundry good things, in her house to haue some.
Good *Aqua composita,* Vinegar tart,
Rose water & Treacle, to comfort the hart. . . .
Conserue of the Barbery, Quinces & such,
with Sirops that easeth, the sickly so much.[16]

With Milton's belabored reminders that we are entrenched in a material world of perishable objects, even if those objects strive for a "life
beyond life," we are brought down from the grandiose dreams of alchemists and back to earth: even an "ethereal and fift essence," even "an
immortality," requires continuous preservative action lest it be "slai[n],"
lest "life" not reproduce itself "beyond life." The escalation of the violence Milton describes, in a dramatic crescendo—homicide, martyr-
dom, massacre—takes on the color of mock epic if we see the continuity between the potential victims and the kinds of items commonly
kept by women to keep households alive and healthy.

Milton thus translates what might be a total transubstantiation of
flesh to word into a physical and approximate process, "the living labours of publick men" clinging to a vegetative existence as "not absolutely dead" books. The "life beyond life" that authors can reach
through their published works is reduced from a triumphant transcendence to the dragged-out extension of worldly existence, a temporary
suspension of death rather than a bold refusal of it: a "life beyond life"
provided for by household medicinal mixing and food preservation
rather than by esoteric sorcery. Books are different from living things
in degree rather than in kind, so that immortality is tempered into longevity, the forbidden fruit of idolatry refigured as the quince conserve
of early modern domestic pharmacopoeia.

Just as books' producers remain trapped in a worldly if prolonged
existence, their consumers too will have to adjust any expectation that
books can provide an escape from their precarious lives. The beneficial
effect of reading is health rather than immortality, and reading, as much
as writing, is in practice closer to the everyday concoction of medicines and home remedies than the elite, ethereal activities of alchemical laboratories. As Milton goes on to explain, books are "imbalm'd and
treasur'd up," "preserv'd and stor'd up" for the purpose of being used
as ingredients in the tempering operations of the judicious reader, for
whom even "the drossiest volume" counts among the "usefull drugs
and materialls wherewith to temper and compose effective and strong
med'cins, which mans life cannot want" (1008). The necessity of gathering available materials, no matter how gross, in order to refine them

into health-giving substances applies as well to vices not contained in books, as part of the holistic regime overseen by God: the provision of passions and pleasures that "rightly temper'd are the very ingredients of vertu." Such unpleasant tempering is also required of the many recipes for home remedies that call for animal excrement, either as an ingredient (combined with walnuts, herbs, and spices in "horse-dung water," good for fevers) or a tempering agent itself, as dunghills were for some the preferred medium for temporarily storing containers of flowers or fruits before or between distillations.[17]

The necessary but undignified work of refining useful material from dross so that it could be made accessible and preserved was also the aim of the daily labors of scholars, editors, anthologists, and commentators, as we saw in the introduction with Erasmus picking his gold off the dunghill and in chapter 2 with Eumnestes desperately trying to get out from under his worm-infested files. Many compilers of early modern printed commonplace books and *florilegia* understood their work to be both vital and deadening in its banality. Theodor Zwinger, a physician and botanist as well as a compiler, made the analogy between bad books and bad plants clear: "There is no herb so vile that it does not contain something useful," he proclaimed, before going on to cite the respective use values of old exempla, new exempla, rare exempla, and common exempla. But he also called the work of compilation "improbus," the word Virgil uses to describe the unrelenting labor that conquers all in the *Georgics*, and "Sisyphean."[18] Carefully arranged like the selections of flowers after which they were named, the designs of anthologies were not meant to be retentive once and for all: their techniques of holding diverse pieces of textual material in variously organized suspensions aimed to inspire rather than obviate similar repetitive labors in their readers, to reproduce their own reproductive labor, to preserve material only so that it can be preserved again.[19]

Considering the seasoned blood samples of *Areopagitica* in the contexts of domestic preservation and editorial labor raises the possibility that their utility to the literary and ethical formation of the reader is not limited to their timely smashing and that they have a value in themselves, precisely *as* preservative agents. Rather than serving as target practice for iconoclasts, these vials hold life in a suspension that is necessary to the continuation of that life. The goal of preserving this material for Milton, as for fellow textual life preservers like Erasmus, Rabelais, and Montaigne, is not transcendence but survival, a reproduction of existing forms of life that keeps things as they are, but only by forming them anew: turning a soul, or a batch of walnuts, into a liquid and bottling it up into a "water of life" to last beyond the original material's mortal lifespan. The tempering activity of continuously reforming and reformulating language and material may indeed result, eventually, in some form of transcendence. But in both *Paradise Lost* and *Paradise Regain'd*, paradise can be preserved and effected only through a commitment to the reproductive labor of tempering—reproductive in the metabolic sense of continuously replacing organic material on a cellular level, reconstituting it to maintain it as itself.[20] The constant necessity of this labor makes it georgic; its almost microscopically local character is what makes it domestic.

## Suspending Sublimation: *Paradise Lost*

In *Paradise Lost*, the end of Adam and Eve's labors is to uphold their present condition by keeping the future in suspension. They can stay innocent in Eden only as long as their consciousness begins and ends with doing what they are already doing, maintaining their flesh exactly the way it is, and becoming who they already are.[21] Their eventual failure in this has to do, I will argue, with a tension between a domestic georgic of maintenance and a teleological georgic of progress, a tension best articulated in Raphael's postprandial speech in book 5. When Raphael suggests that Adam and Eve's earthly forms may be one day "by gradual scale sublim'd," their bodies "improv'd by tract of time" (5.483, 498), they become unable to reconcile the life of maintenance work they have led so far with the notion of transcending their current state.

The idea that Adam and Eve are engaged in a kind of spiritual subsistence farming runs counter to readings of the poem as centered on private domestic drama as well as to those that read Milton's Eden as a fully operational laboratory for a public-facing Baconian georgic, either in the sense of political progressivism and scientific pursuit or in the sense of capitalist profit and imperialist expansion. When Adam and Eve's activities in *Paradise Lost* have been recognized as both domestic and georgic, it has usually been in the sense of what we might today call "working on their relationship," with the travails of depoliticized private life taking the place of the heroic public feats of earlier epics as the source of national values.[22] Joanna Picciotto has argued against the view of Adam and Eve's conjugal society as protobourgeois, claiming that their collaboration in the garden models instead the collectivist politics of a public experimentalist community.[23] Rejecting the evacuation of politics from Milton's domestic sphere, Picciotto claims that Milton saw innocent labor as both the means and the ends of restoring paradise to fallen humanity. Picciotto, calling Eden "literally imperfect," likens Milton's attitude toward labor to those of both contempo-

rary experimentalists and political reformers like the Diggers, whose
efforts were focused on improving the land by farming it to its as-yet
unrealized potential in the service of progressively increasing human
knowledge and happiness.[24] Adam and Eve are constantly "reforming"
the garden, which Barbara Lewalski takes to mean that they must "raise
to higher levels of perfection the world which has been made for them,"
with the two of them likewise "growing in perfection," which involves
graduating from pastoral stasis to georgic progress.[25] When Maureen
Quilligan protests that the first couple's work, because it is necessary
to perform on a daily basis, is "apparently insufficient," she echoes Eve's
impatience in book 9 with their failure to meet production goals.[26] And
it is true that Milton's first couple, who readers might expect to sit back
and enjoy their own personal golden age, as yet untouched by the biblical (analogous to the georgic) curse to eat only by the sweat of their
brow, instead spend all day working on the garden, pruning and harvesting, resting only after dutifully attending to their "Gardning labour"
(4.328). On a more practical level, their campaigns against trees' "fruitless imbraces" (5.215) and attempts to arrange botanical marriages suggest an interest in the progress of flowers into fruit, and Adam points
out that their "disburd'ning" of nature makes it "more fruitful," implying that the strategy behind their pruning is to produce greater yields
(5.319–20).

And yet Adam and Eve's domestic georgic succeeds precisely when it
suspends any material improvement of the world. Paradisal labor does
not, as Quilligan would have it, "[fall] short of its goal of reformation,"
because in Eden reform simply means maintaining existing forms, reconstituting them in order to ensure their survival.[27] Restorative and
curative labor on a tract of land need not be conflated with improvement over tract of time. Picciotto, in an important nuance of her account of paradisal progress, sees deferral as central to that progress. In
her reading of the poem's collectivist bent, "the gradual cooperative
striving toward fulfillment brings its own pleasure," in a version of Eve's
"amorous delay" in book 4: "forestalling the subjective satisfaction of
certainty" is as key to the experience of Milton's poem as it was to experimentalist science.[28] But while Picciotto sees this suspension of results as a "dialectical struggle between the intellectual's two bodies"—
one fallen and privatized, the other innocent and collective—I see that
suspension working in Milton less as a heroic *agon* than as a precarious
practice of domestic maintenance.[29]

This maintenance work does not preclude improvement, but that
is not its goal. Adam and Eve's innocent efforts are geared not toward
progress but toward survival, in the sense in which John Berger de-

scribes a culture that "envisages the future as a sequence of repe⸍ acts of survival," without any prospective gain, as opposed to a "cu of progress" that imagines the future as infinite expansion, with production increasing over time.[30] In Eden, where "wanton growth" must be "lop[ped]" and fallen branches must be cleared (4.625–32), the focus is on maintenance, on keeping the garden the way it is, not increasing its productivity; they are already harvesting more than enough fruit.

As they labor in the garden, Adam and Eve perform repetitive tasks that fold future possibility into the present in a way that makes the future, as we might understand it, almost nonsensical. When they work to disentangle those "fruitless imbraces," the embraces remain in the present tense, so that fruitlessness is never more than a false prolepsis, taking place in a future that will never itself come to fruition. Every morning, they arrive at the orchard and set to work

> where any row
> Of Fruit-trees overwoodie reachd too farr
> Thir pamperd boughes, and needed hands to check
> Fruitless imbraces: or they led the Vine
> To wed her Elm; she spous'd about him twines
> Her marriageable arms, and with her brings
> Her dowr th' adopted Clusters, to adorn
> His barren leaves. (5.212–19)

The Virgilian trope of the marriage of the elm with the vine, if it happens at all (the typically Miltonic "or" is ambivalent as to whether this is an additional or an alternative activity to pruning), will yield nothing but a pleasing decoration. The goal here is "to adorn . . . barren leaves," not to make them fruitful, allowing the vine's arms to be suspended in a "marriageable" state without ever having to actually marry anything.[31] Here, Adam and Eve's daily work arranges the world in a way that does nothing more than prevent a nonevent, checking fruitlessness rather than necessarily instantiating fruit. Reform in Eden means ensuring the continuation of an existent state by reconstituting it, or by preemptively reversing its failure, so that paradisal gardening is akin to the metabolic repair of the body. As Karl Marx famously said of the conditions of Milton's poetic labor—an "unproductive worker," he "produced *Paradise Lost* as a silkworm produces silk, as the activation of *his own* nature"— Adam and Eve's workspace is an extension of their bodies, their work a function of their reproduction as persons.[32]

A paradise organized around subsistence, rather than oriented toward progress or perfection, might sound disappointing. For Adam, sometimes it is. In book 5, while Eve is composing a salad inside the bower and her husband is enjoying the sunshine outside, Adam suddenly discerns Raphael arriving on the horizon, and he implores Eve to empty her pantry and pull out all the stops in order to impress their celestial guest. Despite their constant collaboration in the garden, in the narrowest of Eden's rooms it is Eve who arranges things: this is an early division of labor, or rather a division between labor and leisure, in the poem. Eve, chiding her husband's ignorance of domestic economy, reminds him that in an overabundant paradise there is no need to harvest any more than immediately necessary, because they run no risk of scarcity: "small store will serve, where store, / All seasons, ripe for use hangs on the stalk" (5.322–23). Curiously, though, she goes on to qualify this statement: "Save what by frugal storing firmness gains / To nourish, and superfluous moist consumes" (5.324–25). Here Eve makes an exception for the category of fruits that make up her "small store," fruits for which a timely harvest followed by "frugal storing" is advisable, like those that Evelyn describes in his treatise on salad-making as "of hard digestion, and not fit to be eaten altogether *Crude*" and so must be "Pickl'd, *Muriated*, or otherwise prepared" in order to become optimally edible.[33] Eve's aside could thus be read as a hope for a tempered gain, for an improvement redefined as reconstitution: a hope that fruits will become firmer, and thus more properly themselves, when they are preserved, so that they are improved only insofar as they are saved.

We are not, however, given much time to dwell on these fruits' pickled futures. Her minilecture on housekeeping concluded, Eve quickly sets to work on the immediate task of making lunch, promiscuously gathering and carefully ordering her ingredients like an exemplary Xenophonic housewife, executing an improvised salad recipe:

> So saying, with dispatchful looks in haste
> She turns, on hospitable thoughts intent
> What choice to chuse for delicacie best,
> What order, so contriv'd as not to mix
> Tastes, not well joynd, inelegant, but bring
> Taste after taste upheld with kindliest change,
> Bestirs her then, and from each tender stalk
> Whatever Earth all-bearing Mother yields
> In *India* East or West, or middle shoare
> In *Pontus* or the *Punic* Coast, or where
> *Alcinous* reign'd, fruit of all kindes, in coate,
> Rough, or smooth rin'd, or bearded husk, or shell
> She gathers, Tribute large, and on the board

Heaps with unsparing hand; for drink the Grape
She crushes, inoffensive moust, and meathes
From many a berrie, and from sweet kernels prest
She tempers dulcet creams, nor these to hold
Wants her fit vessels pure, then strews the ground
With Rose and Odours from the shrub unfum'd. (5.331–49)

Well-joining her tastes and tempering her creams, Eve the salad artist combines the diverse elements of Eden into a delicate balance. Milton here departs from the culinary chauvinism of recipe book authors like Evelyn, who boasts that the best salads are made "without so much as a Grain of *Exotic Spice*," untainted by "the Luxury of the East," or Gervase Markham, whose English housewife's admirably economical and ecoconscious locavorism is also a xenophobic refusal of both foreign products and foreignness in general.[34] Eve's salad ingredients could be those that would later grow in the East Indies, "or" the West Indies, "or" the Punic Coast, with the Miltonic "or" attesting to how the tempering or mixing of possibilities is also a suspension of multiple temporal and geographical worlds: the present tense, as she "gathers" what the Asian or African or American earth "yields," erases later geopolitical distinctions even as they are evoked.[35]

In a sense, Adam and Eve's marital misunderstanding is like something out of a sitcom: the ignorant husband gesturing vaguely to whatever it is wives do; the unappreciated wife rolling her eyes for the audience's benefit. "This is comedy," Thomas Kranidas declares (approvingly) of this passage.[36] But when Eve, as Diane McColley puts it, "takes her work seriously," we are invited to take it seriously as well.[37] Like the self-reforming moral subject of *Areopagitica* who promiscuously tastes and then tempers a wide range of materials to compose useful and effective medicines, Eve knows to be at once unsparing in her initial selections and careful in her ensuing combinations. Eve's domestic labors may be important, as Ricks claims of the couple's labors in general, because they are imbued with impending tragedy, but they also have the much more immediate value of modeling the Miltonic cultivation of language, the continuous process of correcting excess in order to let what Ricks calls "living tissue" thrive.[38] As Evelyn puts it, glossing Milton's lines about Eve choosing and mixing harmonious tastes to illustrate his own salad-composing philosophy, "the main skill of an artist lies in this," the deictic "this" effectively collapsing Eve's skill of assembling vegetal elements with Milton's skill of strategically setting words off each other, the artistry that the poet describes with the artistry he enacts.[39] The introduction of the idea of inelegant tastes might be less a depressing glimpse into postlapsarian cooking than a careful and controlled correction, on the part of Milton and Eve alike, of negative possibilities with positive ones. Eve's work to keep the garden and its ingredients in a sustainable suspension, "upheld with kindliest change," demonstrates that tempering tastes by correctly mixing them together (or, in some cases, storing them to ripen over time) is precisely what upholds both taste and paradise itself.[40] As Evelyn sums up, after again quoting "our Paradisian Bard" in his description of Eve's hospitality, "Thus, the *Hortulan* Provision of the *Golden Age* fitted all *Places*, *Times*, and *Persons*; and when Man is restor'd to that State again, it will be as it was in the Beginning."[41] This "golden age," unlike the one that precedes Jupiter's curse in the *Georgics*, is provisioned not directly by the garden itself, but by the laborious processing of the garden's fruits.

Adam, meanwhile, remains more concerned with the consumption than the production of food, and soon entreats his guest to dish about the angelic diet. Raphael assures Adam that deviating from his usual fare of mellifluous dews and pearly grain to dine on earthly fruits will not wreak havoc on his digestive system, because the substance of angels and humans differs in degree, not in kind. Appropriately enough for a lunch served in a garden, and in keeping with the rhythms of Edenic life so far, Raphael goes on to use a half-botanical, half-digestive metaphor to illustrate this continuum from human to angel:

> So from the root
> Springs lighter the green stalk, from thence the leaves
> More aerie, last the bright consummate floure
> Spirits odorous breathes: flours and thir fruit
> Mans nourishment, by gradual scale sublim'd
> To vital Spirits aspire, to animal,
> To intellectual, give both life and sense. (5.479–85)

The trees become increasingly ethereal as they rise from their roots up through their stalks, their "more aerie" leaves, and finally the flowers that, like those in the physician John French's foolproof method of distillation, will "yeelde their spirit easily."[42] Raphael goes on to explain how humans, by simply reproducing themselves *as* human through their digestion and assimilation of nutrients, can progress from eating earthly fruits to imbibing the celestial food of heaven. And here he describes how Adam and Eve can themselves gradually sublime into more rarefied, spiritual forms:

> time may come when men
> With Angels may participate, and find
> No inconvenient Diet, nor too light Fare:
> And from these corporal nutriments perhaps
> Your bodies may at last turn all to Spirit,
> Improv'd by tract of time, and wingd ascend
> Ethereal, as wee. (5.493–99)

Now things begin, however haltingly, to shift away from the regimen of preservation, maintenance, and metabolic reproduction—the domain of domestic georgic—and into a new paradigm of progress, improvement, and teleological georgic. "Improv'd" and "sublim'd," Adam and Eve will ("perhaps"!) one day be able to "ascend": this, it seems, is progress. It is also what is earlier insinuated by Eve's oneiric interlocutor as he offers her a corporal nutriment that promises to turn her body to spirit at once: "Thy self a Goddess," the Satanic premonition addresses Eve, "not to Earth confind" (5.78).

Raphael concludes, however, by reminding his listeners to remain "obedient" and to respect the limits currently imposed on them: "Mean while enjoy / Your fill what happiness this happie state / Can comprehend, incapable of more" (5.503–5). The angelic instruction, unlike the Satanic one and like the later injunction to be "lowlie wise," is squarely in the "georgic spirit," to use Anthony Low's preferred phrase, as is Adam's response to the latter: "to know / That which before us lies in daily life, / Is the prime Wisdom" (8.173, 192–94).[43] The couple are told merely to survive space and time, remaining "confind" by their parameters, and perhaps *by* survival—by continuing to sustain themselves on the "corporal nutriments" to which they are already accustomed—only *then* to surpass themselves. The "gradual scale" by which they may eventually be sublimed is so gradual as to be imperceptible. They must, in other words, suspend the idea of progress or improvement, however delicious, and focus for the time being merely on maintenance.[44]

But if Raphael's advice means to enjoin Adam and Eve to be happy with their happy state of self-reproduction, it also introduces a concept of linear progress of which Adam and Eve had, in their collective life, originally been innocent.[45] Time has up till now been an organizational principle of pleasant alternation between day and night, work and rest: "God hath set / Labour and rest, as day and night to men / Successive," Adam had helpfully explained while guiding Eve to bed (4.612–14). But now it is suddenly possible to understand time as an uninterrupted "tract," a narrative with an endpoint. And so too have the daily, cyclical labors of the digestive tract been proleptically flattened and converted into the forward trajectory of history.

Fast-forwarding to book 9, we find Eve on the fast track of this trajectory. Faced with the forbidden fruit, she is seduced by the promise of suddenly subliming:

> what hinders then
> To reach, and feed at once both Bodie and Mind?
> So saying, her rash hand in evil hour
> Forth reaching to the Fruit, she pluck'd, she eat. (9.778–81)

Thus the precise locus of Eve's transgression is not only in *that* she eats, but also in *how* she eats, no sooner ("so saying") announcing her intention than already "reaching" with "rash hand," then plucking, eating, in a frenzied asyndeton, without any tempering, without even a pause for a conjunction. This is not to suggest that eating the fruit would have been inconsequential as long as Eve had first taken some deep breaths and a meditative walk around the garden, but rather that the temporal collapse of the form is inseparable from the content of the act. The whole appeal of the fruit is that eating it will afford instant results, dispensing with all the incremental cultivation, minor self-corrections, and drawn-out suspensions—the daily pruning of branches, the frugal storing—that have been integral to paradisal life. The valorization of efficiency that informs her action—to "feed at once both Bodie and Mind" certainly sounds economical—continues what Quilligan calls the "proto-capitalist" line of reasoning that had led Eve to propose that she and Adam "divide [their] labours" (9.214) in the first place, leaving her alone and vulnerable to Satan.[46] Why drag out the workday by seasoning their labor with conversation and kisses, Eve had protested to her husband, when they could get more done, in less time, apart?

When Eve suggests this, Adam commends his helpmeet on her well-"imployed" thoughts, which indicate her commitment to "studie houshold good" and promote "good workes" in her husband, to the profit of them both:

> Well hast thou motion'd, well thy thoughts imployd
> How we might best fulfill the work which here
> God hath assign'd us, nor of me shalt pass
> Unprais'd: for nothing lovelier can be found
> In Woman, then to studie houshold good,
> And good workes in her Husband to promote. (9.229–34)

If the gendered division of labor in the middle books separates Adam's intellectual commerce with Raphael from Eve's manual labor within the bower, Adam here ascribes "studie" to Eve, as if the most hidden abode of the bower were, like a "closet" in an early modern household, a potential site of both feminine domestic labor and the masculine intellectual labor of study, in either case a repository of secrets.[47] Reacting to feminist criticism that Eve is left out of worthwhile paradisal activities, "relegated" to the boring bower, Barbara Lewalski argues instead that Eve "transcends" her domestic role. Noting that Adam and Eve garden side by side and that Eve overhears almost all of Adam's exchange of ideas with Raphael, Lewalski would save Eve from irrelevance: "Eve, far from being confined to her bower and her domestic concerns while Adam forges forth in the outside world, is imagined to share fully with her mate in the necessary work of that world."[48] But it must also be said that Adam is shut out—or shuts himself out—of the bower, and is unable or unwilling to share fully in the work of the *inside* world, both of the kitchen and of the mentally interior gathering, storing, tempering, and organizing that accompany the housewife's bodily activities.[49] Adam's inability or unwillingness to participate fully in the domestic economy is a failure to conceive of paradisal labor as an activity that is neither fruitless nor directly productive or progressive, but that, for the time being, preserves the world and its fruits through repeated acts of tempering.[50]

Back in book 5, Eve had understood—in a way Adam, so anxious to impress Raphael with conspicuous consumption, had not—that household good, like Milton's poetic labor in Evelyn's gloss, was organized around tempering and preserving available materials, rather than accumulating new ones, and this understanding was intimately tied to her vocation as a domestic laborer. When Eve mentions that some fruits do better in storage, the possibility of any kind of improvement is only an afterthought, a possibility suspended, or saved, as if in parentheses: "Save what by frugal storing firmness gains / To nourish, and superfluous moist consumes." In this aside, Eve imagines gains as coming only when the labor of harvesting has been suspended. C. S. Lewis's famous criticism of the last two books of *Paradise Lost* as an "untransmuted lump of futurity" and thus an "inartistic" inadequacy, a reading since replaced with more charitable evaluations of the ending's poetic success, might be revalued and restored: an "untransmuted" state might be read not as an infelicity but as the preservation of potential, the kind of as-yet-untransmuted lump that, in Milton's simile for Raphael's angelic digestion, "the Empiric Alchemist / Can turn, or holds it possible to turn / . . . to perfet Gold" (5.440–42), where the felt possibility of the alchemist's transmutation is as worthy of mention as his actual ability.[51]

Eve's domestic georgic—where interior labor aims primarily at preservation—offers us a new conception of, or alternative to, Bacon's "Georgics of the mind," the heroic intellectual labor that would lead to the advancement of learning, commerce, and imperial power. It also helps us see Milton's productivity, especially once he became blind, as of a piece with that of the women in his household: his daughters who served as substitute amanuenses during the composition of *Paradise Lost*, among those ready to respond to his call to be "milked" every morning after the nightly visits of the Muse, and his wife, who, Eve-like, prepared ostensibly eyesight-boosting protomacrobiotic meals according to her husband's exacting standards as well as acting as an amanuensis herself.[52] The georgic energies of Milton's unfallen Eve, like those of Milton as well as of his wife and daughters, are focused on maintaining the conditions that make intellectual life possible.[53]

## Reproducing the Incarnation: *Paradise Regain'd*

*Paradise Regain'd* is in a way less a sequel than a second iteration of *Paradise Lost*. Milton's amanuensis Thomas Ellwood's critique of the latter—"Thou has said much here of *Paradise lost*, but what hast thou to say of *Paradise found*?"—was, by Ellwood's account, something the poet "had not thought of," though near the end of *Paradise Lost* Adam is explicitly told he can find a "paradise within thee, happier farr" (12.587), a proclamation repeated in the basic plot structure of *Paradise Regain'd*.[54] Through the Son, *Paradise Regain'd* offers a more sustainable model of subliming by gradual scale than Adam and Eve could imagine. The effect, to readers' eternal disappointment, is even more gradual and less sublime than the model proposed by Raphael and both more georgic and more domestic in character than that of *Paradise Lost*. As the Son—so called with reference as much to Mary, whose "Mothers house" he returns to at the end of the poem (4.639), as to God—greets Satan's frenetic temptations in the wilderness with a series of preternaturally calm refusals, the reader herself may feel tempted to shake the idle hero into action, or at least to sympathize with Satan when he sputters, "What dost thou in this World?" (4.372).[55] Some critics have defended the Son's passivity with reference to Milton's own political position as the only viable option for a righteous person under an unlawful regime. Others have sought to save the Son from the charge of passivity in the first place, reframing his apparent idleness as a form of crypto-heroic action. But like the attempted redemption of Eve's "relegation" to domesticity, this approach passes over the possibility that the Son's interior work could be directed toward provisional maintenance: the incremental preservation of biological and intellectual life that must be performed privately and incessantly until conditions allow for that life to be lived publicly. Rather than trying to convert the Son's stance into a form of legibly productive action, we could look to the Son's reproductive labor that, while conducted individually for now, could prove a model for collective life.

Readers of *Paradise Regain'd* could reasonably expect, upon hearing some celestial trumpet blaring at the beginning of book 1, to witness the Son in heroic action. This expectation might be modified, however, with an awareness of how this "brief epic" is tempered at every turn by elements of the *Georgics*: both poems employ the rare four-book structure, both are written in a middle style that frequently gestures to both epic heights and pastoral humility, and both, particularly if we take the Son as typed on Job, focus their praise on a hardworking farmer-like figure.[56] And the poet quickly clarifies a few lines into book 1 what the ingredients of this epic are: "deeds / Above Heroic, though in secret done" (1.14–15). In Hannah Arendt's terms from *The Human Condition*, this is a blatant contradiction: heroic action is inherently public, defined primarily by the "courage" in "leaving one's private hiding place and showing who one is."[57] Here, with the flight of heroism no sooner announced than discounted with that concessive "though," we are alerted that this poem will be a record less of accomplishment than of modification and correction, with each deed elevated to a state "above heroic" only to be immediately domesticated down to a lower order, epic triumph tempered by and into domestic georgic.

After enduring the spotlight at his baptism, which had turned into a surprise coming-out party for the Son of God, and while "they in Heav'n their Odes and Vigils tun'd" in joyous anticipation of how he will "vanquish by wisdom hellish wiles" (1.182, 175), Jesus abruptly decides to take a meditation retreat. Though his internal dialogue with himself, or God—he is "alone," but with "the Spirit leading"; he is immersed in "his deep thoughts, the better to converse / With solitude" (1.189–91)—is nominally a planning meeting for how he might "publish his God-like office now mature" (1.188), the Son apparently has some maturing work left to do. "Musing and much revolving in his brest," he feels ill-equipped to organize "a multitude of thoughts at once / Awakn'd in me," and he is unable to make his inward state accord with what he has heard about himself, "ill sorting with my present state compar'd" (1.185, 196–97, 200). This internal attempt to sort what is "ill sorting"—a tempering that is a version of the explicitly georgic pruning and explicitly domestic salad-making of Adam and Eve—goes on for more than a hundred lines.

The Son seems to have acquired this habit from his mother, who, by continuously reflecting upon words and signs she has received from her son and elsewhere, works to inure herself to the uncertainty of his current unannounced absence from home. The distressed Mary can only assuage the worried thoughts "rais'd" in her breast after having "clad" them "in sighs" (2.64–65). This swaddling takes the form of an extended speech, an account of the events of her life as a mother and expectant mother, the words of the prophets, and the recent and past actions of her son. She ends by recalling what happened when the twelve-year-old Jesus ran away to the temple and how she "mus'd" upon it afterward:

> What he meant I mus'd,
> Since understand; much more his absence now
> Thus long to some great purpose he obscures.
> But I to wait with patience am inur'd;
> My heart has been a store-house long of things
> And sayings laid up, portending strange events. (2.99–104)

Reframing past events in terms of current ones and adjusting her mental response accordingly, Mary, "second Eve," shares Eve's foresight in saving that which would not, to casual observers, seem to require gathering up and storing away. Furthermore, she echoes Eve in her attention to organizing rather than merely retaining her materials, or rather in her sense that "mere" retention necessarily requires the proper ordering and tempering of materials over time, in order to adapt things and sayings to changing circumstances while still keeping them as themselves. Consciously fashioning herself into a repository rather than unwittingly serving as one, Mary has prepared herself as a fit vessel (it is in part by having protectively "clad" her worries "in sighs" that she can be "inur'd" with patience), and her preparations continue once the storing begins: "pondering oft, and oft to mind / Recalling," "with thoughts / Meekly compos'd" (2.105–8). In the "store-house" of Mary's breast, words are allowed to ripen within the body, so that "what he meant I mus'd, / Since understand," crude language "since" processed into digestibility like the fruit that, Eve explains, "by frugal storing firmness gains / To nourish" (5.324–25). Laboring thus internally, Mary does not, as some critics contend, count herself among those "who only stand and waite."[58] Stanley Fish, who includes Mary in his claim that "waiting is the only action (or nonaction) the characters in *Paradise Regained* ever take," reads as a "declaration of passivity" what I take as an account of internal, reproductive labor, a labor that has defined Mary's existence since the conception of the Son of God and that did not cease after his birth.[59]

An obsession with proper curation and storage, as Dayton Haskin argues, also reflects the methods of Milton himself, who painstakingly "gathered, compared, and synthesized diverse biblical passages" with the intent of forming them into his final epic.[60] Milton's description in *De Doctrina Christiana* of storing up passages into a "treasure [*thesaurum*] which would be a provision for my future life" echoes a wealth of contemporary discourse about "laying up" scriptural treasure and other words of wisdom in literal or figurative "cabinets" as a personal investment in grace or knowledge.[61] It also describes Milton's prescription for biblical reading in *Doctrine and Discipline of Divorce*: since Christ has scattered "the heavenly grain of his doctrine like pearle heer and there, which requires a skilfull and laborious gatherer," readers must take up a vocation of gathering, saving, and storing in order to have access to that doctrine at all (969). In a more collective call to curation, at a political moment when such organizing work felt more immediately possible, Milton envisions in *Areopagitica* "the sad friends of Truth" as together conscripted into "imitating the carefull search that *Isis* made for the mangl'd body of *Osiris*," with the restorative goal of "gathering up" the "hewd" and "scatter'd" pieces of what was once the "perfect shape" of Truth (1017–18). Haskin concludes that the biblical account of Mary's attitude toward the circumstances of Jesus' birth— she kept them (*sunetērei*), putting them together (*sumballousa*) in her heart (Luke 2:19)—affords Mary the poetic role of creation, a role imitated by the Son and meant to be imitated in turn by the actively creative reader.[62]

While critics like Haskin aim to elevate such organizing labors to the status of productive work, the poet's role—like Mary's, the Son's, and the reader's—can be more clearly understood in relation to domestic georgic: as reproductive as it is productive, as reconstitutive as it is creative of something new. The invisible work performed on that which is kept "laid up," so easily confused for a lack of activity or redefined as a heroic form of action, is a modestly reproductive labor that commissions time to help both process and preserve material that might otherwise be lost. To recall Low's definition of the georgic as between private (pastoral) and public (epic) and how the georgic Son mediates between the two—"He works in obscurity, yet his deeds have public results"—these public results never, in the space of the poem, come to fruition.[63] When in the final line the Son "home to his Mothers house private return'd" (4.639), the poem leaves us in doubt as to whether big things will ever come from these small movements. Even if secret, private deeds gesture to public futures, those futures can only be represented as speculative.

Satan, as he tempts the Son throughout the poem, does not understand that ripeness can be a product of such studied composition rather than the inevitable and unwanted result of passing time. He cannot, in other words, conceive of a work of culture that occurs internally and invisibly. In the opening salvo of book 3, as he mounts the argument of the temptation to glory, Satan casts overripeness as the stage that inevitably follows ripeness: "Thy years are ripe, and over-ripe.... / Yet years, and to ripe years judgment mature, / Quench not the thirst of glory, but augment" (3.31, 37–38). A Satanic model of ripening goes from "ripe" to "over-ripe" without any intervening action, without acknowledging the storing and saving practices that can continue beyond the natural process of ripening to prevent superfluity from being consumed. Denise Gigante argues that when Satan says of Jesus that he has "found him, view'd him, tasted him, but find / Far other labour to be undergon" (2.131–32), he "finds him to be something he cannot digest," but perhaps more to the point, Satan is uninterested in digestion or in any tasting or testing that requires internal "labour."[64]

The Son, by contrast, spends the entire poem cultivating an internal practice of cultivation that simply allows him to continue being who he is, "thought following thought, and step by step led on" (1.192), with no discrete destination ever proposed. After some hand-wringing attempts to resolve those "ill sorting" contradictions that had been plaguing him, the Son implicitly acknowledges the merit of his mother's internal interpretive model. Reproducing Mary's compressed narration of his life to him, he recalls how his response was to call upon the scriptural material available to him and thus to confirm his mother's account of his identity:

> This having heard, strait I again revolv'd
> The Law and Prophets, searching what was writ
> Concerning the Messiah, to our Scribes
> Known partly, and soon found of whom they spake
> I am. (1.259–63)

This labor recalls and continues Mary's mental processing, turning thoughts over in her mind without exactly producing anything new, a labor in a way more properly "reproductive" than the new creation of childbirth. She begins her monologue as a way to deal with those "troubl'd thoughts" or "motherly cares and fears" "rais'd" in her mind, which she treats in a correspondingly motherly way, making sure they are adequately "clad" by her sighed speech (2.64–65). And even as she despairs that her conception of her son was a past act that has no bearing on the present, her concern is assuringly answered by its own expression: "O what avails me now that honour high / To have conceiv'd of God" (2.66–67). As with the thoughtful ruminant animals who, in *Paradise Lost*, head "bedward ruminating" (4.352), the distinction between having conceived her child and continuing to conceive of what the future may hold in store for him dissolves.[65]

Meanwhile the Son, processing his thoughts in solitude, begins to ruminate on the prospect of turning incorporeal fare into corporeal substance. Having wandered in the desert for forty days, he only just now realizes he is hungry: "But now I feel I hunger, which declares, / Nature hath need of what she asks" (2.252–53). Despite his slight discomfort, though, the Son is forced to admit that his hunger has no material consequences:

> yet God
> Can satisfie that need some other way,
> Though hunger still remain: so it remain
> Without this bodies wasting, I content me,
> And from the sting of Famine fear no harm,
> Nor mind it, fed with better thoughts that feed
> Mee hungering more to do my Fathers will. (2.253–59)

Jesus is confident that his hunger will continue to be "without this bodies wasting," with no effect on his body. The only explanation for this is that he has really, literally, been fed by "better thoughts." These are not the pleasing thoughts of consolation or distraction, some spiritual food that will figuratively sustain him through, or transcend, the inevitable degradation of his flesh or that will one day prove to be food for poetic thought. Rather, these thoughts will physically and immediately preserve his body, like a miracle weight-loss-prevention formula that counteracts any "harm" or "wasting" by continuously converting incorporeal thoughts into reconstitutive corporeal matter. In other words, he is fed by himself, or by what he has endogenously incorporated from a "Father" to whom he can claim unmediated access. His commerce, in other words, is entirely with himself, from "I feel I hunger" to "I content me."

The "paradise within" is here, to draw upon Michael Schoenfeldt's apt literal-mindedness, "within" in a physiological sense, in the purely self-sustaining body, in a way that both subsumes and nullifies a more

metaphorical kind of inwardness—such that in the Son, counterintuitively and countertypologically, it is the literal that fulfills the figurative.[66] The Son thus reverses the transubstantiating digestion performed by Raphael in *Paradise Lost*, as Adam observes in wonder the
angel's healthy appetite for Eve's earthly food:

> nor seemingly
> The Angel, nor in mist, the common gloss
> Of Theologians, but with keen dispatch
> Of real hunger, and concoctive heate
> To transubstantiate. (5.434–38)

Raphael's quasi-alchemical "transubstantiation" of food into angelic
substance, which occasions the explanation of the cosmic "gradual
scale" discussed in the previous section, is part of what so confuses
Adam and Eve, who had only understood transformative processes, and
time itself, as cyclical. The Son, by continuously completing the other
half of this process of transubstantiation—metabolically turning spirit
into flesh as surely as Raphael turned flesh into spirit—restores a paradisal circularity to time and transformation, recasting these processes
as reproductive rather than productive, as enabling of survival rather
than of progressive sublimation.

　　If the premise of *Paradise Regain'd* is that the Fall was not, contrary to orthodox Christian doctrine, reversed once and for all by the
crucifixion, Milton thus suggests the additional heterodoxy that the
Son's incarnation is achieved not once and for all by his birth but is
rather produced continuously, metabolically, by the ongoing, reproductive sacrament of self-examination.[67] The immediacy of this conversion of word into flesh is not in its instantaneity—the nutritional
value of thoughts is made available only when they have already been
thoroughly thought through—but in the constancy and locality of the
process. Milton's Jesus only gradually comes to the conclusion that
thoughts will sustain him, working through the logical steps: "But
now . . . yet . . . though . . . so." Paradise is thus regained, in Milton's
poem, not by a finite self-sacrifice occurring at a single moment in time
but by a continuous self-reproduction. Likewise incarnation, no more
final than crucifixion, is not achieved once and for all by the divine
birth: Jesus must constantly metabolize spirit, constantly make the
Word flesh. Culturing his stores of textual material into physical sustenance, the Son makes of biblical interpretation a metabolic process that
is both bodily and invisible. It is through this domestic georgic model
that we can understand the Son's literal self-absorption as the conver-

sion of the cultural, cultivating activity of interpretation into the very stuff of natural, biological life. The Son is fed by himself, or by the education he has incorporated from his mother, which—when he thinks about it long enough—amounts to his identity as his Father's Son.

Noting that the "paradise within" promised to Adam and Eve in *Paradise Lost*, and carefully tended to by the Son in *Paradise Regain'd*, is in disturbing parallel to Satan's claim that "the mind is its own place" (1.254), Seth Lobis contrasts Adam and Eve's innocent georgic—their local "tending" of each other and the garden's lesser life forms—with Satan's dark georgic, which "tends" in the sense of tension or stretching to greater ambitions.[68] If Satan, particularly in *Paradise Regain'd*, where he caps off his offer of the Roman Empire with an exhortation to the Son to "aim therefore at no less than all the world" (4.105), tends to imperial overreach, this serves as a reminder that georgics of the mind can be as easily excessive as moderate, as irresponsibly expansive as temperately sustainable. In domestic georgic, ripeness is all, and yet it is never, on its own, enough, as it is always subject to future uncertainty: the "store" that "ripe for use hangs on the stalk" in Eden, and of which Eve sets aside small provision anyway; the Son's "ripe" years, construed—mistakenly, we are led to believe—by Satan as "over-ripe"; and the "field / Of Ceres, ripe for harvest" that Milton compares to the phalanx of angels surrounding Satan and that, the plowman all too rightly fears, may "prove chaff."

# Conclusion

## A WOMAN'S WORK IS NEVER DONE

*There are years, days, hours, minutes, weeks, moments, and other mea-sures of time spent in the production of "not writing." Not writing is work-ing, and when not working at paid work working at unpaid work like caring for others, and when not at unpaid work like caring, caring also for a human body, and when not caring for a human body many hours, weeks, years, and other measures of time spent caring for the mind in a way like reading or learning and when not reading and learning also making things (like garments, food, plants, artworks, decorative items) and when not reading and learning and working and making and carry-ing and worrying also politics.*

ANNE BOYER, "What is 'Not Writing'?"

*The poem was jotted in fragments during children's naps, brief hours in a library, or at 3 a.m. after rising with a wakeful child. I despaired of doing any continuous work at this time, yet I began to feel that my fragments had a common consciousness and a common theme.*

ADRIENNE RICH, "When We Dead Awaken"

This book has argued that encyclopedic and monumental works—the epics of Spenser and Milton, the psychedelic epyllion of Marvell, the sprawling multivolume texts of Rabelais and Montaigne—can, when read in a minor key, reveal the networks of small-scale repetitive labors that sustain their fictional worlds and the worlds of their authors. I have focused on high-canonical male writers to foreground the surprising juxtaposition between their reputations of transcendent literary genius and their preoccupations with annoying menial labor. In briefly turn-ing now to two poems written by women, Mary Collier's "The Woman's Labour" (1739) and Alice Oswald's *Memorial* (2011), both of which put women's manual and affective labor center stage and respond to poems by men, I aim to show how the domestic georgic concerns that persist and recur in canonical literary texts like kidney stones—the returning obsessions with the repetitive labors that sustain worlds—inspire repetitive labors in turn. These labors are corrective as well as preservative, literary as well as critical. In closing, I also want to gesture toward how the recent quasi-literal feminization of humanistic work in the twenty-first century has made intellectual and domestic labor—curatorial work and care work, the sustaining of institutions and the sustaining of bodies, writing and what Anne Boyer calls "not writing"—increasingly interwoven.

In "The Woman's Labour," Collier, a washerwoman who also took on various other seasonal jobs, represents the daily labors of women like her as a laundry list in heroic couplets, supplementing the story left incomplete by fellow laborer-poet Stephen Duck.[1] Male agricultural laborers like Duck, to whose "The Thresher's Labour" (1730) Collier's poem explicitly responds, were subject to work schedules whose apparent variation belied a fundamental monotony, which Duck's diction ploddingly hits home. "Week after Week we this dull Task pursue," grumbles Duck, "Unless when winn'wing Days produce a new: / A new, indeed, but frequently a worse!" (69–70). "A new" follows "a new" just as unchangingly, despite the expectation aroused by the enjambment, as "week" follows "week." But at the end of the day, Duck and his fellow threshers are allowed to rest from their repetitive toils. Every evening, the threshers come home to warm meals and warm beds prepared by their wives—wives who were also working all day in the fields or in the homes of the better-off, which is why their work is truly ceaseless, while Duck's can only be said to be so hyperbolically. In "The Woman's Labour," as the men settle in for supper, Collier's heroic couplets march on relentlessly:

When Ev'ning does approach, we homeward hie,
And our domestic Toils incessant ply:
Against your coming Home prepare to get
Our Work all done, our House in order set;
*Bacon* and *Dumpling* in the Pot we boil,
Our Beds we make, our Swine we feed the while;
Then wait at Door to see you coming Home,
And set the Table out against you come:
Early next Morning we on you attend;
Our Children dress and feed, their Cloaths we mend;
And in the Field our daily Task renew,
Soon as the rising Sun has dry'd the Dew. (74–85)

A parade of commas, colons, and semicolons dilate Collier's sentences to the length of an overscheduled day, the rhyming tasks recalling the nun's account of daily convent life in *Upon Appleton House* ("So through the mortal fruit we boil / The sugar's uncorrupting oil") or the "huswiues affaires" that, in Thomas Tusser's didactic couplets, "hath neuer none ende."[2] Yet the flurry of activity is described as strangely passive, full of waiting, doing nothing more than keeping the home up for the husband's return. Like the full-time housewives whose "unproductive" labor leaves no lasting tangible effects, working-class wives must "against your coming Home prepare"; they "wait at Door to see you coming Home"; they "set the Table out against you come"; in the morning they "on you attend," suggesting an attitude of open-ended subservience more than any discrete tasks.

But even this relatively empty time does not seem to be available for the imagination; it is not the pastoral idle time when the shepherd, while watching his flock, can lazily strum his lyre. For Simone de Beauvoir, this state of constant, diligent vigilance is what makes the modern housewife's existence so pathetic: "It is laden with waiting; . . . there are long moments of passivity and emptiness; most of the time, [tasks] are accomplished in boredom."[3] Waiting provides no leisure for Collier's speaker, and there is no comfort in her tasks' predictability. After her initial description of her second shift, she spends a few lines redescribing the daily work in the fields, and then the cycle repeats: "We must make haste, for when we Home are come, / Alas! we find our Work but just begun," as if upon crossing the threshold of the enjambment she is somehow surprised—"Alas!"—to find herself crowded in by the same old set of vague duties ("So many Things for our Attendance call"; "We all Things for your coming Home prepare") as the previous day (104–5, 106, 109).

In Duck's georgic world, a space, however small and however strenuously denied by the poet, remains for meditation. "No Intermission in our Work we know" is how Duck introduces what amounts to a lengthy intermission in his poem, a negative enumeration of all the pastoral pleasures denied him and his fellow threshers:

> Our Eye beholds no pleasing Object here,
> No cheerful Sound diverts our list'ning Ear.
> The Shepherd well may tune his Voice to sing,
> Inspir'd with all the Beauties of the Spring.
> No Fountains murmur here, no Lambkins play,
> No Linnets warble, and no Fields look gay. (54–59)

Relieved of the mounting pressures of Duck's catalog of "the Toils of each revolving Year; / Those endless Toils which ever grow anew" (8–9), the reader and the speaker alike pause to take in the negative image of an idyllic landscape. If there are no murmuring fountains or gamboling lambs, there is still the leisure to imagine them. Duck goes on to insist that even in sleep the threshers find no refuge: "We then perform our Labours o'er again: / Our mimic Fancy ever restless seems; / And what we act awake, she acts in Dreams" (254–56). But here it is a female figure who is working overtime, as Duck implicitly corrects his claim that it is the men themselves dreamworking the night shift; in fact, it is "she" (Fancy) who "acts," just as at the poem's outset an epic "Muse" is called upon to "prepare" the thresher's song (2, 7). In Collier's museless poem, she who acts while men dream is a far cry from Fancy: mothers, exhausted from working all day in and outside the house, "but little sleep can have, / Because our froward Children cry and rave" (112–13). Yet Collier, like the much later Anne Boyer and Adrienne Rich in the epigraphs above, represents the sleepless anxiety of caregiving, rather than a quiet room of her own, as the circumstance as well as the material for poetic production. She is, after all, writing a poem about the conditions that, according to Beauvoir's theory, should make it impossible to write a poem, and that for Boyer are the conditions for "not writing," which also seem to be the conditions—"working, and when not working at paid work working at unpaid work like caring for others, and when not at unpaid work like caring, caring also for a human body"—for writing a poem called "What Is 'Not Writing'?"[4] The very discontinuity created by the constant interruptions of childcare and other extrapoetic obligations creates a certain continuity with its own momentum, "fragments" taking on "a common consciousness and a common theme," as Rich puts it.[5]

"A Woman's Labour" refuses the pastoralism of "The Thresher's Labour," filling the glancing gaps Duck leaves open for rest and reverie with all the domestic georgic labors that allow for others' rest and reverie. From the other end of the Virgilian sequence of genres, Oswald's *Memorial* demotes Homer's *Iliad* to domestic georgic, denuding the poem of its epic material to reveal the metabolic operations that make epic action possible and memorable. This might also be called, in Hannah Arendt's terms, a depoliticization of epic. All the action in the *Iliad*—the great speeches of great men, disclosing themselves in their particularity, each of them a hero who has left the safe, private space of home to enter into the public world of war—is evacuated. Only labor— "the activity which corresponds to the biological process of the human body" and to "the over-all gigantic circle of nature herself, where no beginning and no end exist and where all natural things swing in changeless, deathless repetition"—remains.[6] If Oswald's original British subtitle, "An Excavation of the *Iliad*," might evoke a heroic georgic—the muscular, singular, and literally groundbreaking archaeological accomplishment of unearthing artifacts from the past—the US edition corrects that connotation: this, the new subtitle clarifies, is merely "A Version of Homer's *Iliad*," one among many in its over twenty-five-hundred-year reception history.[7] Stripping Homer's poem down to a series of miniobituaries, often delivered in deadpan, punctuated by similes describing domestic, agricultural, or natural activity, Oswald iterates epic as domestic georgic.

Oswald's poem, like Collier's with its echoing couplets, is structured by repetition. The initial roll call of all the fatalities recorded by Homer, in an unbroken column of names in all caps that recalls both Maya Lin's Vietnam War Memorial and the Linear B tablets that inventoried royal supplies, is repeated in the second section, where they are sometimes relisted, sometimes afforded a narrative vignette, and interspersed with similes, each of which is printed twice.[8] The last section consists of single similes, suspended in the middle of the page, with only the final simile repeated. Entirely free of punctuation, the poem in some ways embodies the flow and flux of nature and of oral poetry, what Eavan Boland calls, in her afterword, an "image of the *Iliad* as a river, not an inland sea, flowing in and out of song, performance, memory, elegy and human interaction" (89). But *Memorial* also creates stagnant still waters, at least temporarily, both in its repetitions and in its form, the kind of tense, dense affective stuff that for Collier fills in what the outside observer might see as empty time. Take the example of the horse Pedasus, the lone nonhuman whose death is recorded:

> One side had stables and stone water troughs
> They caught a horse in the windy hills
> They put it in the king's paddock
> And called it PEDASUS the Leaper
> The other side had sacks of white barley
> They stole that horse and whipped it into battle
> Pedasus with unquestioning eyes
> Carried and served both sides
> Now the earth is his owner
> Like a drop of fig juice squeezed into milk
> Mysteriously thickens it
> As if a drip of lethargy

Falls into the bucket
And the woman stirring
Stops
Like a drop of fig juice squeezed into milk
Mysteriously thickens it
As if a drip of lethargy
Falls into the bucket
And the woman stirring
Stops (57)

Fed by and laboring for first "one side," then "the other side"—the repeated "they" makes the Greeks indistinguishable from the Trojans,
one side in a world-historic conflict merely a reiteration of the other—
the horse is freed by death from the repetitive cycle of labor only for
labor to begin again with the repeated simile, something like Collier's
return from a day's work of winnowing or washing only to encounter
another set of repetitive labors at home. Lack of end stops notwith-
standing, the poem abruptly "stops" when the woman stirring does,
a stop that seems a stutter step away from the way the milk seizes up
when the fig juice is added as a coagulant. Elsewhere, we learn Ajax
"stopped" and killed Acamas

Like that slow-motion moment
When a woman weighs the wool
Her poor old spider hands
Work all night spinning a living for her children
And then she stops
She soothes the scales to a standstill
Like that slow-motion moment
When a woman weighs the wool
Her poor old spider hands
Work all night spinning a living for her children
And then she stops
She soothes the scales to a standstill (22)

Here again, the sudden stop to a man's life is twice repeated and dilated
in a momentary "standstill" as a woman makes her "living." Arrests of
life are necessary for life to continue, in jittery stops and starts that can
constitute a flow only when observed from afar.

Reading Collier's and Oswald's poems, for all their wit and beauty,
can be a slog. One review of *Memorial* calls it a "rosy-fingered yawn";
another complains that between the "bureaucracy of death" and the

"merely tedious" repeated similes, "the life of the 'Iliad' has vanished here."[9] Even an admirer describes it as "numbing, repetitive, and continually anticlimactic."[10] Collier, when she earns discussion beyond a passing acknowledgment as the first poet of the second shift, is praised for a rendering of life-draining drudgery that is of more sociological than literary interest.[11] The heroic couplet's capacity to hold contradictions in suspension is here flattened into redundancy, with the rhymes repeating or logically extending their predecessors: lie/die; attend/mend; care/prepare; spring/begin; complain/again; renew/dew.[12]

Collier lays mind-numbingly bare the labor that sustains men in their own manual and poetic labor. Oswald does so more subtly, elevating the role of women's labor both in the similes that feature weavers and dairywomen and in the eulogies that evoke mourning mothers and that echo the wailing women who antiphonically answered male poets at archaic Greek funerals. In the ventriloquized lament of Lycaon's mother, her son's name repeats like a mantra as he oscillates between death and life and between war and labor, from "pruning" to "killed" and back to "unkilled" and "pruning":

> Now she can't look at the sea she can't think about
> The bits unburied being eaten by fishes
> He was the tall one the conscientious one
> Who stayed out late pruning his father's fig trees
> Who was kidnapped who was ransomed
> Who walked home barefoot from Arisbe
> And rested for twelve days and was killed
> LYCAON killed Lycaon unkilled Lycaon
> Bending down branches to make wheels
> Lycaon kidnapped Lycaon pruning by moonlight
> Lycaon naked in a river pleading for his life
> Being answered by Achilles No (66)

Those funerary laments were eventually worked into epic poetry, so that in terms of literary history as well as immediate bodily needs Greek women provided for the poetic labor of men.[13] One way of understanding the alternation between the gory deaths and the remembered everyday actions and similes in both *Memorial* and the *Iliad* is that it allows us to see both the men the world has lost and the world those men have lost, most dramatically in Homer in the ekphrasis of Achilles's magnificent shield that seems to represent the entire Mediterranean region and in Oswald in the final simile section, each precious isolated image flitting by with the turn of the page.[14] But the world of labor, of the natural and agricultural cycles to which acts of war are compared, is not only the world men experience aesthetically; it is also what sustains them materially.

As we have glimpsed with Erasmus's *famuli*, Montaigne's valet-secretary, and Milton's dictation-taking daughters, labor that blurs the domestic and the intellectual has long held up the scholarly and literary work of men and continues to do so today. Bruce Holsinger's curation on Twitter of examples of male scholars thanking their wives for typing—and editing, proofreading, and even researching and writing parts of—their manuscripts is at once revelatory and redundant. Each iteration of Holsinger's #ThanksForTyping hashtag, taken from the acknowledgments of academic monographs, both repeats and exacerbates a truth universally acknowledged: "My wife typed the entire manuscript and the subsequent two or three revisions of it, and she also did much of the proofreading";[15] "My wife typed my manuscript drafts as soon as I gave them to her, even though she was caring for our first child . . . and was also teaching part time in the chemistry department";[16] "My wife transcribed the first draft of the manuscript, working from the Black Letter type, sixteenth-century spelling, and wondrous punctuation of the original publications. She has also carried the burden of checking the several drafts through which a large part of this volume has passed";[17] "In addition to enriching my life every day, she has been a superb research assistant, having read almost as many soldiers' letters and diaries as I have. Along with those soldiers, she deserves to be named a co-author"[18] (she was not named a coauthor); "I have to thank my wife for typing the whole of this difficult manuscript in spite of the heavy burden laid on housewives by a six years' war and its oppressive aftermath";[19] "And to my wife for typing, retyping and typing yet again the manuscript."[20] The intellectual labor of the women in these examples, mostly from the mid-twentieth century but up to 1996, runs seamlessly together with their domestic and emotional labor: not only are they required, like Silvia Federici's archetypal housewife, "to service the male worker physically, emotionally, and sexually, to raise his children, mend his socks, patch up his ego when it is crushed," they also must mend his sentences and patch up his citations while "typing, retyping, and typing yet again."[21] This labor is not exactly thankless; they are, after all, literally thanked. But these acknowledgments make it sound like female manual and editorial labors are acts of grace, the answer to a prayer that, like Rabelais's Pantagrueline prognostication that the rich will have wealth and the summer will be warm, could not thinkably go unanswered; they are praised for bearing the "burden" they had no choice but to bear. If wives are now more rarely thanked for typing, in institutions of higher education it is often female professors who are expected to provide care and support for students struggling academically or emotionally, to serve on the university committees that oversee the housekeeping of the institution, and to relieve the burdens on their male colleagues. More generally, academic work in the humanities, increasingly "feminized" as it loses both funding and cultural value, has come to share both the precarity and the affective demands of other forms of service work, from the "labors of love" expected from caregivers to the casualized intellectual labor of online "content creators."[22]

The growing attention in academia and in creative industries to how women's undercompensated labor—domestic, intellectual, or both, or somewhere in between—supports the compensated or better-compensated work of men tends to leave aside the question of how such "support" work should be valued. That question is related to the question of what in this context counts as "work," in Arendt's sense, and what counts as "labor." Which products of the intellect are ends in themselves, and which are merely tools to achieve those ends? Where is the line between a secretary—perhaps one whose paleographic talents transform illegible texts into usable material for her husband—and a collaborator? Should research assistants be named as coauthors? Do translations and critical editions—invaluable for their fields, but often of no value for tenure and job search committees, when and where these still exist—preserve existing knowledge that original scholarship can build on, or do they constitute original scholarship themselves? When two female academics protest that a male colleague and potential coauthor has asked them to "do the tedious housework of gathering sources while he takes credit for the conceptual heavy lifting," does this suggest that gathering sources is real intellectual work that should be valued as such—through a "Wages for the Tedious Housework of Gathering Sources" movement, perhaps—or rather that men should have to do their own tedious, low-value housework?[23] The questions raised by Collier and Oswald, in bringing to the surface the domestic georgic labors elided or crowded out by Duck and Homer, are inverted versions of these: they represent rather than perform the maintenance of men, but in casting themselves as somewhat reduplicative versions of male-authored originals, their works run a similar risk of being dismissed as below the bar of original intellectual production. Is "The Woman's Labour," at times a point-by-point refutation of "The Thresher's Labour," devalued when read as a kind of supplement or appendix to Duck's? Is *Memorial* a derivative imitation of the *Iliad*? What separates the production from the reproduction of knowledge or of literary forms? "The housekeeper's immediate goals are only means, not real ends," Beauvoir declares, "and they reflect no more than anonymous projects"; this is what "dooms her wholly to the general and inessential."[24] But for Collier and Oswald, as well as for the male authors studied in this book, domestic georgic cultivates meaning out of means; its endlessness is inseparable from its open-endedness.

# ACKNOWLEDGMENTS

I wrote this book with the help of the many people who sustained and transformed my thinking at the University of California, Berkeley, and at the University of Chicago, through virtual or temporary community, and especially as I completed the manuscript in the summer of 2020, at home.

I received vital support and guidance from my mentors at Berkeley. This project began in a seminar with Timothy Hampton my first year of graduate school, when I still wanted to be a modernist; he showed me how rich and strange the Renaissance was, but also how it might in part be domesticated. Anne-Lise François, Victoria Kahn, and Jeffrey Knapp helped me to cultivate both precision and open-endedness and to see and articulate the stakes of what I was doing. Joanna Picciotto has worked with me through every iteration of this book. She has given me a model of intellectual labor I will always strive to live up to.

At the University of Chicago, the intellectual communities of the Renaissance Workshop, the Society of Fellows, and the English department helped make this book what it is. Meghanne Barker, Aaron Benanav, Miguel Caballero, Mara Caden, Alexis Chema, Timothy Harrison, Michèle Lowrie, Kaneesha Parsard, Basil Salem, David Simon, Adam Spanos, and Richard Strier have provided crucial feedback. Thanks to Steve Rings and Deb Neibel for keeping the Society of Fellows going. Special thanks to Joshua Scodel for reading every chapter, for commenting with such incredible care, and for asking what my jocular tone is doing for me.

I have presented versions of this book's chapters at the annual meetings of the Renaissance Society of America, the American Comparative Literature Association, and the Modern Language Association. In these venues and elsewhere, I enjoyed productive exchanges, sometimes fleeting but long fermenting, with Frances Dolan, Richard Halpern, Aaron Kunin, Anahid Nersessian, Nigel Smith, and William West. Katherine Ibbett has helped me out of more than one pickle.

Thank you to Barry McCrea and Peter Brooks for first teaching me about endings and their suspension, and to my students in the Greece and Rome Core for transforming texts every year anew.

My research has received material support from the Townsend Center for the Humanities at UC Berkeley, the Bancroft Library, the Mellon Foundation, the Folger Shakespeare Library, and the University of Chicago Society of Fellows. Without the work that goes into creating and maintaining digital databases like Google Books, Gallica, Early English Books Online, and the Folger Shakespeare Library's online manuscript collection, my work would have been more difficult or, especially during pandemic-related library closures, impossible. Earlier versions of two chapters have been published as "Sustaining Fiction: Preserving Patriarchy in Marvell's *Upon Appleton House*," *Studies in Philology* 114, no. 3 (Summer 2017): 641–61, and "Irritating Montaigne," *Montaigne Studies* 30 (Winter 2018): 111–23.

Thank you to Alan Thomas and Randolph Petilos at the University of Chicago Press for overseeing this book's publication and to George Roupe for scrupulous copyediting. The two readers for the Press provided generous and catalytic feedback, the enzymes that helped me digest my thoughts into something close to a final form.

The idea behind this book comes in a way from my mother, Martha Kadue, whose own academic work asked questions about how institutions put a price on women's "labors of love." My father, David Kadue, has spared me countless infelicities by line editing this manuscript. I am grateful for all the love, support, and strong opinions about puns and punctuation that they both have given me.

Thank you, finally, to the friends who have helped me metabolize my thinking about preservative labor over yearslong conversations: Sophia Azeb, Paco Brito, Keith Budner, Kathryn Crim, Jordan Greenwald, Stephen Haswell Todd, Jessie Hock, Marianne Kaletzky, Abram Kaplan, Julia Nelsen, Emily O'Rourke, Jane Raisch, Jennifer Row, Lynn Xu, and Esther Yu. Ramsey McGlazer taught me everything I know about repetition. I could not have done without his constant correction. Ross Lerner has read, reread, and immeasurably improved this manuscript, and while he has not done any typing, he has done more than half the housework. It is a source of ever new delight to share domestic and intellectual life with him.

# NOTES

## Introduction

1. Francis Bacon, *New Atlantis,* in *The Major Works,* ed. Brian Vickers (Oxford: Oxford University Press, 1996), 480–83.

2. Hannah Arendt, *The Human Condition* (Chicago: University of Chicago Press, 1958), 41, 207, 101, 100. Arendt acknowledges a fundamental commonality between labor and action: both are futile, or "unproductive" in the terms of political economy. But labor's futility is deadening—the same task performed over and over, rote production fated for its immediate consumption—while that of action is the condition for meaningful human life: any attempt to obviate action's "futility, boundlessness, and uncertainty of outcome" and short-circuit its "authentic, non-tangible, and always utterly fragile meaning" into a calcified end product reduces human actors to mere "craftsmen," *praxis* to *poiēsis* (195, 196). Elsewhere in her writing, Arendt comments on how something like labor ensures that human ideas, artifacts, and institutions endure, as in her description of thinking as "sheer activity" and "like Penelope's web; it undoes every morning what it has finished the night before" in *The Life of the Mind* (New York: Harcourt, 1978), 72, 88; or her praise of "care" as a cultural principle (the faculty of taste "takes care of the beautiful"; the Roman *cultura animi* "makes man fit to take care of the things of the world" and precisely for that reason "has something to do with politics") in "The Crisis in Culture: Its Social and Its Political Significance," in *Between Past and Future* (New York: Penguin, 1968), 221, 211.

3. Hannah Woolley, *The queen-like closet; or, Rich cabinet stored with all manner of rare receipts for preserving, candying & cookery* (London, 1670), 14.

4. "Take green Walnuts in the beginning of *Iune,* beat them in a Mortar, and distil them in an ordinary Still, keep that Water by it self, then about Midsummer gather some more, and distill them as you did before, keep that also by it self, then take a quart of each and mix them, together, and distil them in a Glass Still, and keep it for your use" (Woolley, *The queen-like closet,* 13).

5. In the section of the introduction to her book *The Usurer's Daughter: Male Friendship and Fictions in Sixteenth-Century England* (London: Routledge, 1994) entitled "The Housewife and the Humanist," Lorna Hutson explains the role played by the figure of the housewife in the male humanist's construction of himself as a successful governor of his world. My interest is in how male humanists constructed themselves not over and

against but *as* housewives, even when their daily activities were as far removed from cooking, cleaning, and household task management as they are in Hutson's account.

6. Patricia Parker, *Literary Fat Ladies: Rhetoric, Gender, Property* (New York: Methuen, 1987), 104.

7. *Les lettres d'Estienne Pasquier* (Avignon, 1590), book 10, fol. 424, "A. M. Regnier, President en l'Election de Soissons," qtd. in Evelyne Berriot-Salvadore, *Les femmes dans la société française de la Renaissance* (Geneva: Droz, 1990), 162. Here and elsewhere when a published English translation was not available, translations from French are my own.

8. Bacon, *Advancement of Learning,* in *The Major Works*, 140. Brian Vickers maintains that Bacon and his followers, long accused of harboring antihumanist hostilities, were more continuous with humanism than has been assumed. The received idea of Bacon's contempt for the humanist emphasis on *verba* over *res*, empty *copia* over weighty knowledge, seems to Vickers to be based entirely on a single passage from *Advancement of Learning* hinging on the charge that, with the critique of scholasticism and the rise of philology, "men began to hunt more after words than matter." But far from dismissing the humanist project out of hand, Vickers argues, Bacon was merely intervening in a long-standing debate within humanism. Bacon was as much a believer in the necessity of moving past superficial stylistic imitation and restoring a correspondence between *res* and *verba* as such bona fide humanists as Gabriel Harvey and Roger Ascham. "The Myth of Francis Bacon's 'Anti-Humanism,'" in *Humanism and Early Modern Philosophy*, ed. Jill Kraye and M. W. F. Stone (London: Routledge, 2000), 143–44, 149.

9. Richard Mulcaster, *Positions wherin those primitive circumstances be examined, which are necessarie for the training up of children, either for skill in their booke, or health in their bodie* (London, 1581), 186, 185, 184.

10. François Rabelais, *Œuvres complètes*, ed. Jacques Boulenger and Lucien Scheler (Paris: Gallimard, 1955), 211; Rabelais, *Gargantua and Pantagruel*, trans. and ed. M. A. Screech (New York: Penguin, 2006), 33. English quotations from *Pantagruel, Gargantua, The Third Book, The Fourth Book*, and the *Pantagrueline Prognostication* come from this edition and will hereafter be cited parenthetically by page number.

11. See Michel Jeanneret on how, in sixteenth-century France, the proliferation of print, multiplicity of religious viewpoints, "discovery" and exploration of new lands, and growing circulation of ancient texts, while certainly causes of excitement, also led to a fear of excess: "la menace de la démesure." "Débordements rabelaisiens," *Nouvelle Revue de Psychanalyse 43* (Spring 1991): 110. For a general account of the anxiety caused by early modern "information overload," see Ann Blair, *Too Much to Know: Managing Scholarly Information before the Information Age* (New Haven, CT: Yale University Press, 2011).

12. Anthony Low, *The Georgic Revolution* (Princeton, NJ: Princeton University Press, 1985). By David Scott Wilson-Okamura's account, "Many poems modeled on the *Georgics*" appeared in the sixteenth century, "but 'georgic' was not established yet as a separate genre; it was the name of a book (as in the phrase 'Virgil's third georgic') but not of a mode or kind"; there were "commentaries on the *Georgics,* but not theories of georgic poetry." *Virgil in the Renaissance* (Cambridge: Cambridge University Press, 2010), 77. See also Alastair Fowler, "The Beginnings of English Georgic," in *Renaissance Genres: Essays on Theory, History, and Interpretation*, ed. Barbara Kiefer Lewalski (Cambridge, MA: Harvard University Press, 1986), and Andrew McRae, *God Speed the Plough: The Representation of Agrarian England, 1500–1660* (Cambridge: Cambridge University Press, 1996). In sixteenth-century France, according to L. P. Wilkinson, the *Georgics* was usu-

ally regarded as a "technical didactic poem," though it was beloved by Montaigne. *The "Georgics" of Virgil: A Critical Survey* (Cambridge: Cambridge University Press, 1969), 293.

13. Francesco Petrarca, "The Ascent of Mont Ventoux," in *The Renaissance Philosophy of Man*, ed. Ernst Cassirer, Paul Oskar Kristeller, and John Herman Randall Jr., trans. Hans Nachod (Chicago: University of Chicago Press, 1948), 38. Wilkinson notes that though Petrarch quotes Virgil's *Georgics* much more frequently than earlier medieval authors like Dante or Chaucer, he never emulated the *Georgics* in his own poetry, and in this case the quotation is a misquotation, using the present tense that was "the generalised form favoured by the *florilegia*" rather than the past tense of the original (*The "Georgics" of Virgil*, 290).

14. Low, *The Georgic Revolution*, 4, 8. "Farming is a heroic activity" is Low's gloss on "Labor omnia vicit / improbus et duris urgens in rebus egestas" (8).

15. Erasmus, *Collected Works of Erasmus, Literary and Educational Writings*, ed. Craig R. Thompson, vol. 24, *Copia: Foundations of the Abundant Style: De duplici copia verborum ac rerum Commentarii duo*, trans. and ed. Betty I. Knott (Toronto: University of Toronto Press, 1978), 295; *Des. Erasmi Roterod. De utraq verborum ac rerum copia lib. II* (London, 1660), sig. A3r-A3v. In the *Ciceronianus*, Erasmus imagines successful rhetoric as a complex metabolic operation that appears like spontaneous parthenogenic reproduction, commending imitation that "transfers what it finds into the mind itself, as into the stomach, so that transfused into the veins it appears to be a birth of one's intellect, ... so that the reader does not recognize an insertion taken from Cicero, but a child born from one's brain, just as they say Pallas was born from Jupiter's, bearing a lively image of its parent." Qtd. in G. W. Pigman, "Versions of Imitation in the Renaissance," *Renaissance Quarterly* 33, no. 1 (Spring 1980): 8–9.

16. As Terence Cave explains, the tradition of manuscript copying "preserved the written materials of the Latin world while converting one of its most fertile concepts from a context of dynamically deployed energies . . . to one of endless repetition." *The Cornucopian Text: Problems of Writing in the French Renaissance* (Oxford: Clarendon, 1979), 4.

17. Joachim Du Bellay, *Les Regrets, précédé de Les Antiquités de Rome et suivi de La Défense et Illustration de la Langue française* (Paris: Gallimard, 1967), 207–8.

18. Bacon, *Advancement of Learning*, 255.

19. Thomas Sprat, *The History of the Royal Society of London, for the Improving of Natural Knowledge* (London, 1734), 24–25.

20. "An Account given to the Society of The Performances of the Georgicall Committee," in Michael Hunter, *Establishing the New Science: The Experience of the Early Royal Society* (Woodbridge: Boydell, 1989), 113.

21. Bacon, *Advancement of Learning*, 245.

22. David O. Ross emphasizes the political violence that characterized most of Virgil's life, too often ignored by commentators before him, and concludes, "I admit to reading Virgil as a poet of deep pessimism: I cannot see that it could be otherwise." *Virgil's Elements: Physics and Poetry in the "Georgics"* (Princeton, NJ: Princeton University Press, 1987), 5. Richard Thomas has a harsher interpretation of "Labor omnia vicit" than Low: "The meaning is 'Insatiable toil occupied all areas of existence'—not a comfortable notion." Virgil, *Georgics*, vol. 1, books I–II, ed. Richard F. Thomas (Cambridge: Cambridge University Press, 1988), 92–93.

23. See, for example, Jacob Burckhardt, *The Civilization of the Renaissance in Italy*, trans. S. G. C. Middlemore (New York: Macmillan, 1914); Thomas M. Greene, *The Light in*

*Troy: Imitation and Discovery in Renaissance Poetry* (New Haven, CT: Yale University Press, 1982); and Leonard Barkan, *Unearthing the Past: Archaeology and Aesthetics in the Making of Renaissance Culture* (New Haven, CT: Yale University Press, 1999). In *Periodization and Sovereignty: How Ideas of Feudalism and Secularization Govern the Politics of Time* (Philadelphia: University of Pennsylvania Press, 2008), Kathleen Davis describes the narrative of secularization overtaking an ecclesiastical society as capitalism triumphed over feudalism as a remarkably unexamined assumption, having "taken on the self-evidentiary status of common sense" (2).

24. Greene, *The Light in Troy*, 92.

25. Stephen Greenblatt, *The Swerve: How the World Became Modern* (New York: Norton, 2011).

26. Stephen Best and Sharon Marcus, "Surface Reading: An Introduction," *Representations* 108, no. 1 (Fall 2009): 5–6. David Kurnick characterizes this description of the critic, and the accompanying prescription for an alternative "attentive" reader, as "melodrama": "One critic, emphatically masculinized, threatens to overpower a vulnerable text to whose actual content he pays no heed—unless another critic intervenes to rescue it, to attend to it with the modest, patient responsiveness of the perfect mother or nurse." "A Few Lies: Queer Theory and Our Method Melodramas," *ELH* 87, no. 2 (Summer 2020): 358–59. To my mind Best and Marcus don't present the text as something in need of motherly care and tenderness but rather *intellectual* "care" and "attentiveness." Values espoused by Best and Marcus that Kurnick associates with femininity— "modesty, openness, attention, curiosity, receptiveness" (358), as well as "care" in the sense of *cura*—were also shared, as Joanna Picciotto shows, by emphatically masculine seventeenth-century experimentalists for whom the acceptance of individual "epistemological limitations" was a necessary component of collective progress in knowledge production. *Labors of Innocence in Early Modern England* (Cambridge, MA: Harvard University Press, 2010), 467.

27. Louis Montrose proposes that scholars unhappy with their institutional situations in the early 1980s took a different recourse, choosing an affiliation with "leisure" rather than "activism and labor," in Best and Marcus's terms. Rather than attempting to muscle their way into the market with georgic swagger, they found that writing about the pastoral mode could be a refuge from "an increasingly technocratic academy and society," so that "the study of pastoral may have become a metapastoral version of pastoral." "Of Gentlemen and Shepherds: The Politics of Elizabethan Pastoral Form," *ELH* 50, no. 3 (Autumn 1983): 415. Anne-Lise François suggests we might read the move from the heroism of high theory to the more modest imperatives of surface reading as a downshift from georgic to pastoral. "Late Exercises in Minimal Affirmatives," in *Theory Aside*, ed. Jason Pott and Daniel Stout (Durham, NC: Duke University Press, 2014), 45. A "domestic georgic" mode of criticism might retain that modesty without disavowing the work it requires.

28. Elaine Leong argues that culinary and medicinal recipe development in early modern England, often associated in recent scholarship with literate women, should be understood as "a series of collaborative household-wide endeavors, filled with continuing gender and class-related negotiations" involving "husbands and wives, fathers and daughters, and mistresses and servants"; at the same time, both prescriptive literature and actual correspondence and account books suggest that household management was "mainly up to the wife." *Recipes and Everyday Knowledge: Medicine, Science, and the Household in Early Modern England* (Chicago: University of Chicago Press, 2018), 10, 15, 49.

Sara Pennell makes a similar case about the crossing of gender and class lines in the early modern kitchen, noting that the head cook in an aristocratic household would have been a man. *The Birth of the English Kitchen, 1600–1850* (London: Bloomsbury, 2016), 130.

29. Elizabeth Mazzola and Corinne S. Abate, "Introduction: 'Indistinguished Space,'" in *Privacy, Domesticity, and Women in Early Modern England,* ed. Corinne S. Abate (Burlington, VT: Ashgate, 2003), 6–7. For the French housewife, see Berriot-Salvadore, *Les femmes dans la société française de la Renaissance,* 159–60. For twentieth-century feminist theories of reproductive labor, see Mariarosa Dalla Costa and Selma James, *The Power of Women and the Subversion of the Community* (Bristol: Falling Wall, 1975); Silvia Federici, "Wages against Housework," in *Revolution at Point Zero: Housework, Reproduction, and Feminist Struggle* (Oakland: PM, 2012); Leopoldina Fortunati, *The Arcane of Reproduction: Housework, Prostitution, Labor and Capital,* trans. Hilary Creek (New York: Automedia, 1995).

30. Berriot-Salvadore, *Les femmes dans la société française de la Renaissance,* 160.

31. For a study of Erasmus's live-in servant-secretary corps, see Franz Bierlaire, *La Familia d'Erasme: Contribution à l'histoire de l'humanisme* (Paris: J. Vrin, 1968), and for dictation more generally, Ann Blair, "Early Modern Attitudes toward the Delegation of Copying and Note-Taking," in *Forgetting Machines: Knowledge Management Evolution in Early Modern Europe,* ed. Alberto Cevolini (Leiden: Brill, 2016). For the theory that Montaigne dictated the *Essais,* see George Hoffmann, *Montaigne's Career* (Oxford: Clarendon, 1998), 46–58. Barbara Lewalski imagines Milton's daughters must have read to their father when more qualified amanuenses were not available or affordable; she cites Edward Phillips's sympathetic account of how Mary and Deborah "were Condemn'd to the performance of Reading" in languages they could pronounce but not understand, which must have been "a Tryal of Patience, almost beyond endurance." Milton's widow, Elizabeth, also claimed to have filled in as his amanuensis. *The Life of John Milton: A Critical Biography* (Malden, MA: Blackwell, 2000), 408–9, 672n63. For the role of wives, household servants, and other "invisible technicians" in experimentalists' intellectual labor, see chapter 8 of Steven Shapin, *A Social History of Truth: Civility and Science in Seventeenth-Century England* (Chicago: University of Chicago Press, 1994).

32. Laura Lunger Knoppers, *Politicizing Domesticity from Henrietta Maria to Milton's Eve* (Cambridge: Cambridge University Press, 2011), 145.

33. Louise Labé's preface to her *Sonets* exhorts women to lift their sights up from their distaffs and spindles ("élever un peu leurs esprits pardessus leurs quenouilles et fuseaux") through writing, thus proving themselves as fit companions to men in public as in domestic affairs ("tant ès affaires domestiques que publiques"). *Œuvres poétiques,* ed. Françoise Charpentier (Paris: Gallimard, 2006), 94. In Margaret Cavendish's *Poems and Fancies* (London, 1653), poems such as "Nature's Cook," "A Posset for Nature's Breakfast," and "A Bisk for Nature's Table" insist on relationships between natural philosophy, feminized culinary labor, and poetry. "To the Reader" of that volume evokes a general kinship between poetic *oikonomia* and household management: "For, *Housewifery* is a discreet *Management,* and ordering all in *Private.* . . . It is just as in *Poetry:* for good *Husbandry* in *Poetry,* is, when there is great store of *Fancy* well order'd, not only in fine *Language,* but proper *Phrases,* and significant *Words.*" Ann Rosalind Jones discusses how both Isabella Whitney and Catherine des Roches "invoke accepted forms of women's work— domestic labor, whether paid or unpaid—to compensate for their own unconventional employment as professional writers." *The Currency of Eros: Women's Love Lyric in Europe, 1540–1620* (Bloomington: Indiana University Press, 1990), 8.

34. Katharine Eisaman Maus argues that male writers in the Renaissance often compared their own intellectual production to pregnancy and childbirth while "at the same time making clear . . . that the figure was an analogy, that processes of mind and body cannot be confused or conflated." "A Womb of His Own: Male Renaissance Poets in the Female Body," in *Sexuality and Gender in Early Modern Europe: Institutions, Texts, Images,* ed. James Grantham Turner (Cambridge: Cambridge University Press, 1993), 275.

35. In this my focus differs from that of Michael McKeon, for whom "formal domestication," like the Christian hermeneutic of accommodation, is a way of reading great things writ small: "The clarification of, or solution to, problems in the greater sphere is programmatically sought within the lesser sphere," and in seventeenth-century England that lesser sphere was very often the household, making the process of domestication twofold: "The realm of the domestic itself possesses a distinctive exemplarity." I am interested less in how authors sought to domesticate "the great, the distant, the worldly, the strange, or the foreign by 'bringing it home'" than in how authors saw those concerns as already at home, fundamentally domestic in character. *The Secret History of Domesticity: Public, Private, and the Division of Knowledge* (Baltimore: Johns Hopkins University Press, 2007), 323, 326.

36. John Milton, *Areopagitica,* in *The Riverside Milton,* ed. Roy Flannagan (Boston: Houghton Mifflin, 1998), 999.

37. John Dod and Robert Cleaver, *A godlie forme of householde gouernment for the ordering of priuate families, according to the direction of Gods word* (London, 1598), 170.

38. Dod and Cleaver, *A godlie forme of householde gouernment,* 170–71.

39. Mary Astell, *An Essay in Defence of the Female Sex, in a Letter to a Lady, written by a Lady* (London, 1721), 76–77.

40. Arendt, *The Human Condition,* 9, 204.

41. Olivier de Serres, *Le théâtre d'agriculture et mesnage des champs* (Paris, 1600), 26. In Rabelais's and Montaigne's lifetimes, France did not experience the same proliferation of recipe books addressed to women as England did in the late sixteenth and throughout the seventeenth century. At the same time, domestic manuals marketed to men, like Serres's *Théâtre,* were explicit about the fact that preservative culinary labor was the province of women, and recipes for confectionery would have likely been followed by the mistress of an estate.

42. Glossing W. H. Auden's claim that "poetry makes nothing happen," François proposes that "nothing" should be understood precisely as an event. While François understands this event as ordained by grace, my interest lies in "nothings" that, however slight, are always tied up with, and weighed down by, questions of labor. *Open Secrets: The Literature of Uncounted Experience* (Stanford, CA: Stanford University Press, 2008), xv.

43. Greene, *Light in Troy,* 82–84; Kathy Eden, *Hermeneutics and the Rhetorical Tradition: Chapters in the Ancient Legacy and Its Humanist Reception* (New Haven, CT: Yale University Press, 2005), 41. Pigman outlines the divergence of Macrobius's model of imitation from that of Seneca. For Macrobius, imitation was about arrangement, not about transformation; his bees simply gathered and did not synthesize, in what Pigman calls "redistributive reproduction" ("Versions of Imitation," 6). In Seneca's exemplum of synthetic bees, presented as a model of active reading and original style, this process is purely metabolic and unconscious: "We see that nature does this in our bodies without any effort on our part." *Selected Letters,* trans. Elaine Fantham (Oxford: Oxford University Press, 2010), 156.

44. A version of this tension has played out in recent history in the role of the house-

wife itself. In 1976 Betty Ford lobbied for the replacement of the word "housewife" with "homemaker" to "show our pride in having made the home and family our life's work," and twenty-first-century cultural commentators and lifestyle bloggers insist on a sharp distinction between (unpaid) "homemakers," who spiritually and creatively uphold the household, and (paid) "housekeepers," who do the tedious chores that physically maintain it. As the writer Ester Bloom, after quoting Ford, puts it, "Homemaking is not the same thing as housekeeping. Though it may also include certain mundane but necessary domestic tasks, homemaking, as I envision it, is less about scrubbing toilets and more about that old saying 'Home is where the heart is.' Homemaking is about creating and maintaining a healthy and loving environment for everyone in the family . . . and fostering your family's relationship to the wider community." "Reclaiming 'Homemaker,'" *Slate*, April 29, 2014, https://slate.com/human-interest/2014/04/stay-at-home-mom -needs-to-go-lets-bring-back-homemaker.html. Blogger Lara Neves, who also quotes Ford, is more blunt: "Housekeeping isn't even the most important part of making a home. You can always hire someone to do your housekeeping for you, but you cannot pay someone to make your home for you. That is up to you." "I Choose to Be a Homemaker, Not a Housekeeper," Overstuffed Life: Simple Solutions for Busy Moms, Sept. 2, 2015, https://www.overstuffedlife.com/2015/09/elevating-the-term-homemaker.html.

45. Richard Helgerson, *Self-Crowned Laureates: Spenser, Jonson, Milton, and the Literary System* (Berkeley: University of California Press, 1983), 8. Picciotto notes how the slippage between temporary, bodily labor and enduring, meaningful work appears in the phrase "intellectual labor" itself. In our modern understanding of intellectual labor, the cyclicality and futility of labor have been completely flattened into a linear conception of work: the intellectual laborer is expected to make linear progress, advance toward truth (or at least greater knowledge), and produce "works" (*Labors of Innocence*, 2). In her account of an earlier understanding of this concept in early modern experimentalism's collapse of the means and ends of paradisal labor, Picciotto makes a distinction between the individual's uncertainty and the collective's progress. While I find this account both persuasive and productive, I want to emphasize the extent to which, for the authors I consider, even potential contributions to collective progress could be more like domestic drudgery than heroically purgatorial labor.

46. Ben Jonson, "To the Memory of My Beloved Master William Shakespeare, and What He Hath Left Us" (lines 59–61) and "Epistle to Selden" (line 76), in *Ben Jonson*, vol. 8, *The Poems; The Prose Works*, ed. C. H. Herford, Evelyn Simpson, and Percy Simpson (Oxford: Clarendon, 1947), 392, 161.

47. For Raymond Williams, pastoral and related genres involve a "magical extraction of the curse of labour" through "a simple extraction of the existence of laborers," so that landowners can see themselves as inhabiting an Eden that naturally reproduces itself. *The Country and the City* (Oxford: Oxford University Press, 1975), 32. See also Montrose, "Of Gentlemen and Shepherds," and Virginia Krause, *Idle Pursuits: Literature and Oisiveté in the French Renaissance* (Newark: University of Delaware Press, 2003). Krause focuses on leisure rather than labor, categorizing both embroidery and public service as that which "transcended" straightforwardly useful work (16).

48. Wendy Wall, *Recipes for Thought: Knowledge and Taste in the Early Modern Kitchen* (Philadelphia: University of Pennsylvania Press, 2015), 168.

49. Wall, *Recipes for Thought*, 187.

50. Patricia Fumerton, *Cultural Aesthetics: Renaissance Literature and the Practice of Social Ornament* (Chicago: University of Chicago Press, 1991), 135.

51. John Murrell, *A Delightfull Daily Exercise for Ladies and Gentlewomen* (London, 1621); *La Pratique de faire toutes confitures* (Lyon, 1558); Hugh Plat, *The Garden of Eden, or, An accurate Description of all Flowers and Fruits now growing in England, with particular Rules how to advance their Nature and Growth, as well in Seeds and Hearbs, as the secret ordering of Trees and Plants* (1608; London, 1659); *Petit traicte contenant la maniere de faire toutes confitures* (Paris, 1545); *The Compleat Cook: or, The Whole Art of Cookery* (London, 1694); Sir Kenelm Digby, *Choice and experimented receipts in physick and chirurgery, as also cordial and distilled waters and spirits, perfumes, and other curiosities* (London, 1675); *A Closet for Ladies and Gentlewomen, or, The Art of Preserving, Conserving, and Candying* (London, 1611).

52. Leong, *Recipes and Everyday Knowledge*, 11.

53. See, for example, Gail Kern Paster, *The Body Embarrassed: Drama and the Disciplines of Shame in Early Modern England* (Ithaca, NY: Cornell University Press, 1993), 113–62; Natasha Korda, *Shakespeare's Domestic Economies: Gender and Property in Early Modern England* (Philadelphia: University of Pennsylvania Press, 2002), 52–53; Wendy Wall, "Just a Spoonful of Sugar: Syrup and Domesticity in Early Modern England," *Modern Philology* 104, no. 2 (Nov. 2006): 149. One reason why culinary labor has proved so productive for scholarship on drama may be that a recipe, insofar as it is both enduring and repeatable, is somewhat like a play text. Though not specifically focused on domestic labor, Richard Halpern's work on tragedy and political economy has suggested that, despite Arendt's identification of action as the human activity most evoked by tragic drama, a play like *Hamlet*—with its constant interior revolving and constant references to the inexorability of the biological life cycle—has much more to tell us about labor than action. *Eclipse of Action: Tragedy and Political Economy* (Chicago: University of Chicago Press, 2017), chapter 4.

54. Wendy Wall, *Staging Domesticity: Household Work and English Identity in Early Modern Drama* (Cambridge: Cambridge University Press, 2002), 19–21.

55. Kim F. Hall, "Culinary Spaces, Colonial Spaces: The Gendering of Sugar in the Seventeenth Century," in *Feminist Readings of Early Modern Culture: Emerging Subjects*, ed. Valerie Traub, M. Lindsay Kaplan, and Dympna Callaghan (Cambridge: Cambridge University Press, 1996), 170, 180.

56. Simone de Beauvoir, *The Second Sex*, trans. Constance Borde and Sheila Malovany-Chevallier (New York: Vintage Books, 2011), 480.

57. Beauvoir, *The Second Sex*, 481.

58. Beauvoir, *The Second Sex*, 639. Much recent work, including Wall's *Recipes for Thought* and Leong's *Recipes and Everyday Knowledge*, points to how at least for some practitioners, early modern housework was technical knowledge in a meaningful sense.

59. For studies of the importance of temperance and related virtues in the Renaissance, see Joshua Scodel, *Excess and the Mean in Early Modern English Literature* (Princeton, NJ: Princeton University Press, 2002), and Todd Reeser, *Moderating Masculinity in Early Modern Culture* (Chapel Hill: University of North Carolina Press, 2006).

60. Milton, *Areopagitica*, in *The Riverside Milton*, 1008.

61. Wilson-Okamura, *Virgil in the Renaissance*, 78. See also Ross, *Virgil's Elements*, for the thematic importance of the tempering of elements in the *Georgics*.

62. Kevis Goodman, *Georgic Modernity and British Romanticism: Poetry and the Mediation of History* (Cambridge: Cambridge University Press, 2004), 29.

63. Ross's study of the *Georgics* emerges from his understanding of the poem as "concerned above all with irrational destruction, with uneasy balances between opposing elements, and with the unreality of hopeful visions" (*Virgil's Elements*, 4).

64. "nec tamen, haec cum sint hominumque boumque labores / versando terram experti, nihil improbus anser / Strymoniaeque grues et amaris intiba fibris / officiunt aut umbra nocet." *The Georgics of Virgil*, trans. David Ferry (New York: Farrar, Straus and Giroux, 2005), 1.118–21.

65. "quod nisi et adsiduis herbam insectabere rastris / et sonitu terrebis aves et ruris opaci / falce premes umbras votisque vocaveris imbrem, / heu magnum alterius frustra spectabis acervum / concussaque famem in silvis solabere quercu" (*Georgics*, 1.155–59).

66. "labor omnia vicit, / improbus, et duris urgens in rebus egestas" (*Georgics*, 1.145–46).

67. Melissa Schoenberger, *Cultivating Peace: The Virgilian Georgic in English, 1650–1750* (Lewisburg, PA: Bucknell University Press, 2019). Schoenberger notes that classicists have long taken Virgil's pessimism seriously, but early modernists have generally been late to the game.

68. Goodman, *Georgic Modernity*, 3–4.

69. Sianne Ngai, *Ugly Feelings* (Cambridge, MA: Harvard University Press, 2005).

70. Erasmus, "Letter to John Botzheim," in Margaret Mann Phillips, *The "Adages" of Erasmus: A Study with Translations* (Cambridge: Cambridge University Press, 1964), xv; Erasmus, *Erasmi opus epistolarum*, vol. 1, *1484–1514*, ed. Percy Stanford Allen (Oxford: Oxford University Press, 1992), 37.

71. Erasmus, "The Labors of Hercules," in *Collected Works of Erasmus*, vol. 34, trans. and ed. R. A. B. Mynors (Toronto: University of Toronto Press, 1992), 170; Erasmus, *Adagiorum chiliades Des. Erasmi Roterodami quatuor cum dimidia ex postrema authoris recognitione* (Venice, 1536), 571.

72. Erasmus, Letter to Pope Leo X, 21 May 1515, qtd. in Simon Goldhill, *Who Needs Greek? Contests in the Cultural History of Hellenism* (Cambridge: Cambridge University Press, 2002), 20.

73. Goldhill, *Who Needs Greek?*, 20–21.

74. Lisa Jardine, *Erasmus, Man of Letters: The Construction of Charisma in Print* (Princeton, NJ: Princeton University Press, 1993), 44, 43.

75. Erasmus, "The Labors of Hercules," 172. Those monstrous errors were compounded, according to Kathy Eden, by "the monstrous ingratitude of his reading public." *Friends Hold All Things in Common: Tradition, Intellectual Property, and the "Adages" of Erasmus* (New Haven, CT: Yale University Press, 2001), 159.

76. Erasmus, "The Labors of Hercules," 173–74; Erasmus, *Adagiorum chiliades*, 572-73.

77. Erasmus, "The Labors of Hercules," 172; Erasmus, *Adagiorum chiliades*, 572.

78. Erasmus, *Adagiorum chiliades, 619.*

79. In Jeffrey Knapp's account of English writers' scripture-based strategy to exalt themselves through humility, "toys" and "trifles" are common epithets to signal the (apparent) irrelevance of literature, as in Sidney's professed embarrassment at the "triflingness" of his "ink-wasting toy," the *Apology for Poetry*. Qtd. in Knapp, *An Empire Nowhere: England, America, and Literature from "Utopia" to "The Tempest"* (Berkeley: University of California Press, 1994), 6.

80. Walter Lynne, *The vertuous scholehouse of ungracious women* (n.d.), sig. A8v, qtd. in Hutson, *The Usurer's Daughter*, 203. In Hutson's gloss: "The work of women indoors cannot compete with the expansiveness of the propitious oratorical occasion for which the prudent man in the marketplace is ready" (203).

81. Arendt, *The Human Condition*, 101.

82. Erasmus, "The Labors of Hercules," 174; Erasmus, *Adagiorum chiliades, 573.*

83. Adam Smith, *An Inquiry into the Nature and Causes of the Wealth of Nations,* ed. Edwin Cannan (Chicago: University of Chicago Press, 1976), 352. For Arendt, Smith's leveling of "menial services" with the professions that "furnished ancient thinking with examples for the highest and greatest activities of man" is a symptom of the "all-important degradation of action and speech" that characterizes modernity (*The Human Condition,* 207).

84. Halpern, *Eclipse of Action,* 36; Smith, *Wealth of Nations,* 352.

85. Erasmus, "The Labors of Hercules," 174; Erasmus, *Adagiorum chiliades,* 573. Ancient sources did not always portray Hercules as a paragon of masculine strength and virility; in Ovid's *Heroides* Iole dresses Hercules in women's clothes and makes him do women's work, and Lucian's elderly, infirm, and comical "Gallic Hercules" was an important figure for Renaissance French humanists. For the latter, see Robert E. Hallowell, "Ronsard and the Gallic Hercules Myth," *Studies in the Renaissance* 9 (1962): 249, and for an extensive study, Marc René Jung, *Hercule dans la littérature française du XVIe siècle* (Geneva: Droz, 1966).

86. For the impact of Spenser's day job as a secretary on his poetic office, see Richard Rambuss, *Spenser's Secret Career* (Cambridge: Cambridge University Press, 1993).

87. Lawrence Stone, *The Crisis of the Aristocracy, 1558–1641* (Oxford: Clarendon, 1965), 214. The secretiveness involved in both high-value "service" and low-value domestic labor makes it an unstable signifier across historical periods with regard to gender. Writing about gender and affective labor in Henry James, Sianne Ngai argues that male characters who are conscripted into informal service arrangements in James's late novels are implicitly feminized: "The overarching character of this work continues to be broadly thought of as feminine, due to its resemblance to 'kin work' and the socializing work of building relationships rather than activities associated with manufacturing or craft. . . . The very covertness of work starts to give off a feminine signal." "Henry James's 'Same Secret Principle,'" *Henry James Review* 41, no. 1 (Winter 2020): 48. Of course, "building relationships" is also the work of male-dominated spheres like politics and business, and "covertness" is a key job requirement for military personnel, private investigators, and spies, generally gendered masculine in the cultural imagination.

88. Roger Ascham, *The Scholemaster,* ed. Edward Arber (London: A. Constable, 1897), 45–46.

89. Erasmus, *A Declaration on the Subject of Early Liberal Education for Children / De pueris statim ac liberaliter instituendis declamatio,* trans. Beert C. Verstraete, in *The Erasmus Reader,* ed. Erika Rummel (Toronto: University of Toronto Press, 1990), 66.

90. Greene, *Light in Troy,* 86.

91. Greene, *Light in Troy,* 86, 95.

92. Jardine, *Erasmus,* 23, 26.

93. Cave, *Cornucopian Text,* xi.

94. Michel de Montaigne, *The Complete Essays of Montaigne,* trans. Donald M. Frame (Stanford, CA: Stanford University Press, 1958), 736, 725.

95. Montaigne, *Complete Essays,* 2, 751.

# Chapter One

1. "Vous ne mettres pas a mal la semence . . . mais avises vous que si vous bouillez la chair avec l'escorce, fault que vous ostes la chair . . . mais traites le doucement quil ne se brise . . . & gardes de le brusler: car si un personnaige n'est un peu exercité a la façon

diceluy, il se brusle." Nostradamus, *Excellent & moult utile opuscule à touts necessaire, qui desirent avoir cognoissance de plusieurs exquises receptes, divisé en deux parties* (Lyon, 1555), 133–36.

2. V.-L. Saulnier, "Médecins de Montpellier. Au temps de Rabelais," *Bibliothèque d'Humanisme et Renaissance* 19, no. 3 (1957): 445–46.

3. Michel Jeanneret, "Les paroles dégelées (Rabelais, *Quart Livre*, 48–65)," *Littérature* 17, no. 1 (1975): 20.

4. Rabelais, *Œuvres complètes*, 550. Quotations from *Pantagruel, Gargantua, Le Tiers Livre, Le Quart Livre*, and the *Pantagrueline Prognostication* come from this edition and will hereafter be cited parenthetically by page number.

5. Edwin Duval, *The Design of Rabelais' "Quart Livre de Pantagruel"* (Geneva: Droz, 1998), 60, 61.

6. Lawrence D. Kritzman, *The Rhetoric of Sexuality and the Literature of the French Renaissance* (Cambridge: Cambridge University Press, 1991), 182.

7. Kritzman, *Rhetoric of Sexuality*, 183–84. Relatedly, Floyd Gray sees Rabelais's exhaustive lists as deadening sequences of reification. The anatomy of Quaresmeprenant, for example, is more like a series of autopsies: "Le texte s'arrête, donc se détruit, à chaque instant. . . . A chaque ligne donc, nous assistons à une mort du texte," successive nails in the coffin of the idea that Quaresmeprenant could be anything other than a negative force in the narrative. *Rabelais et le comique du discontinu* (Paris: Champion, 1994), 36.

8. Jeanneret, "Débordements rabelaisiens," 107. Others agree that the last authentic book especially is not quite as "Rabelaisian" as Rabelais's earlier output, in terms of *mots* as well as *mets*. Jean-Claude Mühlethaler notes the shift in mealtime moods over the four books from "joyeuse convivialité" to something "de plus en plus dégradée." "Des mets et des maux. Aspects et enjeux de la dévaluation de la table à la Renaissance," *Romanische Forschungen* 108 (1996): 404. Thomas Greene, commenting on how the *Quart Livre* ends with Panurge's perhaps too-literal scatological conclusion to a book full of ingestion, admits that the volume lacks a certain *je ne sais quoi*: "Some vital Rabelaisian element runs thinner. One hardly knows what to call it," the characters "thinner" in more ways than one. *Rabelais: A Study in Comic Courage* (Englewood Cliffs, NJ: Prentice-Hall, 1970), 99. M. A. Screech finds that this book swaps out jokes for plodding pedantry, "explaining so many matters which the earliest books simply laughed at or passed over lightly." *Rabelais* (Ithaca, NY: Cornell University Press, 1979), 414.

9. "Le mode euphorique du *très*," "la tonalité maléfique du *trop*." Jeanneret, "Débordements rabelaisiens," 105.

10. Todd Reeser comments on the range of meanings of this virtue in early modern France: *le moyen, la moderation, la mediocrité, le meilieu, la moyenne mesure* all fell somewhere between excess and lack. Having aroused increased interest with the 1533 translation of Aristotle's *Nicomachean Ethics* into French (and multiple Latin editions), moderation became an important if often undefined aspect of ideal masculinity in the Renaissance (*Moderating Masculinity*, 12, 31).

11. Jeanneret, "Débordements rabelaisiens," 123.

12. "Le sphinx ou la chimère, un monstre à cent têtes, à cent langues, un chaos harmonique, une farce de portée infinie, une ivresse lucide à merveille, une folie profondément sage." Jules Michelet, *Histoire de France au seizième siècle: La réforme* (Paris: Calmann-Lévy, 1898), 354.

13. Rabelais's cavalier attitude toward women's bodies, from Gargamelle's tripe-covered childbirth to the humiliation of the "lady of Paris," would also not seem conso-

nant with a thoughtfulness about gendered and reproductive labor. Perhaps the best that can be said of Rabelais's views on women is that he didn't have any; Floyd Gray points to the "gleeful indifference" with which Rabelais puts caricatures of feminist and anti-feminist positions in his characters' mouths. *Gender, Rhetoric, and Print Culture in French Renaissance Writing* (Cambridge: Cambridge University Press, 2000), 29.

14. "L'outrance est recyclée dans le processus régénérateur des énergies naturelles. . . . Tout circule et se transforme." Jeanneret, "Débordements rabelaisiens," 107. Duval's insistence that Rabelais's books have a "design" is up against not only the vulgar deconstructionist sense that the "text" does not obey bibliographic borders but also the widespread idea, here articulated by Jeanneret, that in the sixteenth century, as opposed to the classification-obsessed ages that came directly before and after it, the goal of learning was not to organize, but simply to "accueillir la variété la plus grande" and to produce works that were "polyphoniques, volontiers fragmentaires ou centrifuges" (116). In a similar spirit, V.-L. Saulnier, invoking Rabelais's abhorrence of all things petrified, concludes, "Rabelais n'a cessé de répéter que le naturel compte d'abord, le naturel qu'il faut diriger et non pas contraindre. Edifier, au lieu d'entasser. Comme on encourage la croissance d'un être vivant, l'aidant seulement à s'ossifier, au lieu de momifier, fossiliser ou figer la vie." "Hommes pétrifiés et pierres vives (autour d'une formule de Panurge)," *Bibliothèque d'Humanisme et Renaissance* 22 (1960): 395.

15. This important point is raised by Gérard Defaux, who argues that the univocity of meaning, far from shutting down the signifying play of language, is in fact the necessary precondition for the kind of "exploitation polysémique" that Jeanneret finds so fundamental to the Rabelaisian text. "A propos de paroles gelées et dégelées (*Quart Livre*, 55–56): 'plus hault sens' ou 'lectures plurielles'?," in *Rabelais' Incomparable Book: Essays on His Art*, ed. Raymond C. La Charité (Lexington, KY: French Forum, 1986), 172.

16. Jeanneret, "Débordements rabelaisiens," 110.

17. Charles Estienne, *L'agriculture et maison rustique*, trans. Jean Liebault (Paris, 1570), 161. When Nostradamus introduces the second section of his treatise on cosmetics and confitures, he acknowledges his readers belonging to the "sexe feminin," who he knows are always on the lookout for new tips and tricks and are eager to keep their cabinets stocked with all manner of confectionery: the entire gender, he claims, "continuellement est cupide de savoir & entendre choses de nouvelleté, et tenir leur cabinet pourveu de plusieurs sortes de confitures" (*Excellent & moult utile opuscule*, 125).

18. Reeser notes the surprising paucity of references in the Pantagrueline books to the hero's moderation, a quality one might expect to see emphasized in the life story of a product of humanist pedagogy. He concludes that Rabelais's strategy could be "simultaneously to represent and not to represent moderation, to focus on moderation as what it is not—excess and lack" (*Moderating Masculinity*, 184, 186). The virtue's "creation through negativity" makes moderation a "byproduct" of immoderation (186) or, to put it another way, "a discursive fiction" (22). Duval sees Frere Jan and Panurge, as Pantagruel's double *comes* (epic companion), as "opposing and perfectly balanced extremes of character between which the *mediocritas* of Pantagruel's own character may be defined" (*Design*, 81).

19. Mühlethaler notes the importance in classical and Renaissance sources of the fragile balance of gustatory moderation—"le plaisir de la table comporte le risque de démesure et de désordre"—though without explaining how exactly it was supposed to be maintained ("Des Mets et Des Maux," 397).

20. Diane Desrosiers-Bonin, *Rabelais et l'humanisme civil,* Etudes rabelaisiennes no. 27 (Geneva: Droz, 1992), 71–72.

21. As Timothy Hampton notes in his discussion of the semantic range of "altération," which could refer to simple thirst, physiological corruption, the deleterious effects of the passions, or the redemptive transformation of love, "Both the state of imbalance and the process that seeks to redress that imbalance are expressed, in Renaissance French, with the same technical term." "Strange Alteration: Physiology and Psychology from Galen to Rabelais," in *Reading the Early Modern Passions,* ed. Gail Kern Paster, Katherine Rowe, and Mary Floyd-Wilson (Philadelphia: University of Pennsylvania Press, 2004), 281–82.

22. Thomas Greene, "The Hair of the Dog That Bit You: Rabelais' Thirst," in *Rabelais' Incomparable Book,* ed. Raymond C. La Charité (Lexington, KY: French Forum, 1986), 193; emphasis in original.

23. As Diane Desrosiers-Bonin puts it, "Comme le Christ, il remplit une mission salvatrice dans la mesure où il vient, sous le signe du vin, altérer, c'est-à-dire réformer, rendre à leur nature originelle ceux qu'il rencontrent." That *altérer* can mean either to alter or to make thirsty requires the constant application, when writing about the phenomenon in Rabelais, of such qualifying, tempering *c'est-à-dires. Rabelais et l'humanisme civil,* 62, 60.

24. The original alteration in Pantagruel's race resulted from their consumption of medlars, fruits which must be altered into a state beyond ripeness in order to be eaten and which caused, in the case of Pantagruel's ancestors, a body-altering swelling of all the limbs and organs. Rabelais, *Œuvres complètes,* 194–96.

25. Greene, *Comic Courage,* 68, 69–70.

26. See Duval on differences between the canonical 1552 and the hastily published 1548 version of the prologue, which was more in keeping with the tone and content of the previous prologues (*Design,* 49). Greene suggests that the Rabelaisian prologue has aged like a fine wine, or vinegar, the "preposterous spiel of the *Pantagruel* Prologue" mellowing into "the subtler boast of these riper and wiser texts" (*Comic Courage,* 84).

27. Ken Albala, *Eating Right in the Renaissance* (Berkeley: University of California Press, 2002), 245; Nostradamus, *Excellent & moult utile opuscule,* 140. Early modern French-Latin and French-English dictionaries attest to the range of meanings for "conficte." Jean Nicot, *Le Thresor de la langue francoyse* (Paris, 1606): "Se confire en son sel, ou autre chose, Combibere"; "Confire les vices qu'on a de nature avec une malice acquise, Condire vitia naturae"; "Confit en joyeusetez, Sale conditus et facetiis." Randle Cotgrave, *A Dictionarie of the French and English Tongues* (London, 1611): "Confire. To preserve, confect, soake, or steepe in; also, to season, relish, or giue savor unto"; "Confis: m. Any thing that hath beene soaked, or steeped; any pickled, or preserved thing."

28. Nostradamus, *Excellent & moult utile opuscule,* 126–27.

29. As Greene points out, the drought into which Pantagruel is born, and the accompanying "alteration" of Utopia's thirsty inhabitants, is what sets off the chain of further alterations that constitute Rabelais's text ("Hair of the Dog," 182).

30. Greene describes Pantagruelist *mediocrité* as "vital" and as a "healing power," the principle that ties together what would otherwise be "an inorganic jumble of vaguely related scenes" (*Comic Courage,* 87). This harmonization of elements that makes the story cohere could also be understood as seasoning, with moderation performing the function of salt in cooking.

31. The episode perhaps most exemplary for Cave of the general Rabelaisian theme of plenitude undercut by the threat of lack is the overcompensating description of Gargantua's *braguette*: "A movement towards plenitude and presence is established, but is constantly threatened by the possibility of inversion or subversion, whether thematically or rhetorically; once again, the distinction between lists or repetitions carrying a thematically positive sign and those with a negative sign may seem, within a linguistic perspective, to be a mirage rather than the affirmation of a value-system" (*Cornucopian Text*, 199). Similar conclusions have been reached by Kritzman ("The plenitude that Rabelais strives for is, by its very nature, empty," *Rhetoric of Sexuality*, 187) and Gray, who says of the Rabelaisian text in general, "ayant rempli la page, entraîné par un certain souci de contradiction, il se préoccupe de l'aérer, de le vider" (*Rabelais et le comique*, 17).

32. "Premierement vous prendrez .v. cens de nois nouvelles environ la saint Jehan—et gardez que l'escorche ne le noyau ne soient encores formez, et que l'escorche ne soit encores trop dure ne trop tendre—et les pelez tout entour et puis les perciez en troiz lieux tout oultre, ou en croix, et puis les mectez tremper en eaue de Saine ou de fontaine et la changier chascun jour, et les fault tremper de .x. a .xii. jours (et lesquelles deviennent comme noires) et que au macher vous n'y puissiez assavourer aucun amertume, et puis les mectre boulir une onde en eaue doulce par l'espace de dire une miserelle, ou tant comme vous verrez qu'il appartendra a ce qu'elles ne soient trop dures ne trop moles." *Le Menagier de Paris*, ed. Georgine E. Brereton and Janet M. Ferrier (Oxford: Clarendon Press, 1981).

33. *Le Menagier de Paris*, 268. Nicot's *Dictionaire Francois-Latin* (Paris, 1584) gives "moderare" and "temperare" as possible definitions of "gouverner." Wendy Wall has emphasized the extent to which early modern English recipe books, rather than giving precise ingredient types, amounts, and cooking times, explicitly call upon the judgment of the (usually female) reader, instructing her to use however much of something as she sees fit, for example. "Literacy and the Domestic Arts," *Huntington Library Quarterly* 73, no. 3 (Sept. 2010): 383–412. Julia Lupton argues for an affinity between the judgment required in cooking and judgment as a political faculty in "Thinking with Things: Hannah Woolley to Hannah Arendt," *postmedieval* 3 (2012): 63–79.

34. Nostradamus, *Excellent & moult utile opuscule*, 129–30.

35. Rabelais's interest in the miracle of keeping the world together anticipates an increased focus on preservation in early modern political thought. When the sixteenth-century Italian political theorist Giovanni Botero asked, "Quelle œuvre est plus grande d'agrandir ou de conserver un Estat?," his answer was that the conservation of the state was not only a greater task than that of expansion but was "almost superhuman": "C'est sans doute que l'œuvre est plus grande de le conserver pource que les choses humaines naturellement vont quasi ores défaillant, ores croissant. . . . De manière que de les tenir arrestees, & quand elles ont pris leur accroissement, les conserver en sorte qu'elles ne diminuent et viennent à cheoir, c'est une entreprise d'une singulière valeur, et quasi par dessus l'homme." (Clearly it is a greater task to conserve a state, because human affairs wax and wane. . . . To keep them stable when they have become great and to conserve them so that they do not decline and fall is an almost superhuman undertaking.) Giovanni Botero, *Raison et gouvernement en dix livres*, trans. Gabriel Chappuys (Paris, 1599), 8; Botero, *The Reason of State*, trans. P. J. and D. P. Waley (New Haven, CT: Yale University Press, 1956), 5–6. Qtd. in Katherine Ibbett, *The Style of the State in French Theater, 1630–1660: Neoclassicism and Government* (Burlington, VT: Ashgate, 2009), 68. Ibbett also traces the redefinition of the verb *conserver* from the end of the sixteenth century—

when only God could conserve human life—to the end of the eighteenth century, when it was the prince who was responsible for the conservation of the state's citizens (75).

36. As Timothy Hampton notes in his description of the interplay of popular and learned medical knowledge in the account of Gargantua's birth, Rabelais's frequent deployments of "series of side steps," where each definition of a word requires a supplemental definition, present divergent discourses as "narratively interlocked," dramatizing "the process through which humanist learning appropriates for literary form the raw material" of the wider (often feminine) world. What Hampton calls the humanist's "discursive domestication of the female voice and body" could be extended to the male domestication of the female domestic discourses contained in recipe books. "The Fallen Fundament: Jargon, Gender, and Literary Authority in the Birth of Gargantua," in *Esprit Généreux, Esprit Pantagruélicque: Essays by His Students in Honor of François Rigolot*, ed. Reinier Leushuis and Zahi Zalloua (Geneva: Droz, 2008), 164, 171, 172.

37. François Rigolot, *Les Langages de Rabelais* (Geneva: Droz, 1996), 152. The plant becomes more and more extraordinary through narrative build: "Herbe banale au départ, objet d'étude du botaniste et du philologue, elle se charge peu à peu de toutes les qualités, de toutes les craintes, de tous les espoirs de l'humanité" (150). Greene expresses a similar sentiment, assuring us that in "what appears the most wayward and opaque of Rabelaisian digressions," where botanical facts are "so exactly and—it must be confessed—tiresomely catalogued," a redemptive transformation is in fact taking place (*Comic Courage*, 78).

38. Rigolot, *Langages*, 149.

39. Prompted by the term "royalle" in Gaster's feast day menu, Timothy Tomasik comments on the culinary dimension of "reduction" in the sixteenth century. Bread was the standard thickener in medieval cooking, but a recipe in *La Fleur de toute cuysine* for "saulce royalle" calls instead for reducing the sauce through boiling, anticipating the reduction-heavy cuisine of the seventeenth century: "boutez tout bouillir en un beau pot jusques quil soit diminue quasi de la moytie." "Fishes, Fowl, and *La Fleur de toute cuysine*: Gaster and Gastronomy in Rabelais's *Quart Livre*," in *Renaissance Food from Rabelais to Shakespeare: Culinary Readings and Culinary Histories*, ed. Joan Fitzpatrick (Burlington, VT: Ashgate, 2010), 35.

40. Nicot, *Thresor de la langue francoyse*, s.v. "reduction."

41. Jacques Derrida, "What Is a 'Relevant' Translation?," trans. Lawrence Venuti, *Critical Inquiry* 27, no. 2 (Winter 2001): 195.

42. Desrosiers-Bonin reminds us how, as Barthes's use of him as "le code de référence littéraire du vin" in *S/Z* attests, the association of Rabelais with wine has become automatic (*Rabelais et l'humanisme civil*, 53).

43. Giovanni Battista Cavigioli, *La Vertu et propriété de vinaigre* (Poitiers, 1541), sig. A4r–A4v. Cavigioli goes on to accuse vinegar skeptics of being blind to the point of blasphemy ("si aveugles qu'ilz n'ont pas grande creance en Dieu nostre pere") if they fail to see all the ways in which God's creations, vinegar evidently among them, can cure us (sig. A5r).

44. Cavigioli, *La Vertu*, sig. A3v.

45. Galen, *On the Natural Faculties*, trans. A. J. Brock (Cambridge, MA: Harvard University Press, 1916), 209, 211.

46. Estienne, *Maison rustique*, 215.

47. *Secrets de divers autheurs approuvez* (Paris, 1619), n.p.

48. Cave, *Cornucopian Text*, 201.

49. Florence Weinberg, "Layers of Emblematic Prose: Rabelais' Andouilles," *Sixteenth Century Journal* 26, no. 2 (Summer 1995): 376.

50. Cave, *Cornucopian Text*, 5.

51. Erasmus, *Collected Works of Erasmus, Literary and Educational Writings*, vol. 24, 307.

52. Greene, *Comic Courage*, 75.

53. Jeanneret, "Débordements rabelaisiens," 113.

54. Seneca, *Epistles*, trans. Richard M. Gummere (Suffolk: Loeb Classical Library, 1917), 278–79.

55. Columella, *On Agriculture*, vol. 3, *Books 10–12: On Trees*, Loeb Classical Library 408, trans. E. S. Forster and Edward H. Heffner (Cambridge, MA: Harvard University Press, 1955), 190–91.

56. John Hale, in *The Civilization of Europe in the Renaissance* (New York: Simon and Schuster, 1993), sees awakening words as a metaphor for the revival of ancient texts in the temperate intellectual climate of the Renaissance, though Reeser notes that Pantagruel and his humanist-educated crew fail to understand what the words mean, which would hardly be a flattering portrait of philology (*Moderating Masculinity*, 165). Screech points to the thawing words that appear in Castiglione's *Book of the Courtier*, Aristotle's *On Interpretation*, Plato's *Cratylus*, Ammonius Hermaeus, Celio Calcagnini, commentaries on Roman law, and the Bible (*Rabelais*, 411, 416, 434).

57. Among these is Screech, who takes seriously Pantagruel's hypothesis that the frozen words are the byproduct of *logoi* that dwell in a platonic realm of virtue and have dripped down "comme catarrhes," or, as Screech puts it in a slippage from medical to medicinal terminology, "distillations" (*Rabelais*, 424). Screech sees this as part of a trickle-down cosmology: "The world is seen as the ultimate recipient of the waste matter of the universe. The off-scourings, excrements and material rejects of the higher spheres sink down naturally on to our round world" (425). If these are, as Screech calls them, "globules of truth" (426), we might think more of "globules" than "truth" when they are compared to chronic mucus.

58. Duval, *Design*, 38, 39n.

59. Judith H. Anderson emphasizes the sense of process congealed in what she translates as "crystallized sweetmeats," noting that *"perlée* means 'crystallized' in this context and suggests human making—more exactly, confecting," as well as "the notion of substance within": a *dragée*, or sweetmeat, was a nut or seed entombed in layers of crystallized syrup. *Words That Matter: Linguistic Perception in Renaissance English* (Stanford, CA: Stanford University Press, 1996), 239.

60. Jeanneret, "Les paroles dégelées," 16.

61. Jeanneret, "Les paroles dégelées," 17, 19.

62. Jeanneret, "Les paroles dégelées," 20.

63. Jeanneret, "Les paroles dégelées," 20.

64. For André Tournon, Rabelaisian language exists only in living exchange: "La vérité ne tombe pas du ciel, elle réside dans l'échange des paroles et des gestes." "De l'interprétation des 'motz de gueule,'" in *Hommage à François Meyer* (Aix-en-Provence: Publications de l'Université de Provence, 1983), 147. Reeser finds the would-be word-fixing narrator washed away by an inevitable flow: "The fluidity of words that cannot be held in the hand parallels the fluidity of etymology" (*Moderating Masculinity*, 168). For Screech, the Platonic intertext of the *Cratylus* establishes "Rabelais as an Heraclitean, accepting the doctrine that everything in the universe is in a state of flux" (*Rabelais*, 425).

65. Greene, *Light in Troy*, 92; Timothy Hampton, *Writing from History: The Rhetoric of Exemplarity in Renaissance Literature* (Ithaca, NY: Cornell University Press, 1990), 37.

66. Aaron Kunin, "Shakespeare's Preservation Fantasy," *PMLA* 124, no. 1 (Jan. 2009): 92–93.

67. Jennifer Summit has made a claim for the preservation of cultural artifacts in medieval libraries as something like a primary form of culture making, describing libraries as "dynamic institutions that actively processed, shaped, and imposed meaning on the very materials they contained" rather than passive receptacles. *Memory's Library: Medieval Books in Early Modern England* (Chicago: University of Chicago Press, 2008), 15. While Summit's approach aims to show that work long considered merely retentive was, on the contrary, actively transformative, I aim to trouble the distinction between retention and transformation on which her study relies.

68. Eden, *Hermeneutics and the Rhetorical Tradition,* 41.

69. Hutson, *Usurer's Daughter,* 48.

70. Hampton, "Fallen Fundament," 173.

71. Hampton, "Fallen Fundament," 173.

72. Screech, *Rabelais*, 418.

73. Jeanneret, "Débordements rabelaisiens," 117.

74. If, as Rabelais declares in the prologue to the *Tiers Livre,* his book is a "tonneau inexpuisible"—with the implication, for Jeanneret, that reading is "une opération sans fin"—it is only because readers keep refilling it. Jeanneret argues that the text poses a "défi permanent qui maintient vivante la productivité du texte," but the "défi" does not keep the text running by itself ("Débordements rabelaisiens," 123).

75. Cave points to Quintilian's stipulation that *copia* should not be "a store of inert goods": "There is no greater folly," Quintilian warns in book X of the *Institutiones oratoriae,* "than the rejection of the gifts of the moment." And yet Quintilian is careful to preface this with a qualifying reminder that "it is essential to bring with us into court a supply of eloquence which has been prepared in advance in the study (*paratam dicendi copiam*) and on which we can confidently rely" (qtd. in Cave, *Cornucopian Text,* 7).

# Chapter Two

1. Edmund Spenser, *The Faerie Queene*, ed. A. C. Hamilton, with Hiroshi Yamashita, Toshiyuki Suzuki, and Shohachi Fukuda, 2nd ed. (New York: Routledge, 2007), II.ix.33. Hereafter cited parenthetically by book, canto, and stanza number.

2. Federici, "Wages against Housework," 15. In his influential study of the pre–Civil War English nobility, some of the reasons Lawrence Stone cites for placing "the real watershed between medieval and modern England" between 1580 and 1620 are that it was "then that usury was first openly legislated for, that interest rates fell to modern levels, that the joint stock company began to flourish, that colonies of Englishmen were established across the seas . . . ; then that capitalist ethics, population growth, and monetary inflation undermined old landlord-tenant relationships and old methods of estate management." *Crisis of the Aristocracy,* 15–16. See also Louis Montrose, "Spenser's Domestic Domain: Poetry, Property, and the Early Modern Subject," in *Subject and Object in Renaissance Culture,* ed. Margreta de Grazia, Maureen Quilligan, and Peter Stallybrass (Cambridge: Cambridge University Press, 1996), 97, and Don E. Wayne, *Penshurst: The Semiotics of Place and the Poetics of History* (Madison: University of Wisconsin Press, 1984), 19. Montrose cites Wayne's work on Jonson's country house poem, which has a

presiding housewife at its center, as evidence of how the "new" English aristocracy of the prerevolutionary period, replacing the nobility ruined by the Wars of the Roses, developed an ideology of the "home" that we might associate more with the bourgeoisie than with the old feudal aristocratic order that Jonson (and Spenser) are purported to represent. Administrators rather than warriors, these aristocrats were more "bourgeois" than one might think, "an agrarian capitalist class with strong links to the trading community, and with investments in incipient mining and manufacturing enterprises and in the earliest colonialist ventures in the New World" (Wayne, *Penshurst*, 24–25).

3. In his reading of Redcrosse's battle with the dragon and its aftermath, Ross Lerner argues that "in his conversion to an 'organ' [of divine might], Redcrosse comes to allegorize the *un*fashioning of 'vertuous and gentle discipline.'" *Unknowing Fanaticism: Reformation Literatures of Self-Annihilation* (New York: Fordham University Press, 2019), 38. Though Lerner's focus on how fanaticism unmakes persons in *The Faerie Queene* differs from my focus on how domestic labor remakes them, I am indebted to his analysis of the poem's struggle to assign a stable allegorical meaning to characters, or literary authority to a poet, whose agency may well be derived from a source outside of them.

4. Thomas Tusser, *Fiue hundreth points of good husbandry vnited to as many of good huswiferie* (London, 1573), 66.

5. Montrose, "Spenser's Domestic Domain," 83–84.

6. Jeff Dolven, "Besides Good and Evil," *SEL* 57, no. 1 (Winter 2017): 16.

7. Federici, "Wages against Housework," 20; Tusser, *Fiue hundreth points*, 66.

8. Patricia Parker, *Inescapable Romance: Studies in the Poetics of a Mode* (Princeton, NJ: Princeton University Press, 1979), 60, 87.

9. Jonathan Goldberg, *Endlesse Worke: Spenser and the Structures of Discourse* (Baltimore: Johns Hopkins University Press, 1981), xii.

10. William Sessions, "Spenser's Georgic," *ELR* 10, no. 2 (Spring 1980): 237. Alastair Fowler sees things differently, noting that Spenser "also uses georgic to humble the pretensions of epic," bringing such heroic declarations down to earth ("The Beginnings of English Georgic," 112).

11. Michael Schoenfeldt, *Bodies and Selves in Early Modern England: Physiology and Inwardness in Spenser, Shakespeare, Herbert, and Milton* (Cambridge: Cambridge University Press, 1999), 45.

12. Hutson, *The Usurer's Daughter*, 21.

13. Hutson, *The Usurer's Daughter*, 21.

14. Montrose, "Spenser's Domestic Domain," 97.

15. Gentian Hervet, *Xenophons treatise of housholde* (London, 1537), sig. 29v.

16. Beauvoir, *The Second Sex*, 483.

17. Hervet, *Xenophons treatise*, sigs. 26v–27r.

18. Kenelm Digby, *Observations on the 22. Stanza in the 9th. Canto of the 2d. Book of Spencers Faery Queen* (London, 1643).

19. Angus Fletcher, *The Prophetic Moment: An Essay on Spenser* (Chicago: University of Chicago Press, 1971), 18, 13.

20. Fletcher, *Prophetic Moment*, 17.

21. Fletcher, *Prophetic Moment*, 19.

22. Fletcher, *Prophetic Moment*, 21. For the beginning of the ideological separation between the domestic and commercial spheres in the sixteenth century, see Korda, *Shakespeare's Domestic Economies*, 72.

23. Henry Smith, *A preparative to mariage, the summe whereof was spoken at a contract, and inlarged after* (London, 1591), 67.

24. Federici, "Wages against Housework," 15.

25. Shapin, *A Social History of Truth*; Blair, "Early Modern Attitudes"; Bierlaire, *La Familia d'Erasme*.

26. While it is true that aristocrats would generally speaking be proud to have a large and visible retinue as a sign of their wealth, a ceremonial display of servants does not necessarily imply comfort with the fact that one would be powerless to perform basic daily tasks without them. Stone suggests such displays were beginning to fall out of fashion around Spenser's time. He charts a marked decline in the size of large households from hundreds in the mid-fifteenth century down to "between 30 and 50" by the mid-seventeenth, as tastes changed in favor of smaller retinues and as young gentlemen who made up the higher ranks of servants began to find the role "socially humiliating" (*Crisis of the Aristocracy*, 213, 214). The cookery book author Robert May, writing after the Restoration, reminisces about his first job as a cook in a great house, "where were four Cooks more" besides himself and his father, going on to bemoan how the decline in kitchen staffing led to not only a decline in culinary production but also a total breakdown of charity, piety, and general morality. "The Author's Life," in *The accomplisht cook, or, The art & mystery of cookery wherein the whole art is revealed in a more easie and perfect method than hath been published in any language* (1660; London, 1685).

27. Spenser, "Letter to Raleigh," in *The Faerie Queene*, 716.

28. Spenser, "Letter to Raleigh," 714.

29. Schoenfeldt, *Bodies and Selves*, 52.

30. John Hughes, "An Essay on Allegorical Poetry" (1715), in *Edmund Spenser: The Critical Heritage*, ed. R. M. Cummings (New York: Barnes and Noble, 1971), 267–68, qtd. in Schoenfeldt, *Bodies and Selves*, 52.

31. Jonathan Sawday, *The Body Emblazoned: Dissection and the Human Body in Renaissance Culture* (New York: Routledge, 1995), 164.

32. Harry Berger Jr., *The Allegorical Temper: Vision and Reality in Book II of Spenser's "Faerie Queene"* (New Haven, CT: Yale University Press, 1957), 74. Jeff Dolven, reading Spenser through the lens of Alexander Kluge and Oskar Negt's *History and Obstinacy*, sees bodily recovery—including sleep and nourishment—as forms of "obstinacy" that count as labor, requiring discipline and exertion. "Obstinate Spenser," *Spenser Review* 47, no. 1 (Winter 2017), http://www.english.cam.ac.uk/spenseronline/review/item/47.1.2.

33. Berger, *Allegorical Temper*, 74.

34. Russ Leo, "The Species-Life of Worldlings," *Spenser Studies* 30 (2015): 219.

35. Leo, "Species-Life," 219–220.

36. Rambuss, *Spenser's Secret Career*, 68.

37. Thomas Herron reads Error's vomiting up of paper in book I, usually glossed as the repudiation of false Catholic doctrine, as the frustrated rejection of the legal filings that sought to protect the native Irish from planters like Spenser. In other words, Spenser may have felt just as materially encumbered by the bureaucratic red tape that threatened his colonial estate—an explicitly spatial reminder that the ideology of the home as a sacred space can entail the oppression of those outside "the home"—as he felt spiritually encumbered by heresy. *Spenser's Irish Work: Poetry, Plantation, and Colonial Reformation* (Aldershot: Ashgate, 2007), 132, 137.

38. Goldberg, *Endlesse Worke*, xii, 1.

39. Alan Stewart and Garrett Sullivan, "'Worme-Eaten, and Full of Canker Holes': Materializing Memory in *The Faerie Queene* and *Lingua*," *Spenser Studies* 17 (2003): 223.

40. Qtd. in Stewart and Sullivan, "'Worme-Eaten,'" 223.

41. Arendt, *The Human Condition*, 101.

42. Arendt, *The Human Condition*, 101.

43. James Kuzner summarizes two chapters of his *Open Subjects: English Renaissance Republicans, Modern Selfhoods, and the Virtue of Vulnerability* (Edinburgh: Edinburgh University Press, 2011) as arguing that "Spenser and Shakespeare . . . imagine social experiences wherein vulnerability can become a definite good" (125).

44. Joseph Campana, *The Pain of Reformation: Spenser, Vulnerability, and the Ethics of Masculinity* (New York: Fordham University Press, 2014), 11. Campana refers to Stephen Greenblatt, *Renaissance Self-Fashioning: From More to Shakespeare* (Chicago: University of Chicago Press, 1980), and Cynthia Marshall, *The Shattering of the Self: Violence, Subjectivity, and Early Modern Texts* (Baltimore: Johns Hopkins University Press, 2003).

45. Campana, *Pain of Reformation*, 142.

46. Stewart and Sullivan, "'Worme-Eaten,'" 228.

47. This emptying of agency in the banal act of eating is perhaps a more mundane version of what Lerner identifies as the ambiguous unmaking of Redcrosse as a grammatical and agential subject in book I (*Unknowing Fanaticism*, 33–37).

48. Fletcher, *Prophetic Moment*, 22–23; Tusser, *Fiue hundreth points*, 70.

49. Thomas Dawson, *The good huswifes jewell wherein is to be found most excellent and rare deuises for conceits in cookerie . . . Whereunto is adjoyned sundry approued reseits for many soueraine oyles, and the way to distill many precious waters, with diuers approued medicines for many diseases* (London, 1587), sigs. 23r–v. Some collections do distinguish between culinary and medicinal recipes, but the same recipe might appear under both categories.

50. Gervase Markham, *The English house-wife, Containing the inward and outward vertues which ought to be in a compleate woman* (London, 1631), 1, 4.

51. Linda Gregerson, "Spenser's Georgic: Violence and the Gift of Place," *Spenser Studies* 22, no. 1 (Jan. 2007): 186.

52. Hugh Plat, *Delightes for ladies to adorn their persons, tables, closets, and distallatories: with beauties, banquets, perfumes and waters* (London, 1600), sig. A2v. In the following lines of this prefatory poem, Plat describes casting animals in marzipan and sugar plate in terms that evoke the reproductions of plants and animals through "casting from life" documented by Pamela Smith: compare "Each bird and fowle so moulded from the life; / And after cast in sweet compounds of Art, / As if the flesh and forme with nature gave, / Did still remaine in every lim and part" to the work of the sixteenth-century goldsmith Wenzel Jamnitzer, who would kill a small animal through a kind of pickling process, "immersing it in vinegar and urine so that it was not deformed by blows, and then posing it in a lifelike manner," making a mold in a kiln which burned out the organic material, and filling the mold with metal to create a replica of the animal (*The Body of the Artisan*, 74–75).

53. John Partridge, *The Treasurie of commodious conceits, & hidden secrets and may be called, the huswives closet, of healthfull provision* (London, 1573), n.p.

54. Richard Bradley, *The Country Housewife and Lady's Director, in the management of a house, and the delights and profits of a farm* (London, 1732), 113.

55. Bacon, *New Atlantis*, 482–83, 480.

56. Wall, *Recipes for Thought*, 170.

57. *Oxford English Dictionary*, s.v. "dew, n."

58. Miriam Jacobson, *Barbarous Antiquity: Reorienting the Past in the Poetry of Early Modern England* (Philadelphia: University of Pennsylvania Press, 2014), 68. Plat highlights the continuum between confectionary and ink, between preservation through culinary and textual means, when in the "flowers candied as they grow" recipe below he gives the instruction to "make gum water as strong as for Inke, but make it with Rosewater" (*Garden of Eden*, 42).

59. Cookery book of Ann Goodenough (ca. 1700–ca. 1775), Folger W.a.332, 40, qtd. in Wall, *Recipes for Thought*, 170; Plat, *Garden of Eden*, 43.

60. C. S. Lewis, *The Allegory of Love: A Study in Medieval Tradition* (London: Oxford University Press, 1938), 326.

61. Qtd. in Wall, *Staging Domesticity*, 51.

62. *The ladies cabinet opened, wherein is found hidden severall experiments in preserving and convserving, physicke, and surgery, cookery, and huswifery* (London, 1639); Plat, *Delightes for ladies*, sig. A3v.

# Chapter Three

1. Michel de Montaigne, *Les Essais*, ed. Pierre Villey and Verdun-Louis Saulnier (Paris: PUF, 2004), 33. Hereafter cited parenthetically by page number.

2. Krause, *Idle Pursuits*, 166. For an analysis of Montaigne's method as a more commercial double-entry bookkeeping ("debiting" and "crediting" ancient sources; correcting rather than deleting erroneous entries in the account book), see Philippe Desan, *L'imaginaire économique de la Renaissance* (Paris: Presses de l'Université de Paris-Sorbonne, 2002), 128–31.

3. Erasmus, "The Labors of Hercules," 173. See the introduction for a more extensive account of Erasmus's slog.

4. Montaigne, *Complete Essays*, 721. Hereafter cited parenthetically by page number.

5. Pierre Charron, *De la sagesse, trois livres* (Paris, 1797), 525. Charron went on to concede precisely Montaigne's point: "C'est une occupation qui n'est pas difficile . . . mais elle est empeschante, penible, espineuse, à cause d'un si grand nombre d'affaires; lesquels, bien qu'ils soyent petits et menus, toutesfois, pource qu'ils sont drus, espais et frequens, faschent et ennuyent. Les espines domestiques piquent, pource qu'elles sont ordinaires; mais si elles viennent des personnes principales de la famille, elles rongent, ulcerent, et sont irremediables." (It is not a difficult occupation . . . but it is burdensome, exacting, and thorny, because of the great number of tasks, which, even though they are small and petty, still—because they are copious, oppressive, and frequent—cause anger and annoyance. The domestic thorns prick because they are ordinary; but if they come from the principal members of the family, they gnaw, gall, and are irreversible.)

6. Olivier de Serres, preface to *Le théâtre d'agriculture*, n.p. Tom Conley, quoting this passage along with Serres's reflections on how much time for study his country retreat has allowed, concludes, "In times of calamity and in the give-and-take of war and peace, in the midst of uncertainty and occasional calamity, care of an estate . . . becomes a meditation on an inner space that the author 'manages' through reading and writing." "Reading Olivier de Serres circa 1600: Between Economy and Ecology," in *Early Modern Écologies: Beyond English Ecocriticism*, ed. Pauline Goul and Phillip John Usher (Amsterdam: Amsterdam University Press, 2020), 258. Recent interest in the cultural impact of practical works like Serres's might complicate claims like Jonathan Dewald's that "no country ideology seems to have ensued" from the French aristocracy's interest in country-house

life, as it did in England. *Aristocratic Experience and the Origins of Modern Culture: France, 1570–1715* (Berkeley: University of California Press, 1993), 21.

7. In a striking negative enumeration, Montaigne claims not to know anything about running a farm, from telling crops apart to caring for sick livestock to making wine: "Ny ne sçay la difference de l'un grain à l'autre, ny en la terre, ny au grenier, . . . ny à peine celle d'entre les choux et les laictues de mon jardin. Je n'entens pas seulement les noms des premiers outils du mesnage, ny les plus grossiers principes de l'agriculture, et que les enfans sçavent; ᴮmoins aux arts mechaniques, en la trafique et en la connoissance des marchandises, diversité et nature des fruicts, de vins, de viandes; ny à dresser un oiseau, ny à medeciner un cheval ou un chien. ᴬ . . . il n'y a pas un mois qu'on me surprint ignorant dequoy le levain servoit à faire du pain, ᶜet que c'estoit que faire cuver du vin" (652). As Hoffmann points out, this was an overstatement (*Montaigne's Career*, 23). Serres assigns the "gouvernement des Vins" to the "maistre" because, he asserts, wine is a man's drink ("aimans les hommes telle liqueur, tous-jours mieux que les femmes"), but the cellar provides enough worry for both man and wife ("du souci à l'un & à l'autre") for the reasons he describes in this chapter's epigraph (*Théâtre d'agriculture*, 832). For the distinction between the concept of *bon mesnage* as applied to women and to men, see Jonathan Patterson, *Representing Avarice in Late Renaissance France* (Oxford: Oxford University Press, 2015), 170, as well as chapter 2. Estate management enthusiasts like Serres, while going out of their way to acknowledge the crucial role of the wife, were primarily concerned with the male householder. But even the political theorist Jean Bodin saw good housewives as necessary to the stability of the state, which relied on the "droit gouvernement de plusieurs mesnages" (upright government of many households), each of which "ne sera pas accomplie de tout poinct sans femme" (will not be complete in each and every respect without a wife) (qtd. in *Representing Avarice*, 111).

8. As Hampton points out, drawing attention to Montaigne's declaration in "De l'experience" that he has learned to mistrust his gait and strives to regulate it, self-regulation tends to be "deferred to an indefinite future: 'je m'attens à la reigler'" (*Writing from History*, 189).

9. Beauvoir, *The Second Sex*, 639.

10. Beauvoir, *The Second Sex*, 483.

11. See, for example, Ann Hartle, *Michel de Montaigne: Accidental Philosopher* (Cambridge: Cambridge University Press, 2003), and Richard Regosin, "Prudence and the Ethics of Contingency in Montaigne's *Essais*," in *Chance, Literature, and Culture in Early Modern France*, ed. John D. Lyons and Kathleen Wine (New York: Routledge, 2016). John D. Lyons calls attention to how Montaigne understands contingency as both mundane and high-stakes: "One's tastes and opinions vary unaccountably from one day to the next," and "political, military and judicial doctrines are all the result of chance and subject to it." *The Phantom of Chance: From Fortune to Randomness in Seventeenth-Century French Literature* (Edinburgh: Edinburgh University Press, 2011), ix, x.

12. Jean Starobinski is typical in this regard: "Montaigne is in no doubt as to the correct moral choice: insistence on veracity remains his unvarying standard of judgment. . . . Such is his concern for honesty that it is untouched even by his recognition of the mutability of all things." *Montaigne in Motion*, trans. Arthur Goldhammer (Chicago: University of Chicago Press, 1985), 4.

13. Philippe Desan discusses how Montaigne's recent popularization has included the French media crediting him with inventing the concepts of the "blog" and the "selfie." *The Oxford Handbook of Montaigne* (Oxford: Oxford University Press, 2016), 5. Sarah

Bakewell, in her popular *How to Live: or, A Life of Montaigne in One Question and Twenty Attempts at an Answer* (London: Chatto and Windus, 2010), asserts that Montaigne took pleasure in the randomness of his writing process: "He was delighted to see his work come out so unpredictably" (8).

14. "Je n'ay plus faict mon livre que mon livre m'a faict, livre consubstantiel à son autheur, d'une occupation propre, membre de ma vie; non d'une occupation et fin tierce et estrangere comme tous autres livres" (665) (I have no more made my book than my book has made me—a book consubstantial with its author, concerned with my own self, an integral part of my life; not concerned with some third-hand, extraneous purpose, like all other books [504]).

15. Elizabeth Guild, *Unsettling Montaigne: Poetics, Ethics and Affect in the "Essais" and other Writings* (Cambridge: D. S. Brewer, 2014), 2.

16. Guild, *Unsettling Montaigne*, 183.

17. Ngai, *Ugly Feelings*, 207.

18. Ngai, *Ugly Feelings*, 6.

19. Ngai, *Ugly Feelings*, 3, 5.

20. Hoffmann, *Montaigne's Career*, especially chapter 1.

21. Annette Baier, "What Emotions Are About," *Philosophical Perspectives* 4 (1990): 3, qtd. in Ngai, *Ugly Feelings*, 179.

22. Ngai, *Ugly Feelings*, 175, 191.

23. Aristotle, *The Nicomachean Ethics*, trans. Terence Irwin (Indianapolis: Hackett, 1985), 106, qtd. in Ngai, *Ugly Feelings*, 175; emphasis in original.

24. Ngai, *Ugly Feelings*, 175.

25. Ngai, *Ugly Feelings*, 175. Ngai is writing about a very different literary text and social and political context from Montaigne's, and I do not mean to suggest any equivalence between Montaigne and Larsen or her fictional character. But I do find Ngai's diagnosis of the misguided expectation of Larsen's readers that affect can and must "legibly, unambiguously, and immediately" respond to social and political realities to be instructive: "Irritation's radical *in*adequacy—its stubborn 'offishness' or incommensurateness with respect to objects . . . calls attention to a symbolic violence in the principle of commensurability itself, when there is an underlying assumption that an appropriate emotional response to racist violence exists, and that the burden lies on the racialized subject to produce that appropriate response legibly, unambiguously, and immediately" (188).

26. Juan Luis Vives, *The Passions of the Soul: The Third Book of De Anima et Vita*, trans. Carlos G. Noreña (Lewiston, NY: Edwin Mellen, 1990), 60.

27. Johann Gottfried Herder, "On the Cognition and Sensation of the Human Soul," in *Philosophical Writings*, trans. and ed. Michael N. Forster (Cambridge: Cambridge University Press, 2002), 189, 190. For an account of the relationship between irritation and poetics in Herder's essay, see Amanda Jo Goldstein, "Irritable Figures: Herder's Poetic Empiricism," in *The Relevance of Romanticism: Essays on German Romantic Philosophy*, ed. Dalia Nassar (Oxford: Oxford University Press, 2014).

28. Steven Goldsmith, *Blake's Agitation: Criticism and the Emotions* (Baltimore: Johns Hopkins University Press, 2013), 43, 49; Jean-François Lyotard, "Judiciousness in Dispute, or Kant after Marx," trans. Cecile Lindsay, in *The Lyotard Reader*, ed. Andrew Benjamin (Cambridge: Basil Blackwell, 1989), 327–28, qtd. in Goldsmith, *Blake's Agitation*, 49.

29. Goldsmith, *Blake's Agitation*, 56.

30. Melissa Gregg and Gregory J. Seigworth, "An Inventory of Shimmers," in *The*

*Affect Theory Reader,* ed. Gregg and Seigworth (Durham, NC: Duke University Press, 2010), 2.

31. David Quint, *Montaigne and the Quality of Mercy: Ethical and Political Themes in the "Essais"* (Princeton, NJ: Princeton University Press, 1998), ix.

32. Guild, *Unsettling Montaigne,* 21.

33. Ngai, *Ugly Feelings,* 1.

34. Ngai, *Ugly Feelings,* 2.

35. Ngai, *Ugly Feelings,* 7.

36. Timothy Hampton, "Difficult Engagements: Private Passion and Public Service in Montaigne's *Essais,*" in *Politics and the Passions, 1500–1850,* ed. Victoria Kahn, Neil Saccamano, and Daniela Coli (Princeton, NJ: Princeton University Press, 2006), 34, 35.

37. The skeptic's paradoxical affirmation of doubt effectively purges itself along with its doubt, "ny plus ny moins que la rubarbe qui pousse hors les mauvaises humeurs et s'emporte hors quant et quant elle mesmes" (527).

38. If Montaigne's emphasis on minor inconveniences suggests that he does not view the household as an analogy to the state, his attitude anticipates that of the duc de Rohan about colonial power in the mid-seventeenth century: "Bref, cette puissance est plus fâcheuse que solide" (In sum, this power is more troubling than solid). Katherine Ibbett, quoting Rohan's remark, calls it "broadly typical of French writing about the difficulties of running an empire" (*The Style of the State,* 71).

39. Cotgrave, *Dictionarie of the French and English Tongues,* s.v. "exasperer."

40. Smith, *Wealth of Nations,* 352.

41. Cave, *Cornucopian Text,* 276.

42. Guild points out that minor features like repetitions and hesitations leave traces of Montaigne's "unsettled" affect but identifies her own focus as the broad workings of "figuration," including irony, anamorphosis, and "highly charged" motifs (*Unsettling Montaigne,* 3). By contrast, I attend to small formal traces as signs of affect's role not as a big mover and shaker in Montaigne's writing but as an iterative, irritating, and (temporarily) maintaining presence.

43. Alison Calhoun, "Redefining Nobility in the French Renaissance: The Case of Montaigne's *Journal de Voyage,*" *MLN* 123, no. .4 (Sept. 2008): 840, 843.

44. Michel de Montaigne, *Journal de voyage,* ed. Fausta Garavini (Paris: Gallimard, 1982), 331, qtd. in Calhoun, "Redefining Nobility," 845.

45. Montaigne's relation to his only child to survive past infancy could itself be described as casual; Léonore barely warrants mention in the *Essais.*

46. For evidence that Montaigne may have dictated the first edition of the *Essais* to a secretary, and the reluctance of scholars attached to the myth of Montaigne's solitary genius to entertain this possibility, see Hoffmann, *Montaigne's Career,* 46–58.

47. What Elaine Scarry attributes to secondhand accounts of pain—"When one hears about another person's physical pain, the events happening within the interior of that person's body may seem to have the remote character of some deep subterranean fact, belonging to an invisible geography that, however portentous, has no reality because it has not yet manifested itself on the visible surface of the earth"; "to have pain is to have great certainty; to hear that another person has pain is to have doubt"—sounds like Montaigne's experience of his own pain, which, for all its immediacy, he holds at arm's length in his writing, and which breeds endless uncertainty. *The Body in Pain: The Making and Unmaking of the World* (Oxford: Oxford University Press, 1985), 3, 7.

48. Qtd. in Greene, *Light in Troy,* 98.

49. David Carroll Simon, *Light without Heat: The Observational Mood from Bacon to Milton* (Ithaca, NY: Cornell University Press, 2018), 149. Margreta de Grazia identifies a similar shift from the recursive to the linear senses of terms, a shift that seems to coincide with "modernity": "Hegel's Reformation and Marx's revolution have both abandoned the reiterative force of their prefixes. Both terms, though once designating recursivity, are now taken to delineate irreversible linearity." For both Hegel and Marx, "the mole is featured as the epic hero of world history; like Aeneas, it braves hardship while moving toward a promised future," a figuration that ignores the fact that in nature, "the mole burrows to seek not an exit but food. . . . Hegel took the liberty of redesigning its trajectory, straightening out its helter-skelter burrowing. . . . Once recast as a progressive struggle against earth and toward liberating air and sun, the mole's naturally erratic course looks unnaturally teleological." *"Hamlet" without Hamlet* (Cambridge: Cambridge University Press, 2007), 27, 25, 29.

50. Montaigne accentuates his own available leisure by going back and adding a B-text revision directly following this sentence to point out that the fifth book of the *Aeneid* seems to him most perfect (410).

51. Richard Regosin, commenting on how the feminine is a "diverse and potentially disruptive element that the *Essais* cannot fully admit nor fully master," notes that this is one of three moments in the *Essais*, "all specific moments when Montaigne treats the composition of his text," when "he addresses women readers as if to implicate the female in its conception." *Montaigne's Unruly Brood: Textual Engendering and the Challenge to Paternal Authority* (Berkeley: University of California Press, 1996), 8.

52. Starobinski, *Montaigne in Motion*, 6–7.

53. For Montaigne's relationship with Marie de Gournay, see Philippe Desan, *Montaigne: A Life*, trans. Steven Randall and Lisa Neal (Princeton, NJ: Princeton University Press, 2017), 532–39.

54. Starobinski, *Montaigne in Motion*, xi. (Montaigne souhaite un *suffisant lecteur*, qui saura imaginer, à partir des *Essais*, les *infinis essais* dont ce livre offre le prétexte [*Montaigne en mouvement*, 9].)

# Chapter Four

1. William Kerrigan, "Marvell and Nymphets," *Greyfriar* 27 (1986): 3–21, 3. Kerrigan goes so far as to claim that "[Marvell's] famous lyrics are pedophilic, such that this is an erotic genre predicted and implied by the poetry, and by the same token the pedophilia is poetic, such that the lyrics draw into their own excellence the troubled logic that creates and sustains this erotic genre" (8).

2. John Rogers, "The Enclosure of Virginity: The Poetics of Sexual Abstinence in the English Revolution," in *Enclosure Acts: Sexuality, Property, and Culture in Early Modern England*, ed. John Michael Archer and Michael Burt (Ithaca, NY: Cornell University Press, 1994), 243; Andrew Marvell, "The Picture of Little T. C. in a Prospect of Flowers," in *The Poems of Andrew Marvell*, ed. Nigel Smith (Harlow: Pearson Longman, 2003), 9–10. Subsequent quotations from this poem will be cited parenthetically by line number.

3. Virgil, *Georgics*, 3.40, 46.

4. Joseph Summers glosses "Reform the errors of the spring" and the subsequent lines as follows: "At first it seems, or perhaps would seem to a child, an almost possible command. . . . But the thing which should be 'most' procured ['that violets may a longer age endure'] is impossible for the human orderer even within his small area. . . . Spring

is full of errors; the decorative details suggest exactly how far nature fails to sustain human visions of propriety, delight, and immortality." "Marvell's 'Nature,'" *ELH* 20, no. 2 (June 1963): 132.

5. Plat, *Garden of Eden*, 51, 65, 66, 89, 52, 96–97.

6. Hannah Woolley, *The Accomplishd ladies delight* (London, 1686), 5.

7. Marvell likely wrote "The Picture of Little T. C." at his patron Lord Fairfax's estate, Nun Appleton, which was both the subject matter and the site of composition of *Upon Appleton House*. This period was a kind of "meantime" for Marvell's career as well: as Nigel Smith posits in his dating of the poem to 1652, "Before this period, [Marvell] was either abroad or engaged in London poetry and politics; after this period, he was preoccupied with the search for patronage and in the writing of political verse." Introduction to "The Picture of Little T. C. in a Prospect of Flowers," in *The Poems of Andrew Marvell*, 112.

8. Diane Purkiss, "Marvell, Boys, Girls, and Men: Should We Worry?," in *Gender and Early Modern Constructions of Childhood,* ed. Naomi J. Miller and Naomi Yavneh (Burlington, VT: Ashgate, 2011), 189.

9. Margarita Stocker, *Apocalyptic Marvell: The Second Coming in Seventeenth-Century Poetry* (Brighton: Harvester, 1986), xiv.

10. Wendy Wall, "Forgetting and Keeping: Jane Shore and the English Domestication of History," *Renaissance Drama* 27 (1996): 125.

11. Dod and Cleaver, *A godlie forme of householde gouernment*, 171; Hannah Woolley, *The Gentlewoman's Companion; or, a Guide to the Female Sex* (London, 1675), 108. Woolley's first phrase seems to have been lifted verbatim from the section on household husbandry in Samson Lennard's translation of Montaigne's disciple Pierre Charron's *De la sagesse, Of wisdome three books written in French by Peter Charro[n] Doctr of Lawe in Paris* (London, 1608), 456. Charron emphasizes that "to take good heed lest the goods in the house bee spoiled . . . doth especiallie belong to the woman, to whom *Aristotle* giues this authoritie and care" (456).

12. Hervet, *Xenophons treatise of housholde*, sigs. 29v, 26v.

13. Aemilia Lanyer, "A Description of Cooke-ham," lines 201–2, in *The Poems of Aemilia Lanyer: Salve Deus Rex Judæorum*, ed. Susanne Woods (Oxford: Oxford University Press, 1993), 138; Ben Jonson, "To Penshurst," lines 85–90, in *Ben Jonson*, 96. Lanyer's poem, addressed to a female patron referred to as "Mistris of that Place" (line 11), is unusual in its emphatic lack of governing male figures, which makes its resonance with spiritual discourses of housewifery all the more striking. For a detailed account of how remote household management could ensure "all things" were "nigh" when the mistress "was far," see chapter 2 of Leong, *Recipes and Everyday Knowledge*.

14. Derek Hirst and Steven N. Zwicker, *Andrew Marvell, Orphan of the Hurricane* (Oxford: Oxford University Press, 2012), 28–29.

15. Xenophon, Οἰκονομικός, in *Xenophontis opera omnia*, vol. 2, 2nd ed. (Oxford: Clarendon, 1921), 8.20.

16. Valerie Traub, "The New Unhistoricism in Queer Studies," *PMLA* 128, no. 1 (Jan. 2013): 21.

17. Hirst and Zwicker, *Orphan of the Hurricane*, 52, 50.

18. Jonathan Goldberg and Madhavi Menon, "Queering History," *PMLA* 120, no. 5 (Oct. 2005): 1608–17; Carla Freccero, *Queer/Early/Modern* (Durham, NC: Duke University Press, 2006). Goldberg and Menon explain that "to produce queering as an object of our scrutiny would mean the end of queering itself, a capitulation to a teleology . . . 'at once heterosexual and heterosexualizing'" (1608–9). Freccero goes so far as to argue

that "all textuality, when subjected to close reading, can be said to be queer" (5). I cite these examples not as representative of queer theory but simply as one tendency within the larger field. As David Kurnick points out, "The description of queer theory as always and everywhere devoted to values of instability and 'play' is one way of trivializing its claims" to political relevance and moral seriousness ("A Few Lies," 349), and that is not my intent.

19. Andrew McRae, "The Green Marvell," in *The Cambridge Companion to Andrew Marvell*, ed. Derek Hirst and Steven N. Zwicker (Cambridge: Cambridge University Press, 2011), 122; Rosalie Colie, *"My Ecchoing Song": Andrew Marvell's Poetry of Criticism* (Princeton, NJ: Princeton University Press, 1970), 5; Nigel Smith, *Andrew Marvell: The Chameleon* (New Haven, CT: Yale University Press, 2010).

20. Stocker takes on this blurry image of Marvell, what she calls "the central cliché of Marvell studies," bluntly: "The essential purpose of this book," she announces early in *Apocalyptic Marvell*, "is to alter radically the received image of Andrew Marvell . . . as a difficult, elusive, elegant, poised—one might say even etiolated—poet" (viii).

21. Timothy Morton, "Guest Column: Queer Ecology," *PMLA* 125, no. 2 (2010): 280, qtd. in Marjorie Swann, "Vegetable Love: Botany and Sexuality in Seventeenth-Century England," in *The Indistinct Human in Renaissance Literature*, ed. Jean E. Feerick and Vin Nardizzi (New York: Palgrave Macmillan, 2012), 153. Stephen Guy-Bray seeks to evacuate the version of "vegetable love" we see in "The Garden" of any metaphoricity at all: "Instead of wanting to procreate like trees," as Thomas Browne famously did, "the speaker of Marvell's poem wants to have sex with them." "Animal, Vegetable, Sexual: Metaphor in John Donne's 'Sappho to Philaenis' and Andrew Marvell's 'The Garden,'" in *Sex before Sex: Figuring the Act in Early Modern England*, ed. James M. Bromley and Will Stockton (Minneapolis: University of Minnesota Press, 2013), 205.

22. Hirst and Zwicker, *Orphan of the Hurricane*, 46; J. M. Wallace, *Destiny His Choice: The Loyalism of Andrew Marvell* (Cambridge: Cambridge University Press, 1981), 232, 244; Hirst and Zwicker, *Orphan of the Hurricane*, 46; Wallace, *Destiny His Choice*, 233; Jonathan Crewe, "The Garden State: Marvell's Poetics of Enclosure," in *Enclosure Acts: Sexuality, Property, and Culture in Early Modern England*, ed. John Michael Archer and Michael Burt (Ithaca, NY: Cornell University Press, 1994), 283.

23. Raymond Williams calls *Upon Appleton House* a "truly transitional" poem, "a complication of feeling between an old order and a new" that exposes "the folly of assimilating all country-house poems to a single tradition, as if their occupants were some kind of unbroken line," when in reality the "order" the country house represents "was being continually reconstituted by the political and economic formation of a new aristocracy and then a new agrarian capitalism" (*The Country and the City*, 58). In this way, the disjointedness of the poem condenses and lays bare the uneasy progression of an aristocratic order that strove to present itself as unbroken. Christopher Kendrick expands Williams's analysis in his framing of Appleton House as a "capitalist manor" and of the poem's "manorial capitalism" (29) in "Agons of the Manor: 'Upon Appleton House' and Agrarian Capitalism," in *The Production of English Renaissance Culture*, ed. David Lee Miller, Sharon O'Dair, and Harold Weber (Ithaca, NY: Cornell University Press, 1994).

24. Lee Edelman, *No Future: Queer Theory and the Death Drive* (Durham, NC: Duke University Press, 2004), 114; Louis Montrose, *The Purpose of Playing: Shakespeare and the Cultural Politics of the Elizabethan Theatre* (Chicago: University of Chicago Press, 1996), 8.

25. R. Howard Bloch, *Etymologies and Genealogies: A Literary Anthropology of the French Middle Ages* (Chicago: University of Chicago Press, 1983), 174.

26. Somewhat similarly, Jeffrey Knapp has shown how Spenser's pastoral relapses could, if only negatively and temporarily, serve as incitement to empire. "Error as a Means of Empire in the *Faerie Queene* 1," *ELH* 54, no. 4 (Winter 1987): 801–34, 803. Patricia Parker also identifies this dynamic, in more explicitly generic terms, in *The Faerie Queene*, which "seems to be exploring the implications of this opposition [between lyric and epic] in its very form—narrative in its forward, linear quest and yet composed out of lyric stanzas that, like the enchantresses within it, potentially suspend or retard" (*Literary Fat Ladies*, 66). For Parker, the opposition between forward motion and suspension amounts to a suspension in itself; she identifies in Spenser "a simultaneously aesthetic and moral uneasiness about the seductiveness of lyric 'charm,' even if that charm is an inseparable part of the attraction of his own poetry, its own tantalizingly suspending instrument" (66). Where Parker keeps the ends of this ambivalence open—and I will expand on the implications of her argument at the end of this chapter—I argue that when early modern poetry acts as such a suspended and suspending instrument, it is often functioning conservatively.

27. "To the victors belongs epic, with its linear teleology; to the losers belongs romance, with its random or circular wandering. Put another way, the victors experience history as a coherent, end-directed story told by their own power; the losers experience a contingency that they are powerless to shape to their own ends." David Quint, *Epic and Empire: Politics and Generic Form from Virgil to Milton* (Princeton, NJ: Princeton University Press, 1993), 9.

28. Best and Marcus, "Surface Reading," 16.

29. Marvell, *Upon Appleton House, To My Lord Fairfax*, in *The Poems of Andrew Marvell*, 85–86. Hereafter cited by line number.

30. Edelman, *No Future*, 2.

31. Diane Purkiss, "Thinking of Gender," in *The Cambridge Companion to Andrew Marvell*, ed. Derek Hirst and Steven N. Zwicker (Cambridge: Cambridge University Press, 2011), 69.

32. Other recipes include "To take away Freckles and Scars in the Face"; "To make the Face fresh and Ruddy"; "To make the Face youthful"; "An excellent Beautifyer for the face used by the Venetian Ladies." Woolley, *Accomplishd ladies delight*, 102, 103, 104.

33. John Murrell, *A Delightfull Daily Exercise for Ladies and Gentlewomen* (London, 1621).

34. Woolley, *The queen-like closet*, 14.

35. Richard Halpern, *Shakespeare's Perfume: Sodomy and Sublimity in the Sonnets, Wilde, Freud, and Lacan* (Philadelphia: University of Pennsylvania Press, 2002), 14. Halpern accounts for this seeming unsexiness by gesturing to the discourse of alchemy, the sublimation of corporeal (and feminine-coded) impurities performed by men in closed-off rooms. At the same time, some alchemists saw clear connections between their work and that of women. Thomas Vaughan said of the alchemical refinement of base matter that in fact "*women* are fitter for it than men, for in such things they are more neat and patient, being used to a small *Chimistrie* of Sack-possets, and other finicall *Sugar-sops*." *Magia adamica or the antiquitie of magic* (London, 1650), 118. For a study of analogies of housewifery to alchemy and chemistry as well as women's actual involvement in these practices (including Vaughan's wife), see Jayne Elisabeth Archer, "Women and Chymistry in Early Modern England: The Manuscript Recipe Book (c. 1616) of Sarah Wigges," in *Gender and Scientific Discourse in Early Modern European Culture*, ed. Kathleen P. Long (Burlington, VT: Ashgate, 2010).

36. Wendy Wall counters Halpern's dismissal of culinary preservation as boring with her analysis of "a domestic discourse in which function and pleasure are unusually intertwined." "Distillation: Transformations in and out of the Kitchen," in *Renaissance Food from Rabelais to Shakespeare: Culinary Readings and Culinary Histories*, ed. Joan Fitzpatrick (Burlington, VT: Ashgate, 2010), 102. As Patricia Fumerton discusses with regard to the "void," an elaborate dessert course served in private aristocratic banqueting houses, some confectionery was made to be destroyed—edible plates and cups that could be broken up and consumed along with their contents or sugar sculptures designed to be shattered in food fights—rather than preserved, making the void primarily a feast for the eyes, as well as fodder for aristocratic class identity (*Cultural Aesthetics*, 132–33).

37. Amy L. Tigner, "Preserving Nature in Hannah Woolley's *The Queen-Like Closet; or Rich Cabinet*," in *Ecofeminist Approaches to Early Modernity*, ed. Jennifer Munroe and Rebecca Laroche (New York: Palgrave Macmillan, 2011), 135, 132; Fumerton, *Cultural Aesthetics*, 112, 124; Hall, "Culinary Spaces," 175.

38. Manuscript receipt book of Penelope Jephson (1671), Folger V.a.396, fol. 45r.

39. Korda, *Shakespeare's Domestic Economies*, 72.

40. As Korda puts it, "The social stratification of nunneries, their replication of domestic and architectural aspects of gentry households, together with their often extensive property holdings and commercial dealings, make it difficult to conceive of them as 'green worlds' removed from the marketplace. Rather, the evidence suggests that nuns were sophisticated, hands-on managers of their domestic economies," generating income from both rents and commercial interests, including the sale of goods (*Shakespeare's Domestic Economies*, 165).

41. William Salmon, *The family dictionary, or, Houshold companion wherein are alphabetically laid down exact rules and choice physical receipts for the preservation of health . . . directions for making oils, ointments, salves, . . . chymical preparations, physical-wines, ales and other liquors and descriptions of the virtues of herbs, fruits, flowers . . . and parts of living creatures used in medicinal potions, . . . likewise directions for cookery, . . . also the way of making all sorts of perfumes . . . together with the art of making all sorts of English wines, . . . the mystery of pickling and keeping all sorts of pickles . . .* (London, 1695), n.p.

42. Lena Cowen Orlin, "Three Ways to Be Invisible in the Renaissance: Sex, Reputation, Stitchery," in *Renaissance Culture and the Everyday*, ed. Patricia Fumerton and Simon Hunt (Philadelphia: University of Pennsylvania Press, 1999), 191, 198.

43. Hirst and Zwicker, *Orphan of the Hurricane*, 47.

44. *Oxford English Dictionary*, s.v. "spinster, n." The word was originally (from 1380) appended to the names of women to indicate their occupation, but by 1617 also referred to their status as unmarried.

45. Fumerton, *Cultural Aesthetics*, 132, 124–25.

46. Hirst and Zwicker have seen in the abbess and her outspoken nuns, who use their overactive tongues both to seduce Isabel and to attempt to defend their fortress (*Orphan of the Hurricane*, 256), a possible echo of the problematically outspoken current Lady Fairfax, who was banned from Charles I's trial after heckling the court not once but twice and whose nagging was perhaps responsible for her husband's resignation of his command in the army (27).

47. Hirst and Zwicker connect the legal language of "The Picture of Little T. C." to the girl's genealogical connection to the famous lawyer (*Orphan of the Hurricane*, 51). Dan Wayne designates Coke's dictum as an "alternate subtitle" to his *Penshurst: The Semiotics of Place and the Poetics of History* because of its encapsulation of the ideology

of the domestic (16). Orlin attributes the proverbial status of the phrase to the post-Reformation "glorification of the individual household" and concurrent decline of actual feudal fortresses, suggesting that "the perceived decline of the castle as a functional architectural form released it to the realm of proverb, metaphor, and even of legal pronouncement," namely Coke's. *Private Matters and Public Culture in Post-Reformation England* (Ithaca, NY: Cornell University Press, 1994), 2.

48. Purkiss, "Thinking of Gender," 69.

49. Picciotto notes that here Marvell emphasizes the labor involved in producing and maintaining textiles: "The artisanal effort of dyeing becomes continuous with the laundering of silks by human hands. . . . Each instant of perception is infused with an awareness of the pains spent to produce it" (*Labors of Innocence*, 358–59).

50. Orlin explains that while for upper-class women "needlework" usually meant embroidery, leaving more practical textile work to lower-class women, some authors insisted, often citing exemplary women from Greek and Roman antiquity, that "even gentlewomen should know how to spin and weave," and "'needlework,' writ large, performed as a universal signifier, an occupational topos for women across all class boundaries" ("Three Ways to Be Invisible," 187).

51. Simon, *Light without Heat*, 142, 131.

52. Orlin, "Three Ways to Be Invisible," 191; Dympna Callaghan, "Looking Well to Linens: Women and Cultural Production in *Othello* and Shakespeare's England," in *Marxist Shakespeares*, ed. Jean E. Howard and Scott Cutler Shershow (New York: Routledge, 2001), 55. For an exploration of how needlework, as a kind of labor that complements contemplation, fit into a moral program of secular monasticism for women in early modern France, see Krause, *Idle Pursuits*, 88–90.

53. Hirst and Zwicker, *Orphan of the Hurricane*, 53.

54. Thorstein Veblen, *The Theory of the Leisure Class: An Economic Study of Institutions* (New York: Macmillan, 1912), 58, qtd. in Korda, *Shakespeare's Domestic Economies*, 56.

55. Korda, *Shakespeare's Domestic Economies*, 56–57. Korda assimilates Veblen's views on housewifery to Jean Baudrillard's in *For a Critique of the Political Economy of the Sign*, trans. Charles Levin (St. Louis: Telos, 1981). Smith, *Wealth of Nations*, 351–52.

56. As Kim Hall puts it, recipe books with titles like *The queen-like closet* "preserve the fiction that they are writing for aristocratic audiences, offering their upwardly-mobile women readers a peek into the status competitions and consumption patterns they wished to emulate" ("Culinary Spaces," 171).

57. Leah S. Marcus, *The Politics of Mirth: Jonson, Herrick, Milton, Marvell, and the Defense of Old Holiday Pastimes* (Chicago: University of Chicago Press, 1989), 128; May, "The Author's Life," in *The accomplisht cook*.

58. William Rabisha, *The whole body of cookery dissected* (London, 1661), 14. Nigel Smith, in explanation of the "jellying stream," calls attention to alchemists' interest in the halcyon's proverbial abilities: "The halcyon was believed to calm seas by making them solid with a substance called *halcyonium*, 'spuma maris concreta' (solidified sea foam)." *Poems of Andrew Marvell*, 238. Typical contemporary recipes for jellied fish, like Rabisha's, suggest that Maria's effects on the world had analogs that were readier to hand.

59. Woolley, *The queen-like closet*, 84; Woolley, *Accomplishd ladies delight*, 40, 43; manuscript cookbook of Susanna Packe (1674), Folger V.a.215, 47. Picciotto also sees in this a mundane analog to apocalyptic vitrification, pointing to how James Howell, in one of Marvell's sources for the poem, compares the "Transubstantiations" and "Lique-

factions" of glassmaking to the sea of glass in Revelation 4:6 and 15:2: "If this small Furnace-fire hath vertue to convert such a small lump of dark Dust and Sand into such a specious clear Body as Crystall, surely, that gran Universall-fire, which shall happen at the day of judgment, may by its violent-ardor *vitrifie* and turn to one lump of Crystall, the whole Body of the Earth." *Epistolae Ho-Elianæ. Familiar Letters Domestic and Forren; Divided into sundry Sections, partly Historicall, Politicall, Philosophicall, Upon Emergent Occasions* (London, 1650), 48, qtd. in Picciotto, *Labors of Innocence*, 363. Here, for Picciotto, "the doctrine of transubstantiation itself is reformed": the workaday operations of a glass factory are "continuous with the transfiguration of creation at the end of history" (363). But while "Howell's thoughts are raised 'to a higher speculation,'" I argue that Marvell's thoughts experience the opposite movement, bringing the apocalypse down to earth.

60. Astell, *Essay in Defence of the Female Sex*, 76–77.

61. *Oxford English Dictionary*, s.v. "halcyon, n."

62. Stocker, *Apocalyptic Marvell*, 60–63. See also John Rogers on Maria's role in transmuting and crystallizing the world's "rude heap" in *The Matter of Revolution: Science, Poetry, and Politics in the Age of Milton* (Ithaca, NY: Cornell University Press, 1996), 101.

63. Colie, *"My Ecchoing Song,"* 269.

64. Hirst and Zwicker, *Orphan of the Hurricane*, 49.

65. Partridge, *Treasurie of commodious conceits*, n.p.

66. Hirst and Zwicker, *Orphan of the Hurricane*, 50; Derek Hirst and Steven N. Zwicker, "Andrew Marvell and the Toils of the Patriarchy: Fatherhood, Longing, and the Body Politic," *ELH* 66.3 (Fall 1999): 634.

67. Edelman, *No Future*, 2–3.

68. Hirst and Zwicker, *Orphan of the Hurricane*, 72.

69. Marcel Proust, *In Search of Lost Time*, vol. 3, *Sodom and Gomorrah*, trans. C. K. Scott Moncrieff and Terence Kilmartin, rev. D. J. Enright (New York: Modern Library, 2003), 3.

70. Derek Hirst and Steven N. Zwicker, "High Summer at Nun Appleton, 1651: Andrew Marvell and Lord Fairfax's Occasions," *Historical Journal* 36, no. 2 (June 1993): 257.

71. Hirst and Zwicker, "High Summer at Nun Appleton," 257.

72. Barry McCrea, *In the Company of Strangers: Family and Narrative in Dickens, Conan Doyle, Joyce, and Proust* (New York: Columbia University Press, 2011), 9–10.

73. McCrea, *In the Company of Strangers*, 10. Northrop Frye defines "the drama of the green world" in Shakesparean romantic comedy as follows: "The action of the comedy begins in a world represented as a normal world, moves into the green world, goes into a metamorphosis there in which the comic resolution is achieved, and returns to the normal world. . . . The green world has analogies, not only to the fertile world of ritual, but to the dream world that we create out of our own desires." "Archetypal Criticism: Theory of Myths," in *Anatomy of Criticism: Four Essays* (Princeton, NJ: Princeton University Press, 1957), 182–83.

74. Parker, *Literary Fat Ladies*, 124–25.

75. William Shakespeare, *A Midsummer Night's Dream*, in *The Riverside Shakespeare*, ed. G. Blakemore Evans (Boston: Houghton Mifflin, 1974), 5.1.18–27.

76. Vitaliy Eyber, *Andrew Marvell's "Upon Appleton House": An Analytic Commentary* (Madison, NJ: Fairleigh Dickinson University Press, 2010), 237.

77. Hirst and Zwicker, "Toils of the Patriarchy," 635.

78. Thomas Barker, *The Country-mans Recreation, or The Art of Planting, Graffing, and Gardening, in Three Books* (London, 1654), 29.

79. William Shakespeare, *The Winter's Tale,* in *The Riverside Shakespeare,* 4.4.92–97.
80. *Oxford English Dictionary,* s.v. "graft, n."
81. Parker, *Literary Fat Ladies,* 125.

# Chapter Five

1. Thomas Elyot, *The boke named the governour* (London, 1537), book 1, chapter 10. Wilkinson finds Elyot's assessment comically inaccurate: "Mere lip-service. How could anyone who really knew the poem characterise it that way?" (*The "Georgics" of Virgil,* 295). David Scott Wilson-Okamura argues that this was nonetheless the primary marker of the poem in the Renaissance: "Instead of labor, what defined the *Georgics* was variety" (*Virgil in the Renaissance,* 78). Fowler asserts that applying the georgic marker to country house poems like *Upon Appleton House* "enables us to appreciate the generic coherence" of that poem ("The Beginnings of English Georgic," 122–23). Colie has catalogued Marvell's allusions to *Georgics* 2 (*"My Ecchoing Song,"* 181).

2. John Milton, *Paradise Lost,* in *The Riverside Milton,* 4.983. All references to Milton's poems are from this edition unless otherwise noted and will be hereafter cited parenthetically by line number.

3. Christopher Ricks, *Milton's Grand Style* (Oxford: Oxford University Press, 1978), 150.

4. In surveying the semantic range of "moderation" and its synonyms, Scodel stresses that one important meaning of "the mean" for Milton, as well as for some contemporaries and for ancient commentators, was the mixing, or tempering, of extremes (*Excess and the Mean,* 7, 80, 94, 101, 271). Joanna Picciotto highlights how, far from "a merely negative virtue," for Milton "temperance is the active art of tempering and composing," a definition with surprising implications: "Innocent temperance actually *requires* promiscuity" (*Labors of Innocence,* 431). This is a broader articulation of Diane Kelsey McColley's reassurance that we need not be alarmed by the "wanton growth" of unfallen Eden in *Paradise Lost,* because "for Milton choosing and ordering amid fertile efflorescence is just what temperance is." *Milton's Eve* (Urbana: University of Illinois Press, 1983), 111.

5. Milton, *Areopagitica,* in *The Riverside Milton,* 1010. All references to Milton's prose are from this edition and will hereafter be cited parenthetically by page number.

6. This textual temperance is central to Dayton Haskin's account in *Milton's Burden of Interpretation* (Philadelphia: University of Pennsylvania Press, 1994), particularly in his reading of *Paradise Regain'd,* discussed below.

7. Scodel, *Excess and the Mean,* 84. See also Schoenberger, *Cultivating Peace,* for an analysis of the role of Virgilian uncertainty in English georgics of the long eighteenth century.

8. Kevis Goodman, "'Wasted Labor'? Milton's Eve, the Poet's Work, and the Challenge of Sympathy," *ELH* 64 (1997): 420. Geoffrey Hartman and Patricia Parker have looked to this passage as a site of abstract suspension disconnected from the material and immediate uncertainty of agricultural labor. For Hartman, the plowman's doubts are overridden by God, "supreme arbiter," who "overbalances the balance" with his golden scales in the following lines in a show of confidence in his creation's longevity; the plowman, it seems, should be worrying about bigger things. "Milton's Counterplot," *ELH* 25, no. 1 (Mar. 1958): 12. Parker looks at the passage formally, seeing "a link between the dilation of Satan," who "collecting all his might dilated stood" (4.986), "and the suspended

'doubt' of one of the poem's famous dilated, or dilatory, epic similes." "Dilation and Delay: Renaissance Matrices," *Poetics Today* 5, no. 3 (1984): 526.

9. Virgil, *Georgics*, 1.45–46.

10. Goodman, "'Wasted Labor?,'" 440.

11. John Evelyn, *Acetaria: A discourse of sallets* (London, 1699), 113.

12. Analyses of the georgic elements of *Paradise Lost* can be found in, among others, Barbara Lewalski, *"Paradise Lost" and the Rhetoric of Literary Forms* (Princeton, NJ: Princeton University Press, 1985); Low, *Georgic Revolution*; Goodman, "'Wasted Labor'?"; Scodel, *Excess and the Mean*; Seth Lobis, "Milton's Tended Garden and the Georgic Fall," *Milton Studies* 55 (2014): 89–111; Andrew Wadoski, "Milton's Spenser: Eden and the Work of Poetry," *SEL* 55, no. 1 (Winter 2015): 174–96. Those who have discussed Eve's domesticity include Barbara K. Lewalski in "Milton on Women—Yet Once More," *Milton Studies* 6 (1975): 3–20, McColley in *Milton's Eve*, and Knoppers in *Politicizing Domesticity*. As I will explain in the next sections, my approach differs from these georgic and domestic readings in focusing on the provisional and iterative, rather than either protobourgeois or politically progressive, nature of both georgic labor and domestic economy in the poem.

13. John D. Schaeffer, "Metonymies We Read By: Rhetoric, Truth and the Eucharist in Milton's *Areopagitica*," *Milton Quarterly* 34, no. 3 (2000): 84.

14. Stanley Fish, *How Milton Works* (Cambridge, MA: Harvard University Press, 2001), 195.

15. Ralph Knevet, *Rhodon and Iris* (London, 1631), qtd. in Wall, "Distillation," 90. James Grantham Turner, pursuant to his claim that the real concerns of *Areopagitica* lie in pornography—in literally promiscuous books rather than figuratively promiscuous reading—sees the arrangement of books-cum-vials as a literary sperm bank. "Libertinism and Toleration: Milton, Bruno and Aretino," in *Milton and Toleration*, ed. Sharon Achinstein and Elizabeth Sauer (Oxford: Oxford University Press, 2007). In my view, the contents of the vials are to be understood more in terms of their suspension than of any discrete future purpose.

16. Tusser, *Fiue hundreth points*, 77.

17. You can find out how "To make Horse-dung Water" in Cookery and pharmaceutical recipes of the Malet family (1700–40), Folger W.a.303, 62–63. A recipe attributed to Elizabeth Grey, Countess of Kent, starts with a sealed glass still filled with honeysuckle berries: "Set it in hot horse-dung eight dayes, distil it in Balm, then when you have drawn the water forth, pour the water into the stuffe again, stop it close, and put it in the dung four and twenty houres" before performing a second distillation. *A choice manual of rare and select secrets in physick and chyrurgery collected and practised by the Right Honorable, the Countesse of Kent, late deceased; as also most exquisite ways of preserving, conserving, candying, &c.* (London, 1653), 160. For an account of the dunghill or compost heap "as a model for creative processes of assemblage," see Frances Dolan, *Digging the Past: How and Why to Imagine Seventeenth-Century Agriculture* (Philadelphia: University of Pennsylvania Press, 2020), 37.

18. Theodor Zwinger, *Theatrum vitae humanae* (Basel, 1586), sig. **4v, **4r, ***6v, trans. and qtd. in Blair, *Too Much to Know*, 187, 209.

19. Blair, *Too Much to Know*, 61.

20. The *Oxford English Dictionary* dates this sense of "reproduction" to the early eighteenth century; "the natural replacement or repair of a lost or damaged part" of an orga-

nism would have in Milton's time been referred to as "the regeneration of the flesh." *S.v.* "reproduction, n.," "regeneration, n."

21. Reading Adam and Eve's unfallen existence as iterative could be seen as a domestication of Regina Schwartz's metaphysical reading in *Remembering and Repeating: Biblical Creation in Paradise Lost* (Chicago: University of Chicago Press, 1988), which argues that in *Paradise Lost*, "the original act is an iteration" (1).

22. Building on Thomas Greene's reading of the poem's emphasis on interiority as looking forward to the bourgeois novel, Scodel sees the couple's "joyful form of self-regulation" as part of Milton's georgification of epic, his shift of the genre's focus from heroic military deeds to the virtuous pleasures (and dangers) of daily conjugal life (*Excess and the Mean*, 256, 283).

23. Picciotto, *Labors of Innocence*, 472. See also Knoppers, *Politicizing Domesticity*, for an argument that "Milton appropriates domesticity in *Paradise Lost* boldly to figure not only domestic but civic virtues essential for political participation and liberty in a Commonwealth, looking back nostalgically, and perhaps defiantly, to the now-lost English Republic" (142–43). While I do not see boldness or defiance in Milton's treatment of Eve's domestic labor, I appreciate Knoppers's subtle analysis of how the mutual regard in Adam and Eve's marriage is undercut by the fact that Adam fails to appreciate her domestic labors (152–53) and her acknowledgment that the path from domestic to civic virtue Milton's picture of domesticity proposes is hardly clear.

24. Picciotto sees seventeenth-century experimentalists and reformers as scrambling the means and ends of restoring Eden, so that, for example, the delving of the Diggers was "not just a means of paradisal recovery": it was "paradise itself." At the same time, the linear orientation of this project was undeniable, "using innovations in applied knowledge to 'quietly improve the Waste and Common Land' in the Baconian confidence that it would soon be 'increased with all sorts of Commodities.'" *Labors of Innocence*, 57–58.

25. Lewalski, "Milton on Women," 7; Lewalski, *"Paradise Lost" and the Rhetoric of Literary Forms*, 196.

26. Maureen Quilligan, "Freedom, Service, and the Trade in Slaves: The Problem of Labor in *Paradise Lost*," in *Subject and Object in Renaissance Culture*, ed. Margreta de Grazia, Maureen Quilligan, and Peter Stallybrass (Cambridge: Cambridge University Press, 1996), 223.

27. Quilligan, "Freedom, Service, and the Trade in Slaves," 223.

28. Picciotto, *Labors of Innocence*, 467–68.

29. Picciotto, *Labors of Innocence*, 405.

30. John Berger, *Pig Earth* (New York: Pantheon, 1979), xix. Adam and Eve's awareness that they will one day have children might suggest a certain kind of linear progress. But they look forward to the prospect of children as a necessary measure to keep up with their overwhelming workload, not to make the garden more productive. The overgrown trees "require / More hands then ours to lop thir wanton growth" (4.629–30); "till more hands / Aid us, the work under our labour grows, / Luxurious by restraint" (9.207–9). The upshot of sexual reproduction seems to be the more comfortable and less stressful reproduction of themselves through labor that they are already performing on a daily basis.

31. In her tracing of the close conceptual ties between ancient Greek tragedy and botany, Ann Michelini explains how Theophrastus and Aristotle called plants "hubristic" that put their surplus resources to producing their own excessive leaves and branches

rather than reproducing by bearing fruit, just as hubristic characters self-aggrandize rather than contributing to society. "Hybris and Plants," *Harvard Studies in Classical Philology* 82 (1978): 38–39. While Adam and Eve's decoration of the elm with the vine creates order rather than excess, it does suggest a model for plant life that does not have fruit as its ultimate goal, where in fact fruits—"adopted Clusters," brought by the vine as her "dowr"—preexist the marriage.

32. Karl Marx, *Capital*, vol. 1, trans. Ben Fowkes (New York: Penguin, 1976), 1044 (emphasis in original). This analogy leaves out the women and other members of Milton's household who provided the mulberry leaves and harvested the silk. Marshall Grossman, reading Marx and Milton together, describes Milton's understanding of his own intellectual and poetic labor—labor characterized by "ease and leasure," but for the direct use of God and the church—as "a theory of surplus value to justify his poetic work as a form of productive labor, albeit labor expropriated to 'good' social use, by a peculiarly divine corporate manager"; "both natural and socially determined labor, at once the 'activation of nature' and the expropriation of capital." "The Fruits of One's Labor in Miltonic Practice and Marxian Theory," *ELH* 59, no. 1 (Spring 1992): 81, 86.

33. Evelyn, *Acetaria*, 113.

34. Evelyn, *Acetaria*, 185, 182. For an analysis of Markham's doubly domestic agenda of "patrolling English practices and insulating the home from the market," with a rhetorical conjunction of the homegrown and the English-made, see Wall, *Staging Domesticity*, 40.

35. This is not to suggest that the implications of Milton's culinary world picture are necessarily less unsavory than those of Evelyn's: the celebration of Eve's omnivorous shopping list could resonate with contemporary endorsements of imperialism, an ideological fantasy of frictionless world trade that occludes the reality of colonial violence and slavery. As Kim Hall has discussed, the consumption of foreign spices like sugar was by the later seventeenth century, when it was increasingly cultivated by enslaved laborers in Barbados, becoming a part of English identity ("Culinary Spaces"). Martin Evans connects Adam and Eve to indigenous people, with Satan and Raphael both bearing traits of colonizers, in *Milton's Imperial Epic: "Paradise Lost" and the Discourse of Colonialism* (Ithaca, NY: Cornell University Press, 1996).

36. Thomas Kranidas, "Adam and Eve in the Garden: A Study of *Paradise Lost*, Book V," *Studies in English Literature, 1500–1900* 4, no. 1 (Winter 1964): 77.

37. McColley, *Milton's Eve*, 110. As far as empowering portraits of Eve as an accomplished cook and thus autonomous agent go, Ann Gulden's takes the cake: "Eve is not merely a passive recipient of the crumbs from Adam's table; she has made the cake, and Adam is not too sure of her ingredients." "Milton's Eve and Wisdom: The 'Dinner-Party' Scene in *Paradise Lost*," *Milton Quarterly* 32, no. 4 (Dec. 1998): 141.

38. Ricks, *Milton's Grand Style*, 143, 52.

39. Evelyn, *Acetaria*, 93.

40. For the implications of Eve's "choice" in this passage for the relationship between freedom and choice in *Paradise Lost*, see Joshua Scodel, "Edenic Freedoms," *Milton Studies* 56 (2015): 161–62.

41. Evelyn, *Acetaria*, 93, 190. My account of Eve's housekeeping differs from those of scholars like Amy Tigner, whose goal in analyzing this scene is "to elucidate how food preparation and consumption in Milton's epic participates in the gendered circumstances of eating in the period" (241), or Kat Lecky, who seeks to correct the association of Eve with domestic labor by connecting her botanical work to that done by male herbalists and experimentalists. My aim is not to show how Milton is responding directly

to culinary or experimentalist cultures, as these scholars have, but rather to show how those cultures shape his poetics on a metabolic level. Tigner, "Eating with Eve," *Milton Quarterly* 44, no. 4 (Dec. 2010): 239–53; Lecky, "Milton's Experienced Eve," *Philological Quarterly* 96, no. 4 (2017): 453–74.

42. John French, *The art of distillation, or, A treatise of the choicest spagiricall preparations performed by way of distillation* (London, 1653), 32.

43. Low, *Georgic Revolution*, 321.

44. Picciotto reads this tension as a clear instance of Milton's experimentalist ethos: "The systematically ambiguous identity of Adam, suspended here between his individual and collective instantiations, prefigures the very dialectic between the intellectual laborer's two bodies that propelled experimental progress," so that "the personal modesty that expresses itself in an individual contentment with 'this happie state' is a necessary condition" of human intellectual progress (*Labors of Innocence*, 468, 467). This necessary condition, however, is not sufficient; Raphael's repeated qualifications—"may," "may," "perhaps" (493, 494, 496)—emphasize the contingency of any promise of progress.

45. This was first observed by William Empson: "Adam and Eve would not have fallen unless God had sent Raphael to talk to them, supposedly to strengthen their resistance to temptation"; Raphael and the Satanic dream are "saying the same thing (that God expects them to manage to get to heaven and that what they eat has something to do with it)." *Milton's God* (New York: New Directions, 1962), 19.

46. Quilligan, "Freedom, Service, and the Trade in Slaves," 225.

47. For examples of closets and cabinets as storage sites for goods and female workspaces as well as "places of high status and male privilege" (296), see Orlin, *Locating Privacy in Tudor London* (Oxford: Oxford University Press, 2007), 296–326.

48. Lewalski, "Milton on Women," 6, 7. In "The Genesis of Gendered Subjectivity in the Divorce Tracts and in *Paradise Lost*," in *Re-Membering Milton: Essays on the Texts and Traditions*, ed. Mary Nyquist and Margaret W. Ferguson, 99–127, (New York: Methuen, 1987), Mary Nyquist has taken issue with the "apologetic tendency" she sees in arguments like Lewalski's: however much readers looking for feminism or formal balance might see Adam and Eve's roles as symmetrical, they are in fact "ordered hierarchically and ideologically" (99–100)—much like those of the husband and wife in contemporary domestic manuals. I agree with this critique of liberal feminist readings that find Eve's early experiences of privacy and autonomy to be "equivalent to a potentially empowering freedom from patriarchal rule" (120), but it overlooks the imaginative possibilities that domestic space offered not only to Eve but also to Milton.

49. Lobis points out that, in anticipatory appreciation of what Eve has accomplished during their separation, Adam "sets out to glorify her labor and does so by undertaking traditional woman's work—weaving," and with his thoughtful flower garland seems to earn the epithet of "domestick *Adam*" afforded him during the separation colloquy, where he speaks with "care" ("Milton's Tended Garden," 102). But Adam's poor sense of timing in adopting a domestic role—Lobis notes "the sad, even awkward, effect that the poem has passed Adam by; he thinks he is still in the familiar georgic mode of book 4" (104)—disqualifies him from ever inhabiting it. As Eve's awareness of the difference between fruits that are better fresh and that which "firmness gains / To nourish" over time (5.324–25) suggests, timing can be everything in housekeeping.

50. After the fall, Adam does exclaim a sudden instinct to preserve, but that instinct is for monumental rather than provisional preservation: "So many grateful Altars I would reare / Of grassie Terfe, and pile up every Stone / Of lustre from the brook, in memo-

rie, / Or monument to Ages" (11.323–26). He desires to set Eden apart as a museum rather than seeking to reinstate daily acts of preservation in the fabric of daily life. In that department, Gulden points out, he is severely lacking: "His ideas on storage are incorrect" ("Milton's Eve and Wisdom," 138).

51. C. S. Lewis, *A Preface to "Paradise Lost"* (London: Oxford University Press, 1961), 129. In documenting Milton's interest in alchemical discourse and its influence on him, Lyndy Abraham reads the concessive "or holds it possible to turn" as an acknowledgment of the gap between divine perfection and human achievement: "This does not mean that Milton is questioning the validity of alchemy, only the possibility of the success of earthly alchemy. . . . The sooty fire of the empiric alchemist is a post-lapsarian fire of 'art,' while Raphael performs his transmutations 'naturally' with 'real . . . concoctive heat.'" "Milton's *Paradise Lost* and 'The Sounding Alchymie,'" *Renaissance Studies* 12, no. 2 (June 1998): 270. But Milton's "or," which gives equal weight to actuality and potential, blurs any bright line between pre- and postlapsarian possibility.

52. Leah Marcus catalogs these and other examples of female transmission and identification through and by Milton in "Milton among Women," *Milton Studies* 51 (2010): 45–62. It is unclear if Milton's daughters did more than read to him (Lewalski is skeptical of their secretarial qualifications), though Stephen Dobranski cites the diverse cast of characters involved in drafting *Paradise Lost*—friends, students, elderly acquaintances, as well as his daughters—as an example of "Milton's collaborative authorship." *Milton, Authorship, and the Book Trade* (Cambridge: Cambridge University Press, 2009), 33. See also Lewalski, *Life of John Milton*, 408–9. Knoppers recounts how Milton's bequest of his possessions to his wife Elizabeth was contingent on her "providing mee such Dishes as I think fitt" (*Politicizing Domesticity*, 142); Lewalski notes that Elizabeth "claimed" to have served as her husband's occasional amanuensis but clearly "could not really meet his scholarly needs" (*Life of John Milton*, 672n63, 412).

53. Picciotto opens her *Labors of Innocence* by identifying the prelapsarian Adam as "the innocent observer," a figure used "to justify experimental science, an emergent public sphere, and the concept of intellectual labor itself," while Eve is on her own "a zealous but incompetent natural philosopher" (1, 475). Only when joined with Adam can Eve participate in the "productive sacrament" of cultivating knowledge (472, 8). For differing accounts of Milton's interest in Eve as an authority figure, see Katherine Eggert, *Showing like a Queen: Female Authority and Literary Experiment in Spenser, Shakespeare, and Milton* (Philadelphia: University of Pennsylvania Press, 2000); Marcus, "Milton among Women"; Gulden, "Milton's Eve and Wisdom"; and Lecky, "Milton's Experienced Eve."

54. Flannagan, introduction to *Paradise Regain'd*, in *The Riverside Milton*, 711.

55. Stanley Fish, "The Temptation to Action in Milton's Poetry," *ELH* 48, no. 3 (Autumn 1981): 516.

56. Louis Martz was the first to make the case for *Paradise Regain'd* as a georgic in "Paradise Regained: The Meditative Combat," *ELH* 27, no. 3 (Sept. 1960): 224–28. Low argues that if the poem is an imitation of the book of Job (which Milton himself had hinted at in *The Reason of Church Government*), this reinforces its status as georgic: Job's story "begins and ends with descriptions of his georgic possessions, it subjects him to georgic tests of storm, disease, and crop failure, and it reduces him to sitting on a dunghill" (*Georgic Revolution*, 324).

57. Arendt, *The Human Condition*, 186.

58. "When I Consider" (sonnet XIX), in *The Riverside Milton*, 256.

59. Fish, *How Milton Works*, 329.

60. Haskin, *Milton's Burden*, 130.

61. John Milton, *The Christian Doctrine*, trans. Charles R. Sumner, in *The Works of John Milton*, ed. James Holly Hanford and Waldo Hilary Dunn (New York: Columbia University Press, 1931–38), 14:8–9, qtd. in Haskin, *Milton's Burden*, 130. For Thomas Harrison's filing system of hanging scraps of text on hooks in a cabinet he called the *Arca studiorum*, see Noel Malcolm, "Thomas Harrison and His 'Ark of Studies': An Episode in the History of the Organisation of Knowledge," *Seventeenth Century* 19 (2004): 196. Some of this gathering might be done by secretaries or other helpers, but as a letter attributed to Francis Bacon instructs Fulke Greville, too much delegating would be counterproductive, and the scholar himself must be the one to synthesize: "I would have you gather the chiefest things, and out of the chiefest Books yourself. . . . For [your collectors] should like labourers bring Stone, Timber, Mortar and other Necessaries to your Building: But you should put them together, & be the Master-workman yourself" (qtd. in Blair, "Early Modern Attitudes," 278).

62. Haskin, *Milton's Burden*, 133.

63. Anthony Low, "Milton, *Paradise Regained*, and Georgic," *PMLA* 98.2 (1983): 168.

64. Denise Gigante, *Taste: A Literary History* (New Haven, CT: Yale University Press, 2005), 39.

65. Mary Carruthers shows how *ruminatio* was a figure for both reading ("the memory is a stomach, the stored texts are the sweet-smelling cud originally drawn from the gardens of books") and writing: Bede tells of the cowherd Caedmon composing poetry "by recollecting it within himself ('rememorandum rerum') and ruminating like a clean animal ('quasi mundum animal ruminendo')." Like Milton, Caedmon was said to thus ruminate at night (though, unlike Milton, accompanied by actual ruminants). *The Book of Memory: A Study of Memory in Medieval Culture* (Cambridge: Cambridge University Press, 1990), 206.

66. The subtitle of Schoenfeldt's *Bodies and Selves in Early Modern England: Physiology and Inwardness in Spenser, Shakespeare, Herbert, and Milton* connects physical and spiritual "inwardness."

67. For an account of the heterodox decentering of the crucifixion in Milton's theology, see Rogers, "Milton's Circumcision," in *Milton and the Grounds of Contention*, ed. Mark R. Kelley, Michael Lieb, and John T. Shawcross (Pittsburgh: Duquesne University Press, 2003).

68. Lobis, "Milton's Tended Garden," 98.

## Conclusion

1. Collier's life as an unmarried woman did not perfectly correspond to that of the overwhelmed wife and mother who narrates her poem. Moira Ferguson suggests in her introduction to Duck and Collier's poems that "so especially downtrodden an existence appears to exasperate Collier and possibly explains her choice in remaining single." *"The Thresher's Labour," Stephen Duck, and "The Woman's Labour," Mary Collier*, introduction by Moira Ferguson (Los Angeles: Clark Memorial Library, 1985), ix. Both poems from this volume will hereafter be cited parenthetically by line numbers.

2. Marvell, *Upon Appleton House*, lines 173–74; Tusser, *Fiue hundreth points*, 66.

3. Beauvoir, *The Second Sex*, 481.

4. Anne Boyer, "What Is 'Not Writing'?," *Garments against Women* (Boise: Ahsahta, 2015), 44.

5. Adrienne Rich, "When We Dead Awaken: Writing as Re-Vision," *College English* 34, no. 1 (Oct. 1972): 24.

6. Arendt, *The Human Condition*, 7, 96.

7. Alice Oswald, *Memorial: An Excavation of the "Iliad"* (London: Faber and Faber, 2011); Oswald, *Memorial: A Version of Homer's "Iliad,"* afterword by Eavan Boland (New York: Norton, 2012). The US edition will hereafter be cited parenthetically by page number.

8. William Logan, "Plains of Blood," review of *Memorial*, by Alice Oswald, *New York Times*, Dec. 21, 2012. https://www.nytimes.com/2012/12/23/books/review/memorial -alice-oswalds-version-of-the-iliad.html.

9. Jason Guriel, "Rosy-Fingered Yawn," *PN Review* 207 (Sept./Oct. 2012), https:// www.pnreview.co.uk/cgi-bin/scribe?item_id=8633; Logan, "Plains of Blood."

10. Paisley Rekdal, "Memorial Time: Poetry, Elegy, and the War Memorial," *Kenyon Review* 40, no. 6 (Nov./Dec. 2018): 110. ("That is the point," Rekdal clarifies.)

11. Ferguson summarizes "The Woman's Labour" as "a bleak picture of the eighteenth-century double shift" (*"The Thresher's Labour,"* ix).

12. As J. Paul Hunter puts it, "Couplets formally involve a careful pairing of oppositions or balances but no formal resolution. There is a notable absence of Hegelian forms of dialectic, and the opposing units are kept in formal tension, rather than being resolved. Rather than privileging one half or the other of the conflict or negotiating a successful compromise, the closed couplet tends to privilege the balancing itself—the preservation and acceptance of difference rather than a working out of modification or compromise." "Form as Meaning: Pope and the Ideology of the Couplet," *Eighteenth Century* 37, no. 3 (Fall 1996): 266.

13. Oswald, *Memorial*, ix. For a discussion of women's roles in Greek lament, as represented in ancient literature including the *Iliad* and in surviving Greek song cultures today, see Gregory Nagy, "Ancient Greek Elegy," in *The Oxford Handbook of the Elegy*, ed. Karen Weisman (Oxford: Oxford University Press, 2010), 21.

14. "Oswald lays the lyric world beside violent death, like someone putting summer flowers in a coffin: a reminder of all that's been lost. . . . The soldiers die in one paragraph, but the world they lose occurs in two." Boland, "Afterword," in Oswald, *Memorial*, 86–87.

15. Bruce Holsinger (@bruceholsinger), "This could not have been written without my wife's anonymity," Twitter, March 25, 2017, 7:17 a.m., https://twitter.com/ bruceholsinger/status/845640885152944128?s=20.

16. Holsinger, "Oh my god maybe for the win," Twitter, March 25, 2017, 7:27 a.m., https://twitter.com/bruceholsinger/status/845643268046106625?s=20.

17. Holsinger, "This one is AMAZING. 'My wife' did his paleography," Twitter, March 26, 2017, 6:12 a.m., https://twitter.com/bruceholsinger/status/845986748274561024?s=20.

18. Laura Ansley (@lmansley), "She is not a co-author on the book," Twitter, March 26, 2017, 2:15 a.m., https://twitter.com/lmansley/status/845927121738514432?s=20.

19. Holsinger, "A peek at an archive of women's academic labor," Twitter, March 25, 2017, 7:05 a.m., https://twitter.com/bruceholsinger/status/845637778251677697?s=20.

20. Holsinger, "typing, retyping, and typing yet again the manuscript," Twitter, March 27, 2017, 7:12 a.m., https://twitter.com/bruceholsinger/status/846364282203897856?s=20.

21. Federici, "Wages against Housework," 15.

22. See, for example, the cluster of essays on "The Changing Profession" in *PMLA* 127, no. 4 (October 2012), a special issue on work, including Margaret Ferguson, "The Let-

ter of Recommendation as Strange Work," and Frieda Ekotto, "Against Representation: Countless Hours for a Professor"; Sarah Brouillette, *Literature and the Creative Economy* (Stanford, CA: Stanford University Press, 2014); and Brouillette, "Academic Labor, the Aesthetics of Management, and the Promise of Autonomous Work," *Nonsite* 9 (May 2013), https://nonsite.org/article/academic-labor-the-aesthetics-of-management-and -the-promise-of-autonomous-work.

23. "So when one asks whether we would like to co-author a paper, undertaking all the translation for it because he does not '*do* languages,' we try to shake it off. He cannot really imagine that we spent years of our adult lives mastering foreign words and grammar just so we could do the tedious housework of gathering sources while he takes credit for the conceptual heavy lifting. (Even his verb choice—'*do*'—makes it sound like this was a hobby, like tourism, as if we just happened to get off on playing with textbooks.) When the co-organizer of an exhibition calls to ask, on a few hours notice, whether he can borrow sheets for the futon on which he volunteered weeks ago to put up a visiting artist—it was just coincidence that he called us and not Patrick or Andrew, right? We want to believe this. And yet, we look at the female faculty who seem to participate in every committee and conference and supervise over half the dissertations in their departments, and we feel afraid." Moira Weigel and Mal Ahern, "Further Materials toward a Theory of the Man Child," *The New Inquiry*, July 9, 2013, https://thenewinquiry.com/ further-materials-toward-a-theory-of-the-man-child/.

24. Beauvoir, *The Second Sex*, 481.

# BIBLIOGRAPHY

Abraham, Lyndy. "Milton's *Paradise Lost* and 'The Sounding Alchymie.'" *Renaissance Studies* 12, no. 2 (June 1998): 261–76.

Albala, Ken. *Eating Right in the Renaissance*. Berkeley: University of California Press, 2002.

Anderson, Judith H. *Words That Matter: Linguistic Perception in Renaissance English*. Stanford, CA: Stanford University Press, 1996.

Archer, Jayne Elisabeth. "Women and Chymistry in Early Modern England: The Manuscript Recipe Book (c. 1616) of Sarah Wigges." In *Gender and Scientific Discourse in Early Modern European Culture*, edited by Kathleen P. Long, 191–216. Burlington, VT: Ashgate, 2010.

Arendt, Hannah. "The Crisis in Culture: Its Social and Its Political Significance." In *Between Past and Future*, 194–222. New York: Penguin, 1968.

———. *The Human Condition*. Chicago: University of Chicago Press, 1958.

———. *The Life of the Mind*. New York: Harcourt, 1978.

Aristotle. *The Nicomachean Ethics*. Translated by Terence Irwin. Indianapolis: Hackett, 1985.

Ascham, Roger. *The Scholemaster*. Edited by Edward Arber. London: A. Constable, 1897.

Astell, Mary. *An Essay in Defence of the Female Sex, in a Letter to a Lady, written by a Lady*. London, 1721.

Bacon, Francis. *The Major Works*. Edited by Brian Vickers. Oxford: Oxford University Press, 1996.

Baier, Annette. "What Emotions Are About." *Philosophical Perspectives* 4 (1990): 1–29.

Bakewell, Sarah. *How to Live: or, A Life of Montaigne in One Question and Twenty Attempts at an Answer*. London: Chatto and Windus, 2010.

Barkan, Leonard. *Unearthing the Past: Archaeology and Aesthetics in the Making of Renaissance Culture*. New Haven, CT: Yale University Press, 1999.

Barker, Thomas. *The Country-mans Recreation, or The Art of Planting, Graffing, and Gardening, in Three Books*. London, 1654.

Baudrillard, Jean. *For a Critique of the Political Economy of the Sign*. Translated by Charles Levin. St. Louis: Telos, 1981.

Beauvoir, Simone de. *The Second Sex*. Translated by Constance Borde and Sheila Malovany-Chevallier. New York: Vintage Books, 2011.

Berger, Harry, Jr.. *The Allegorical Temper: Vision and Reality in Book II of Spenser's "Faerie Queene."* New Haven, CT: Yale University Press, 1957.

Berger, John. *Pig Earth.* New York: Pantheon, 1979.

Berriot-Salvadore, Evelyne. *Les femmes dans la société française de la Renaissance.* Geneva: Droz, 1990.

Best, Stephen, and Sharon Marcus. "Surface Reading: An Introduction." *Representations* 108, no. 1 (Fall 2009): 1–21.

Bierlaire, Franz. *La Familia d'Erasme: Contribution à l'histoire de l'humanisme.* Paris: J. Vrin, 1968.

Blair, Ann. "Early Modern Attitudes toward the Delegation of Copying and Note-Taking." In *Forgetting Machines: Knowledge Management Evolution in Early Modern Europe*, edited by Alberto Cevolini, 265–85. Leiden: Brill, 2016.

———. *Too Much to Know: Managing Scholarly Information before the Information Age.* New Haven, CT: Yale University Press, 2011.

Bloch, R. Howard. *Etymologies and Genealogies: A Literary Anthropology of the French Middle Ages.* Chicago: University of Chicago Press, 1983.

Bloom, Ester. "Reclaiming 'Homemaker.'" *Slate.* April 29, 2014. https://slate.com/human -interest/2014/04/stay-at-home-mom-needs-to-go-lets-bring-back-homemaker .html.

Botero, Giovanni. *Raison et gouvernement en dix livres.* Translated by Gabriel Chappuys. Paris, 1599.

———. *The Reason of State.* Translated by P. J. and D. P. Waley. New Haven, CT: Yale University Press, 1956.

Boyer, Anne. *Garments against Women.* Boise: Ahsahta, 2015.

Bradley, Richard. *The Country Housewife and Lady's Director, in the management of a house, and the delights and profits of a farm.* London, 1732.

Brouillette, Sarah. "Academic Labor, the Aesthetics of Management, and the Promise of Autonomous Work." *Nonsite* 9 (May 2013). https://nonsite.org/article/academic -labor-the-aesthetics-of-management-and-the-promise-of-autonomous-work.

———. *Literature and the Creative Economy.* Stanford, CA: Stanford University Press, 2014.

Burckhardt, Jacob. *The Civilization of the Renaissance in Italy.* Translated by S. G. C. Middlemore. New York: Macmillan, 1914.

Burton, Robert. *The Anatomy of Melancholy: What It Is, with All the Kinds, Causes, Symptoms, Prognostics, and Several Cures of It.* London: Chatto and Windus, 1883.

Calhoun, Alison. "Redefining Nobility in the French Renaissance: The Case of Montaigne's *Journal de Voyage.*" *MLN* 123, no. 4 (Sept. 2008): 836–54.

Callaghan, Dympna. "Looking Well to Linens: Women and Cultural Production in *Othello* and Shakespeare's England." In *Marxist Shakespeares*, edited by Jean E. Howard and Scott Cutler Shershow, 53–81. New York: Routledge, 2001.

Campana, Joseph. *The Pain of Reformation: Spenser, Vulnerability, and the Ethics of Masculinity.* New York: Fordham University Press, 2014.

Carruthers, Mary. *The Book of Memory: A Study of Memory in Medieval Culture.* Cambridge: Cambridge University Press, 1990.

Cave, Terence. *The Cornucopian Text: Problems of Writing in the French Renaissance.* Oxford: Clarendon, 1979.

Cavendish, Margaret. *Poems and Fancies.* London, 1653.

Cavigioli, Giovanni Battista. *La Vertu et propriété de vinaigre.* Poitiers, 1541.

Charron, Pierre. *De la sagesse, trois livres.* Paris, 1797.

———. *Of wisdome three books written in French by Peter Charro[n] Doctr of Lawe in Paris.* Translated by Samson Lennard. London, 1608.

*A Closet for Ladies and Gentlewomen, or, The Art of Preserving, Conserving, and Candying.* London, 1611.

Colie, Rosalie. *"My Ecchoing Song": Andrew Marvell's Poetry of Criticism.* Princeton, NJ: Princeton University Press, 1970.

Columella. *On Agriculture.* Vol. 3, *Books 10–12: On Trees.* Loeb Classical Library 408. Translated by E. S. Forster and Edward H. Heffner. Cambridge, MA: Harvard University Press, 1955.

*The Compleat Cook: or, The Whole Art of Cookery.* London, 1694.

Conley, Tom. "Reading Olivier de Serres circa 1600: Between Economy and Ecology." In *Early Modern Écologies: Beyond English Ecocriticism,* edited by Pauline Goul and Philip John Usher, 223–62. Amsterdam: Amsterdam University Press, 2020.

Cookbook of Susanna Packe. 1674. Folger Shakespeare Library, MS V.a.215.

Cookery book of Ann Goodenough. ca. 1700–ca. 1775. Folger Shakespeare Library, MS W.a.332.

Cookery and pharmaceutical recipes of the Malet family. 1700–1740. Folger Shakespeare Library, MS W.a.303.

Cotgrave, Randle. *A Dictionarie of the French and English Tongues.* London, 1611.

Crewe, Jonathan. "The Garden State: Marvell's Poetics of Enclosure." In *Enclosure Acts: Sexuality, Property, and Culture in Early Modern England,* edited by John Michael Archer and Richard Burt, 270–89. Ithaca, NY: Cornell University Press, 1994.

Dalla Costa, Mariarosa, and Selma James. *The Power of Women and the Subversion of the Community.* Bristol: Falling Wall, 1975.

Davis, Kathleen. *Periodization and Sovereignty: How Ideas of Feudalism and Secularization Govern the Politics of Time.* Philadelphia: University of Pennsylvania Press, 2008.

Dawson, Thomas. *The good huswifes jewell wherein is to be found most excellent and rare deuises for conceits in cookerie, found out by the practise of Thomas Dawson. Whereunto is adjoyned sundry approued reseits for many soueraine oyles, and the way to distill many precious waters, with diuers approued medicines for many diseases. Also certaine approued points of husbandry, very necessarie for all husbandmen to know.* London, 1587.

Defaux, Gérard. "A propos de paroles gelées et dégelées (*Quart Livre,* 55–56): 'plus hault sens' ou 'lectures plurielles'?" In *Rabelais's Incomparable Book: Essays on His Art,* edited by Raymond C. La Charité, 155–77. Lexington, KY: French Forum, 1986.

de Grazia, Margreta. *"Hamlet" without Hamlet.* Cambridge: Cambridge University Press, 2007.

Derrida, Jacques. "What Is a 'Relevant' Translation?" Translated by Lawrence Venuti. *Critical Inquiry* 27, no .2 (Winter 2001): 174–200.

Desan, Philippe. *L'imaginaire économique de la Renaissance.* Paris: Presses de l'Université de Paris-Sorbonne, 2002.

———. *Montaigne: A Life.* Translated by Steven Randall and Lisa Neal. Princeton, NJ: Princeton University Press, 2017.

———, ed. *The Oxford Handbook of Montaigne.* Oxford: Oxford University Press, 2016.

Desrosiers-Bonin, Diane. *Rabelais et l'humanisme civil.* Etudes rabelaisiennes no. 27. Geneva: Droz, 1992.

Dewald, Jonathan. *Aristocratic Experience and the Origins of Modern Culture: France, 1570–1715.* Berkeley: University of California Press, 1993.

Digby, Sir Kenelm. *Choice and experimented receipts in physick and chirurgery, as also cordial and distilled waters and spirits, perfumes, and other curiosities.* London, 1675.

———. *Observations on the 22. Stanza in the 9th. Canto of the 2d. Book of Spencers Faery Queen.* London, 1643.

Dobranski, Stephen B. *Milton, Authorship, and the Book Trade.* Cambridge: Cambridge University Press, 2009.

Dod, John, and Robert Cleaver. *A godlie forme of householde gouernment for the ordering of priuate families, according to the direction of Gods word.* London, 1598.

Dolan, Frances. *Digging the Past: How and Why to Imagine Seventeenth-Century Agriculture.* Philadelphia: University of Pennsylvania Press, 2020.

Dolven, Jeff. "Besides Good and Evil." *SEL* 57, no. 1 (Winter 2017): 1–22.

———. "Obstinate Spenser." *Spenser Review* 47, no. 1.2 (Winter 2017). http://www .english.cam.ac.uk/spenseronline/review/item/47.1.2.

Du Bellay, Joachim. *Les Regrets, précédé de Les Antiquités de Rome et suivi de La Défense et Illustration de la Langue française.* Paris: Gallimard, 1967.

Duck, Stephen, and Mary Collier. *"The Thresher's Labour," Stephen Duck, and "The Woman's Labour," Mary Collier.* Introduction by Moira Ferguson. Los Angeles: Clark Memorial Library, 1985.

Duval, Edwin. *The Design of Rabelais's "Quart Livre de Pantagruel."* Geneva: Droz, 1998.

Edelman, Lee. *No Future: Queer Theory and the Death Drive.* Durham, NC: Duke University Press, 2004.

Eden, Kathy. *Friends Hold All Things in Common: Tradition, Intellectual Property, and the "Adages" of Erasmus.* New Haven, CT: Yale University Press, 2001.

———. *Hermeneutics and the Rhetorical Tradition: Chapters in the Ancient Legacy and Its Humanist Reception.* New Haven, CT: Yale University Press, 2005.

Eggert, Katherine. *Showing like a Queen: Female Authority and Literary Experiment in Spenser, Shakespeare, and Milton.* Philadelphia: University of Pennsylvania Press, 2000.

Ekotto, Frieda. "Against Representation: Countless Hours for a Professor." *PMLA* 127, no. 4 (Oct. 2012): 968–72.

Elyot, Thomas. *The boke named the governour.* London, 1537.

Empson, William. *Milton's God.* New York: New Directions, 1962.

Erasmus. *Adagiorum chiliades Des. Erasmi Roterodami quatuor cum dimidia ex postrema authoris recognitione.* Venice, 1536.

———. *Collected Works of Erasmus.* Vol. 34 (Adages IIviii to IIIiii100). Translated and edited by R. A. B. Mynors. Toronto: University of Toronto Press, 1992.

———. *A Declaration on the Subject of Early Liberal Education for Children / De pueris statim ac liberaliter instituendis declamation.* Translated by Beert C. Verstraete. In *The Erasmus Reader,* edited by Erika Rummel. Toronto: University of Toronto Press, 1990.

———. *Des. Erasmi Roterod. De utraq verborum ac rerum copia lib. II.* London, 1660.

———. *Erasmi opus epistolarum.* Vol. 1, *1484–1514,* edited by Percy Stanford Allen. Oxford: Oxford University Press, 1906, 1992.

Estienne, Charles. *L'agriculture et maison rustique.* Translated by Jean Liebault. Paris, 1570.

Evans, Martin. *Milton's Imperial Epic: "Paradise Lost" and the Discourse of Colonialism.* Ithaca, NY: Cornell University Press, 1996.

Evelyn, John. *Acetaria: A discourse of sallets.* London, 1699.

Eyber, Vitaliy. *Andrew Marvell's "Upon Appleton House": An Analytic Commentary.* Madison, NJ: Fairleigh Dickinson University Press, 2010.

Federici, Silvia. "Wages against Housework." In *Revolution at Point Zero: Housework, Reproduction, and Feminist Struggle*, 15–22. Oakland: PM, 2012.

Ferguson, Margaret. "The Letter of Recommendation as Strange Work." *PMLA* 127, no. 4 (Oct. 2012): 954–62.

Fish, Stanley. *How Milton Works*. Cambridge, MA: Harvard University Press, 2001.

———. "The Temptation to Action in Milton's Poetry." *ELH* 48, no. 3 (Autumn 1981): 516–31.

Fletcher, Angus. *The Prophetic Moment: An Essay on Spenser*. Chicago: University of Chicago Press, 1971.

Fortunati, Leopoldina. *The Arcane of Reproduction: Housework, Prostitution, Labor and Capital*. Translated by Hilary Creek. New York: Automedia, 1995.

Fowler, Alastair. "The Beginnings of English Georgic." In *Renaissance Genres: Essays on Theory, History, and Interpretation*, edited by Barbara Kiefer Lewalski, 105–25. Cambridge, MA: Harvard University Press, 1986.

François, Anne-Lise. "Late Exercises in Minimal Affirmatives." In *Theory Aside*, edited by Jason Potts and Daniel Stout, 34–55. Durham, NC: Duke University Press, 2014.

———. *Open Secrets: The Literature of Uncounted Experience*. Stanford, CA: Stanford University Press, 2008.

Freccero, Carla. *Queer/Early/Modern*. Durham, NC: Duke University Press, 2006.

French, John. *The art of distillation, or, A treatise of the choicest spagiricall preparations performed by way of distillation*. London, 1653.

Frye, Northrop. "Archetypal Criticism: Theory of Myths." In *Anatomy of Criticism: Four Essays*, 131–23. Princeton, NJ: Princeton University Press, 1957.

Fumerton, Patricia. *Cultural Aesthetics: Renaissance Literature and the Practice of Social Ornament*. Chicago: University of Chicago Press, 1991.

Galen. *On the Natural Faculties*. Translated by A. J. Brock. Cambridge, MA: Harvard University Press, 1916.

Gigante, Denise. *Taste: A Literary History*. New Haven, CT: Yale University Press, 2005.

Goldberg, Jonathan. *Endlesse Worke: Spenser and the Structures of Discourse*. Baltimore: Johns Hopkins University Press, 1981.

Goldberg, Jonathan, and Madhavi Menon. "Queering History." *PMLA* 120, no. 5 (Oct. 2005): 1608–17.

Goldhill, Simon. *Who Needs Greek? Contests in the Cultural History of Hellenism*. Cambridge: Cambridge University Press, 2002.

Goldsmith, Steven. *Blake's Agitation: Criticism and the Emotions*. Baltimore: Johns Hopkins University Press, 2013.

Goldstein, Amanda Jo. "Irritable Figures: Herder's Poetic Empiricism." In *The Relevance of Romanticism: Essays on German Romantic Philosophy*, edited by Dalia Nassar, 273–95. Oxford: Oxford University Press, 2014.

Goodman, Kevis. *Georgic Modernity and British Romanticism: Poetry and the Mediation of History*. Cambridge: Cambridge University Press, 2004.

———. "'Wasted Labor'? Milton's Eve, the Poet's Work, and the Challenge of Sympathy." *ELH* 64 (1997): 415–46.

Gray, Floyd. *Gender, Rhetoric, and Print Culture in French Renaissance Writing*. Cambridge: Cambridge University Press, 2009.

———. *Rabelais et le comique du discontinu*. Paris: Champion, 1994.

Greenblatt, Stephen. *Renaissance Self-Fashioning: From More to Shakespeare*. Chicago: University of Chicago Press, 1980.

———. *The Swerve: How the World Became Modern.* New York: Norton, 2011.

Greene, Thomas M. "The Hair of the Dog That Bit You: Rabelais's Thirst." In *Rabelais's Incomparable Book,* edited by Raymond C. La Charité, 181–94. Lexington, KY: French Forum, 1986.

———. *The Light in Troy: Imitation and Discovery in Renaissance Poetry.* New Haven, CT: Yale University Press, 1982.

———. *Rabelais: A Study in Comic Courage.* Englewood Cliffs, NJ: Prentice-Hall, 1970.

Gregerson, Linda. "Spenser's Georgic: Violence and the Gift of Place." *Spenser Studies* 22, no. 1 (Jan. 2007): 185–201.

Gregg, Melissa, and Gregory J. Seigworth. "An Inventory of Shimmers." In *The Affect Theory Reader,* edited by Melissa Gregg and Gregory J. Seigworth, 1–28. Durham, NC: Duke University Press, 2010.

Grey, Elizabeth. *A choice manual of rare and select secrets in physick and chyrurgery collected and practised by the Right Honorable, the Countesse of Kent, late deceased; as also most exquisite ways of preserving, conserving, candying, &c.* London, 1653.

Grossman, Martin. "The Fruits of One's Labor in Miltonic Practice and Marxian Theory." *ELH* 59, no. 1 (Spring 1992): 77–105.

Guild, Elizabeth. *Unsettling Montaigne: Poetics, Ethics and Affect in the "Essais" and Other Writings.* Cambridge: D. S. Brewer, 2014.

Gulden, Ann Torday. "Milton's Eve and Wisdom: The 'Dinner-Party' Scene in *Paradise Lost.*" *Milton Quarterly* 32, no. 4 (Dec. 1998): 137–43.

Guriel, Jason. "Rosy-Fingered Yawn." *PN Review* 207 (Sept./Oct. 2012). https://www.pnreview.co.uk/cgi-bin/scribe?item_id=8633.

Guy-Bray, Stephen. "Animal, Vegetable, Sexual: Metaphor in John Donne's 'Sappho to Philaenis' and Andrew Marvell's 'The Garden.'" In *Sex before Sex: Figuring the Act in Early Modern England,* edited by James M. Bromley and Will Stockton, 195–212. Minneapolis: University of Minnesota Press, 2013.

Hale, John. *The Civilization of Europe in the Renaissance.* New York: Simon and Schuster, 1993.

Hall, Kim F. "Culinary Spaces, Colonial Spaces: The Gendering of Sugar in the Seventeenth Century." In *Feminist Readings of Early Modern Culture: Emerging Subjects,* edited by Valerie Traub, M. Lindsay Kaplan, and Dympna Callaghan, 168–90. Cambridge: Cambridge University Press, 1996.

Hallowell, Robert E. "Ronsard and the Gallic Hercules Myth." *Studies in the Renaissance* 9 (1962): 242–55.

Halpern, Richard. *Eclipse of Action: Tragedy and Political Economy.* Chicago: University of Chicago Press, 2017.

———. *Shakespeare's Perfume: Sodomy and Sublimity in the Sonnets, Wilde, Freud, and Lacan.* Philadelphia: University of Pennsylvania Press, 2002.

Hampton, Timothy. "Difficult Engagements: Private Passion and Public Service in Montaigne's *Essais.*" In *Politics and the Passions, 1500–1850,* edited by Victoria Kahn, Neil Saccamano, and Daniela Coli, 30–48. Princeton, NJ: Princeton University Press, 2006.

———. "The Fallen Fundament: Jargon, Gender, and Literary Authority in the Birth of Gargantua." In *Esprit Généreux, Esprit Pantagruélicque: Essays by His Students in Honor of François Rigolot,* edited by Reinier Leushuis and Zahi Zalloua, 161–76. Geneva: Droz, 2008.

———. "Strange Alteration: Physiology and Psychology from Galen to Rabelais." In

*Reading the Early Modern Passions*, edited by Gail Kern Paster, Katherine Rowe, and Mary Floyd-Wilson, 272–93. Philadelphia: University of Pennsylvania Press, 2004.

———. *Writing from History: The Rhetoric of Exemplarity in Renaissance Literature*. Ithaca, NY: Cornell University Press, 1990.

Hartle, Ann. *Michel de Montaigne: Accidental Philosopher*. Cambridge: Cambridge University Press, 2003.

Hartman, Geoffrey. "Milton's Counterplot." *ELH* 25, no. 1 (Mar. 1958): 1–12.

Haskin, Dayton. *Milton's Burden of Interpretation*. Philadelphia: University of Pennsylvania Press, 1994.

Helgerson, Richard. *Self-Crowned Laureates: Spenser, Jonson, Milton, and the Literary System*. Berkeley: University of California Press, 1983.

Herder, Johann Gottfried. "On the Cognition and Sensation of the Human Soul." In *Philosophical Writings*, translated and edited by Michael N. Forster, 187–244. Cambridge: Cambridge University Press, 2002.

Herron, Thomas. *Spenser's Irish Work: Poetry, Plantation, and Colonial Reformation*. Aldershot: Ashgate, 2007.

Hervet, Gentian. *Xenophons treatise of housholde*. London, 1537.

Hirst, Derek, and Steven N. Zwicker. *Andrew Marvell, Orphan of the Hurricane*. Oxford: Oxford University Press, 2012.

———. "Andrew Marvell and the Toils of the Patriarchy: Fatherhood, Longing, and the Body Politic." *ELH* 66, no. 3 (Fall 1999): 629–54.

———. "High Summer at Nun Appleton, 1651: Andrew Marvell and Lord Fairfax's Occasions." *Historical Journal* 36, no. 2 (June 1993): 247–69.

Hoffmann, George. *Montaigne's Career*. Oxford: Clarendon, 1998.

Howell, James. *Epistolae Ho-Elianæ. Familiar Letters Domestic and Forren; Divided into sundry Sections, partly Historicall, Politicall, Philosophicall, Upon Emergent Occasions*. London, 1650.

Hughes, John. "An Essay on Allegorical Poetry." In *Edmund Spenser: The Critical Heritage*, edited by R. M. Cummings, 248–76. New York: Barnes and Noble, 1971.

Hunter, J. Paul. "Form as Meaning: Pope and the Ideology of the Couplet." *Eighteenth Century* 37, no. 3 (Fall 1996): 257–70.

Hunter, Michael. *Establishing the New Science: The Experience of the Early Royal Society*. Woodbridge: Boydell, 1989.

Hutson, Lorna. *The Usurer's Daughter: Male Friendship and Fictions in Sixteenth-Century England*. London: Routledge, 1994.

Ibbett, Katherine. *The Style of the State in French Theater, 1630–1660: Neoclassicism and Government*. Burlington, VT: Ashgate, 2009.

Jacobson, Miriam. *Barbarous Antiquity: Reorienting the Past in the Poetry of Early Modern England*. Philadelphia: University of Pennsylvania Press, 2014.

Jagose, Annamarie. "Feminism's Queer Theory." *Feminism and Psychology* 19, no. 2 (2009): 157–74.

Jardine, Lisa. *Erasmus, Man of Letters: The Construction of Charisma in Print*. Princeton, NJ: Princeton University Press, 1993.

Jeanneret, Michel. "Débordements rabelaisiens." *Nouvelle Revue de Psychanalyse* 43 (Spring 1991): 105–23.

———. "Les paroles dégelées (Rabelais, *Quart Livre*, 48–65)." *Littérature* 17, no. 1 (1975): 14–30.

Jones, Ann Rosalind. *The Currency of Eros: Women's Love Lyric in Europe, 1540–1620.* Bloomington: Indiana University Press, 1990.

Jonson, Ben. *Ben Jonson.* Vol. 8, *The Poems; The Prose Works,* edited by C. H. Herford, Evelyn Simpson, and Percy Simpson. Oxford: Clarendon Press, 1947.

Jung, Marc René. *Hercule dans la littérature française du XVIe siècle.* Geneva: Droz, 1966.

Kendrick, Christopher. "Agons of the Manor: 'Upon Appleton House' and Agrarian Capitalism." In *The Production of English Renaissance Culture,* edited by David Lee Miller, Sharon O'Dair, and Harold Weber, 13–55. Ithaca, NY: Cornell University Press, 1994.

Kerrigan, William. "Marvell and Nymphets." *Greyfriar* 27 (1986): 3–21.

Knapp, Jeffrey. *An Empire Nowhere: England, America, and Literature from "Utopia" to "The Tempest."* Berkeley: University of California Press, 1994.

———. "Error as a Means of Empire in the *Faerie Queene* 1." *ELH* 54, no. 4 (Winter 1987): 801–34.

Knevet, Ralph. *Rhodon and Iris.* London, 1631.

Knoppers, Laura Lunger. *Politicizing Domesticity from Henrietta Maria to Milton's Eve.* Cambridge: Cambridge University Press, 2011.

Korda, Natasha. *Shakespeare's Domestic Economies: Gender and Property in Early Modern England.* Philadelphia: University of Pennsylvania Press, 2002.

Kranidas, Thomas. "Adam and Eve in the Garden: A Study of *Paradise Lost,* Book V." *Studies in English Literature, 1500–1900* 4, no. 1 (Winter 1964): 71–83.

Krause, Virginia. *Idle Pursuits: Literature and Oisiveté in the French Renaissance.* Newark: University of Delaware Press, 2003.

Kritzman, Lawrence D. *The Rhetoric of Sexuality and the Literature of the French Renaissance.* Cambridge: Cambridge University Press, 1991.

Kunin, Aaron. "Shakespeare's Preservation Fantasy." *PMLA* 124, no. 1 (Jan. 2009): 92–106.

Kurnick, David. "A Few Lies: Queer Theory and Our Method Melodramas." *ELH* 87, no. 2 (Summer 2020): 349–69.

Kuzner, James. *Open Subjects: English Renaissance Republicans, Modern Selfhoods, and the Virtue of Vulnerability.* Edinburgh: Edinburgh University Press, 2011.

Labé, Louise. *Œuvres poétiques.* Edited by Françoise Charpentier. Paris: Gallimard, 2006.

*The ladies cabinet opened, wherein is found hidden severall experiments in preserving and conserving, physicke, and surgery, cookery, and huswifery.* London, 1639.

Lanyer, Aemilia. *The Poems of Aemilia Lanyer: Salve Deus Rex Judæorum.* Edited by Susanne Woods. Oxford: Oxford University Press, 1993.

Lecky, Kat. "Milton's Experienced Eve." *Philological Quarterly* 96, no. 4 (2017): 453–74.

Leo, Russ. "The Species-Life of Worldlings." *Spenser Studies* 30 (2015): 201–28.

Leong, Elaine. *Recipes and Everyday Knowledge: Medicine, Science, and the Household in Early Modern England.* Chicago: University of Chicago Press, 2018.

Lerner, Ross. *Unknowing Fanaticism: Reformation Literatures of Self-Annihilation.* New York: Fordham University Press, 2019.

Lewalski, Barbara K. *The Life of John Milton: A Critical Biography.* Malden, MA: Blackwell, 2000.

———. "Milton on Women—Yet Once More." *Milton Studies* 6 (1975): 3–20.

———. *"Paradise Lost" and the Rhetoric of Literary Forms.* Princeton, NJ: Princeton University Press, 1985.

Lewis, C. S. *The Allegory of Love: A Study in Medieval Tradition.* London: Oxford University Press, 1938.

———. *A Preface to "Paradise Lost."* London: Oxford University Press, 1961.

Lobis, Seth. "Milton's Tended Garden and the Georgic Fall." *Milton Studies* 55 (2014): 89–111.

Logan, William. "Plains of Blood." Review of *Memorial*, by Alice Oswald. *New York Times*, Dec. 21, 2012. https://www.nytimes.com/2012/12/23/books/review/memorial -alice-oswalds-version-of-the-iliad.html.

Low, Anthony. *The Georgic Revolution.* Princeton, NJ: Princeton University Press, 1985.

———. "Milton, *Paradise Regained*, and Georgic." *PMLA* 98, no. 2 (1983): 152–69.

Lupton, Julia Reinhard. "Thinking with Things: Hannah Woolley to Hannah Arendt." *postmedieval* 3 (2012): 63–79.

Lynne, Walter. *The vertuous scholehouse of ungracious women.* N.d.

Lyons, John D. *The Phantom of Chance: From Fortune to Randomness in Seventeenth-Century French Literature.* Edinburgh: Edinburgh University Press, 2011.

Lyotard, Jean-François. "Judiciousness in Dispute, or Kant after Marx." Translated by Cecile Lindsay. In *The Lyotard Reader*, edited by Andrew Benjamin, 324–59. Cambridge: Basil Blackwell, 1989.

Malcolm, Noel. "Thomas Harrison and His 'Ark of Studies': An Episode in the History of the Organisation of Knowledge." *Seventeenth Century* 19 (2004): 196–232.

Marcus, Leah S. "Milton among Women." *Milton Studies* 51 (2010): 45–62.

———. *The Politics of Mirth: Jonson, Herrick, Milton, Marvell, and the Defense of Old Holiday Pastimes.* Chicago: University of Chicago Press, 1989.

Markham, Gervase. *The English house-wife, Containing the inward and outward vertues which ought to be in a complete woman.* London, 1631.

Marshall, Cynthia. *The Shattering of the Self: Violence, Subjectivity, and Early Modern Texts.* Baltimore: Johns Hopkins University Press, 2003.

Martz, Louis. "Paradise Regained: The Meditative Combat." *ELH* 27, no. 3 (Sept. 1960): 223–47.

Marvell, Andrew. *The Poems of Andrew Marvell.* Edited by Nigel Smith. Harlow: Pearson Longman, 2003.

Marx, Karl. *Capital.* Vol. 1, translated by Ben Fowkes. New York: Penguin, 1976.

Maus, Katharine Eisaman. "A Womb of His Own: Male Renaissance Poets in the Female Body." In *Sexuality and Gender in Early Modern Europe: Institutions, Texts, Images*, edited by James Grantham Turner, 266–88. Cambridge: Cambridge University Press, 1993.

May, Robert. *The accomplisht cook, or, The art & mystery of cookery wherein the whole art is revealed in a more easie and perfect method than hath been published in any language.* 1660. London, 1685.

Mazzola, Elizabeth, and Corinne S. Abate. "Introduction: 'Indistinguished Space.'" In *Privacy, Domesticity, and Women in Early Modern England*, edited by Corinne S. Abate, 1–17. Burlington, VT: Ashgate, 2003.

McColley, Diane Kelsey. *Milton's Eve.* Urbana: University of Illinois Press, 1983.

McCrea, Barry. *In the Company of Strangers: Family and Narrative in Dickens, Conan Doyle, Joyce, and Proust.* New York: Columbia University Press, 2011.

McKeon, Michael. *The Secret History of Domesticity: Public, Private, and the Division of Knowledge.* Baltimore: Johns Hopkins University Press, 2007.

McRae, Andrew. *God Speed the Plough: The Representation of Agrarian England, 1500–1660.* Cambridge: Cambridge University Press, 1996.

———. "The Green Marvell." In *The Cambridge Companion to Andrew Marvell*, edited by Derek Hirst and Steven N. Zwicker, 122–39. Cambridge: Cambridge University Press, 2011.

*Le Menagier de Paris*. Edited by Georgine E. Brereton and Janet M. Ferrier. Oxford: Clarendon, 1981.

Michelet, Jules. *Histoire de France au seizième siècle: La réforme*. Paris: Calmann-Lévy, 1898.

Michelini, Ann. "Hybris and Plants." *Harvard Studies in Classical Philology* 82 (1978): 35–44.

Milton, John. *The Christian Doctrine*. Translated by Charles R. Sumner. In *The Works of John Milton*, vols. 14–17. Edited by James Holly Hanford and Waldo Hilary Dunn. New York: Columbia University Press, 1931–38.

———. *The Riverside Milton*. Edited by Roy Flannagan. Boston: Houghton Mifflin, 1998.

Montaigne, Michel de. *The Complete Essays of Montaigne*. Translated by Donald M. Frame. Stanford, CA: Stanford University Press, 1958.

———. *Les Essais*. Edited by Pierre Villey and Verdun-Louis Saulnier. Paris: PUF, 2004.

———. *Journal de voyage*. Edited by Fausta Garavini. Paris: Gallimard, 1982.

Montrose, Louis. "Of Gentlemen and Shepherds: The Politics of Elizabethan Pastoral Form." *ELH* 50, no. 3 (Autumn 1983): 415–59.

———. *The Purpose of Playing: Shakespeare and the Cultural Politics of the Elizabethan Theatre*. Chicago: University of Chicago Press, 1996.

———. "Spenser's Domestic Domain: Poetry, Property, and the Early Modern Subject." In *Subject and Object in Renaissance Culture*, edited by Margreta de Grazia, Maureen Quilligan, and Peter Stallybrass, 83–130. Cambridge: Cambridge University Press, 1996.

Morton, Timothy. "Guest Column: Queer Ecology." *PMLA* 125, no. 2 (2010): 273–82.

Mühlethaler, Jean-Claude. "Des mets et des maux. Aspects et enjeux de la dévaluation de la table à la Renaissance." *Romanische Forschungen* 108 (1996): 396–424.

Mulcaster, Richard. *Positions wherin those primitive circumstances be examined, which are necessarie for the training up of children, either for skill in their booke, or health in their bodie*. London, 1581.

Murrell, John. *A Delightfull Daily Exercise for Ladies and Gentlewomen*. London, 1621.

Nagy, Gregory. "Ancient Greek Elegy." In *The Oxford Handbook of the Elegy*, edited by Karen Weisman, 13–45. Oxford: Oxford University Press, 2010.

Neves, Lara. "I Choose to Be a Homemaker, Not a Housekeeper." Overstuffed Life: Simple Solutions for Busy Moms. Sept. 2, 2015. https://www.overstuffedlife.com/2015/09/elevating-the-term-homemaker.html.

Ngai, Sianne. "Henry James's 'Same Secret Principle.'" *Henry James Review* 41, no. 1 (Winter 2020): 44–76.

———. *Ugly Feelings*. Cambridge, MA: Harvard University Press, 2005.

Nicot, Jean. *Dictionaire Francois-Latin*. Paris, 1584.

———. *Le Thresor de la langue francoyse*. Paris, 1606.

Nostradamus. *Excellent & moult utile opuscule à touts necessaire, qui desirent avoir cognoissance de plusieurs exquises receptes, divisé en deux parties*. Lyon, 1555.

Nyquist, Mary. "The Genesis of Gendered Subjectivity in the Divorce Tracts and in *Paradise Lost*." In *Re-Membering Milton: Essays on the Texts and Traditions*, edited by Mary Nyquist and Margaret W. Ferguson, 99–127. New York: Methuen, 1987.

Orlin, Lena Cowen. *Locating Privacy in Tudor London*. Oxford: Oxford University Press, 2007.

———. *Private Matters and Public Culture in Post-Reformation England.* Ithaca, NY: Cornell University Press, 1994.

———. "Three Ways to Be Invisible in the Renaissance: Sex, Reputation, Stitchery." In *Renaissance Culture and the Everyday,* edited by Patricia Fumerton and Simon Hunt, 183–203. Philadelphia: University of Pennsylvania Press, 1999.

Oswald, Alice. *Memorial: An Excavation of the "Iliad."* London: Faber and Faber, 2011.

———. *Memorial: A Version of Homer's "Iliad."* Afterword by Eavan Boland. New York: Norton, 2012.

Parker, Patricia. "Dilation and Delay: Renaissance Matrices." *Poetics Today* 5, no. 3 (1984): 519–35.

———. *Inescapable Romance: Studies in the Poetics of a Mode.* Princeton, NJ: Princeton University Press, 1979.

———. *Literary Fat Ladies: Rhetoric, Gender, Property.* New York: Methuen, 1987.

Partridge, John. *The Treasurie of commodious conceits, & hidden secrets and may be called, the huswives closet, of healthfull provision.* London, 1573.

Pasquier, Estienne. *Les lettres d'Estienne Pasquier.* Avignon, 1590.

Paster, Gail Kern. *The Body Embarrassed: Drama and the Disciplines of Shame in Early Modern England.* Ithaca, NY: Cornell University Press, 1993.

Patterson, Jonathan. *Representing Avarice in Late Renaissance France.* Oxford: Oxford University Press, 2015.

Pennell, Sara. *The Birth of the English Kitchen, 1600–1850.* London: Bloomsbury, 2016.

*Petit traicte contenant la maniere de faire toutes confitures.* Paris, 1545.

Petrarca, Francesco. "The Ascent of Mont Ventoux." In *The Renaissance Philosophy of Man,* edited by Ernst Cassirer, Paul Oskar Kristeller, and John Herman Randall Jr., translated by Hans Nachod, 36–46. Chicago: University of Chicago Press, 1948.

Picciotto, Joanna. *Labors of Innocence in Early Modern England.* Cambridge, MA: Harvard University Press, 2010.

Phillips, Margaret Mann. *The "Adages" of Erasmus: A Study with Translations.* Cambridge: Cambridge University Press, 1964.

Pigman, G. W. "Versions of Imitation in the Renaissance." *Renaissance Quarterly* 33, no. 1 (Spring 1980): 1–32.

Plat, Hugh. *Delightes for ladies to adorn their persons, tables, closets, and distallatories: with beauties, banquets, perfumes and waters.* London, 1600.

———. *The Garden of Eden, or, An accurate Description of all Flowers and Fruits now growing in England, with particular Rules how to advance their Nature and Growth, as well in Seeds and Hearbs, as the secret ordering of Trees and Plants.* 1608. London, 1659.

*La Pratique de faire toutes confitures.* Lyon, 1558.

Proust, Marcel. *In Search of Lost Time.* Vol. 3, *Sodom and Gomorrah.* Translated by C. K. Scott Moncrieff and Terence Kilmartin, revised by D. J. Enright. New York: Modern Library, 2003.

Purkiss, Diane. "Marvell, Boys, Girls, and Men: Should We Worry?" In *Gender and Early Modern Constructions of Childhood,* edited by Naomi J. Miller and Naomi Yavneh, 182–92. Burlington, VT: Ashgate, 2011.

———. "Thinking of Gender." In *The Cambridge Companion to Andrew Marvell,* edited by Derek Hirst and Steven N. Zwicker, 68–86. Cambridge: Cambridge University Press, 2011.

Quilligan, Maureen. "Freedom, Service, and the Trade in Slaves: The Problem of Labor in *Paradise Lost.*" In *Subject and Object in Renaissance Culture,* edited by Margreta de

Grazia, Maureen Quilligan, and Peter Stallybrass, 213–34. Cambridge: Cambridge University Press, 1996.

Quint, David. *Epic and Empire: Politics and Generic Form from Virgil to Milton.* Princeton, NJ: Princeton University Press, 1993.

———. *Montaigne and the Quality of Mercy: Ethical and Political Themes in the "Essais."* Princeton, NJ: Princeton University Press, 1998.

Rabelais, François. *Gargantua and Pantagruel.* Translated and edited by M. A. Screech. New York: Penguin, 2006.

———. *Œuvres completes.* Edited by Jacques Boulenger and Lucien Scheler. Paris: Gallimard, 1955.

Rabisha, William. *The whole body of cookery dissected.* London, 1661.

Rambuss, Richard. *Spenser's Secret Career.* Cambridge: Cambridge University Press, 1993.

Receipt book of Penelope Jephson. 1671. Folger Shakespeare Library, MS V.a.396.

Reeser, Todd. *Moderating Masculinity in Early Modern Culture.* Chapel Hill: University of North Carolina Press, 2006.

Regosin, Richard. *Montaigne's Unruly Brood: Textual Engendering and the Challenge to Paternal Authority.* Berkeley: University of California Press, 1996.

———. "Prudence and the Ethics of Contingency in Montaigne's *Essais.*" In *Chance, Literature, and Culture in Early Modern France,* edited by John D. Lyons and Kathleen Wine, 125–40. New York: Routledge, 2016.

Rekdal, Paisley. "Memorial Time: Poetry, Elegy, and the War Memorial." *Kenyon Review* 40, no. 6 (Nov./Dec. 2018): 99–112.

Rich, Adrienne. "When We Dead Awaken: Writing as Re-Vision." *College English* 34, no. 1 (Oct. 1972): 18–30.

Ricks, Christopher. *Milton's Grand Style.* Oxford: Oxford University Press, 1978.

Rigolot, François. *Les Langages de Rabelais.* Geneva: Droz, 1996.

Rogers, John. "The Enclosure of Virginity: The Poetics of Sexual Abstinence in the English Revolution." In *Enclosure Acts: Sexuality, Property, and Culture in Early Modern England,* edited by John Michael Archer and Richard Burt, 229–50. Ithaca, NY: Cornell University Press, 1994.

———. *The Matter of Revolution: Science, Poetry, and Politics in the Age of Milton.* Ithaca, NY: Cornell University Press, 1996.

———. "Milton's Circumcision." In *Milton and the Grounds of Contention,* edited by Mark R. Kelley, Michael Lieb, and John T. Shawcross, 188–213. Pittsburgh: Duquesne University Press, 2003.

Ross, David O. *Virgil's Elements: Physics and Poetry in the "Georgics."* Princeton, NJ: Princeton University Press, 1987.

Salmon, William. *The family dictionary, or, Houshold companion wherein are alphabetically laid down exact rules and choice physical receipts for the preservation of health . . . directions for making oils, ointments, salves, . . . chymical preparations, physical-wines, ales and other liquors and descriptions of the virtues of herbs, fruits, flowers . . . and parts of living creatures used in medicinal potions, . . . likewise directions for cookery, . . . also the way of making all sorts of perfumes . . . together with the art of making all sorts of English wines, . . . the mystery of pickling and keeping all sorts of pickles. . . .* London, 1695.

Saulnier, V.-L. "Hommes pétrifiés et pierres vives (autour d'une formule de Panurge)." *Bibliothèque d'Humanisme et Renaissance* 22 (1960): 393–402.

———. "Médecins de Montpellier. Au temps de Rabelais." *Bibliothèque d'Humanisme et Renaissance* 19, no. 3 (1957): 425–79.

Sawday, Jonathan. *The Body Emblazoned: Dissection and the Human Body in Renaissance Culture.* New York: Routledge, 1995.

Scarry, Elaine. *The Body in Pain: The Making and Unmaking of the World.* Oxford: Oxford University Press, 1985.

Schaeffer, John D. "Metonymies We Read By: Rhetoric, Truth and the Eucharist in Milton's *Areopagitica.*" *Milton Quarterly* 34, no. 3 (2000): 84–92.

Schoenberger, Melissa. *Cultivating Peace: The Virgilian Georgic in English, 1650–1750.* Lewisburg, PA: Bucknell University Press, 2019.

Schoenfeldt, Michael. *Bodies and Selves in Early Modern England: Physiology and Inwardness in Spenser, Shakespeare, Herbert, and Milton.* Cambridge: Cambridge University Press, 1999.

Schwartz, Regina. *Remembering and Repeating: Biblical Creation in "Paradise Lost."* Chicago: University of Chicago Press, 1988.

Scodel, Joshua. "Edenic Freedoms." *Milton Studies* 56 (2015): 153–200.

———. *Excess and the Mean in Early Modern English Literature.* Princeton, NJ: Princeton University Press, 2002.

Screech, M. A. *Rabelais.* Ithaca, NY: Cornell University Press, 1979.

*Secrets de divers autheurs approuvez.* Paris, 1619.

Seneca. *Epistles.* Translated by Richard M. Gummere. Suffolk: Loeb Classical Library, 1917.

———. *Selected Letters.* Translated by Elaine Fantham. Oxford: Oxford University Press, 2010.

Serres, Olivier de. *Le théâtre d'agriculture et mesnage des champs.* Paris, 1600.

Sessions, William. "Spenser's Georgic." *ELR* 10, no. 2 (Spring 1980): 202–38.

Shakespeare, William. *The Riverside Shakespeare.* Edited by G. Blakemore Evans et al. 1974. Boston: Houghton Mifflin, 1997.

Shapin, Steven. *A Social History of Truth: Civility and Science in Seventeenth-Century England.* Chicago: University of Chicago Press, 1994.

Simon, David Carroll. *Light without Heat: The Observational Mood from Bacon to Milton.* Ithaca, NY: Cornell University Press, 2018.

Smith, Adam. *An Inquiry into the Nature and Causes of the Wealth of Nations.* Edited by Edwin Cannan. Chicago: University of Chicago Press, 1976.

Smith, Henry. *A preparative to mariage, the summe whereof was spoken at a contract, and inlarged after.* London, 1591.

Smith, Nigel. *Andrew Marvell: The Chameleon.* New Haven, CT: Yale University Press, 2010.

Smith, Pamela. *The Body of the Artisan: Art and Experience in the Scientific Revolution.* Chicago: University of Chicago Press, 2004.

Spenser, Edmund. *The Faerie Queene.* Edited by A. C. Hamilton, with Hiroshi Yamashita, Toshiyuki Suzuki, and Shohachi Fukuda, 2nd ed. New York: Routledge, 2007.

Sprat, Thomas. *The History of the Royal Society of London, for the Improving of Natural Knowledge.* London, 1734.

Starobinski, Jean. *Montaigne in Motion.* Translated by Arthur Goldhammer. Chicago: University of Chicago Press, 1985.

Stewart, Alan, and Garrett Sullivan. "'Worme-Eaten, and Full of Canker Holes': Materializing Memory in *The Faerie Queene* and *Lingua.*" *Spenser Studies* 17 (2003): 215–38.

Stocker, Margarita. *Apocalyptic Marvell: The Second Coming in Seventeenth-Century Poetry.* Brighton: Harvester, 1986.

Stone, Lawrence. *The Crisis of the Aristocracy, 1558–1641.* Oxford: Clarendon, 1965.

Summers, Joseph. "Marvell's 'Nature.'" *ELH* 20, no. 2 (June 1963): 121–35.

Summit, Jennifer. *Memory's Library: Medieval Books in Early Modern England.* Chicago: University of Chicago Press, 2008.

Swann, Marjorie. "Vegetable Love: Botany and Sexuality in Seventeenth-Century England." In *The Indistinct Human in Renaissance Literature,* edited by Jean E. Feerick and Vin Nardizzi, 139–58. New York: Palgrave Macmillan, 2012.

Tigner, Amy L. "Eating with Eve." *Milton Quarterly* 44, no. 4 (Dec. 2010): 239–53.

———. "Preserving Nature in Hannah Woolley's *The Queen-Like Closet; or Rich Cabinet.*" In *Ecofeminist Approaches to Early Modernity,* edited by Jennifer Munroe and Rebecca Laroche, 128–49. New York: Palgrave Macmillan, 2011.

Tomasik, Timothy. "Fishes, Fowl, and *La Fleur de toute cuysine:* Gaster and Gastronomy in Rabelais's *Quart Livre.*" In *Renaissance Food from Rabelais to Shakespeare: Culinary Readings and Culinary Histories,* edited by Joan Fitzpatrick, 25–51. Burlington, VT: Ashgate, 2010.

Tournon, André. "De l'interprétation des 'motz de gueule.'" In *Hommage à François Meyer.* Aix-en-Provence: Publications de l'Université de Provence, 1983.

Traub, Valerie. "The New Unhistoricism in Queer Studies." *PMLA* 128, no. 1 (Jan. 2013): 21–39.

Turner, James Grantham. "Libertinism and Toleration: Milton, Bruno and Aretino." In *Milton and Toleration,* edited by Sharon Achinstein and Elizabeth Sauer, 107–25. Oxford: Oxford University Press, 2007.

Tusser, Thomas. *Fiue hundreth points of good husbandry vnited to as many of good huswiferie.* London, 1573.

Vaughan, Thomas. *Magia adamica or the antiquitie of magic.* London, 1650.

Veblen, Thorstein. *The Theory of the Leisure Class: An Economic Study of Institutions.* New York: Macmillan, 1912.

Vickers, Brian. "The Myth of Francis Bacon's 'Anti-Humanism.'" In *Humanism and Early Modern Philosophy,* edited by Jill Kraye and M. W. F. Stone, 135–58. London: Routledge, 2000.

Virgil. *Georgics.* Vol. 1, books I–II, edited by Richard F. Thomas. Cambridge: Cambridge University Press, 1988.

———. *The Georgics of Virgil.* Translated by David Ferry. New York: Farrar, Straus and Giroux, 2005.

Vives, Juan Luis. *The Passions of the Soul: The Third Book of De Anima et Vita.* Translated by Carlos G. Noreña. Lewiston, NY: Edwin Mellen, 1990.

Wadoski, Andrew. "Milton's Spenser: Eden and the Work of Poetry." *SEL* 55, no. 1 (Winter 2015): 174–96.

Wall, Wendy. "Distillation: Transformations in and out of the Kitchen." In *Renaissance Food from Rabelais to Shakespeare: Culinary Readings and Culinary Histories,* edited by Joan Fitzpatrick, 89–104. Burlington, VT: Ashgate, 2010.

———. "Forgetting and Keeping: Jane Shore and the English Domestication of History." *Renaissance Drama* 27 (1996): 123–56.

———. "Just a Spoonful of Sugar: Syrup and Domesticity in Early Modern England." *Modern Philology* 104, no. 2 (Nov. 2006): 149–72.

———. "Literacy and the Domestic Arts." *Huntington Library Quarterly* 73, no. 3 (Sept. 2010): 383–412.

———. *Recipes for Thought: Knowledge and Taste in the Early Modern Kitchen*. Philadelphia: University of Pennsylvania Press, 2015.

———. *Staging Domesticity: Household Work and English Identity in Early Modern Drama*. Cambridge: Cambridge University Press, 2002.

Wallace, J. M. *Destiny His Choice: The Loyalism of Andrew Marvell*. Cambridge: Cambridge University Press, 1981.

Wayne, Dan E. *Penshurst: The Semiotics of Place and the Poetics of History*. Madison: University of Wisconsin Press, 1984.

Weigel, Moira, and Mal Ahern. "Further Materials toward a Theory of the Man Child." *The New Inquiry*, July 9, 2013. https://thenewinquiry.com/further-materials-toward-a-theory-of-the-man-child/.

Weinberg, Florence. "Layers of Emblematic Prose: Rabelais' Andouilles." *Sixteenth Century Journal* 26, no. 2 (Summer 1995): 367–77.

Wilkinson, L. P. *The "Georgics" of Virgil: A Critical Survey*. Cambridge: Cambridge University Press, 1969.

Williams, Raymond. *The Country and the City*. Oxford: Oxford University Press, 1975.

Wilson-Okamura, David Scott. *Virgil in the Renaissance*. Cambridge: Cambridge University Press, 2010.

Woolley, Hannah. *The Accomplishd ladies delight*. London, 1686.

———. *The Gentlewoman's Companion; or, a Guide to the Female Sex*. London, 1675.

———. *The queen-like closet; or, Rich cabinet stored with all manner of rare receipts for preserving, candying & cookery*. London, 1670.

Xenophon, Οἰκονομικός. In *Xenophontis opera omnia*, vol. 2, 2nd ed. Oxford: Clarendon, 1921.

Zwinger, Theodor. *Theatrum vitae humanae*. Basel, 1586.

# INDEX

academia: female professors, 159–60; as feminized, 160

Aeschylus, 32

affect, 15, 67, 81–85, 95; affective labor, 130–31, 153, 160; affect theory, 15, 84

agitation, 3; affective state of, 81, 83; and irritation, 83; as mental activity, 78, 80; political, 83

alchemy, 133, 192n35, 194n58, 201n51

allegory, in *The Faerie Queene*, 55, 56, 60–61, 70

*alloiosis*, 32

Anderson, Judith H., 180n59

Arendt, Hannah, 1, 10, 89, 155, 165n2; action, 2, 66, 85, 145, 172n53, 174n83; Hercules, labors of, 19; labor, 2, 21, 66, 91, 160; *oikos* and *polis*, distinction between, 85; work (vs. labor and action), 66, 91, 160

aristocracy, 7, 20–21, 123, 181–82n2, 183n26, 185–86n6, 191n23, 193n36

Aristotle, 81, 82–83, 175n10, 180n56, 190n11

Ascham, Roger, 166n8; *The Scholemaster*, 21

Astell, Mary, 10, 120

Auden, W. H., 170n42

Bacon, Francis, 2, 3, 5, 8, 15, 73–74, 166n8, 202n61; *Advancement of Learning*, 6; Baconianism, 6, 97, 129, 135, 198n24; "Georgics of the mind," 6, 144; *New Atlantis*, 2

Bakewell, Sarah, 186–87n13

Bakhtin, Mikhail, 29, 30, 32, 50

Barbados, 199n35

Barkan, Leonard, 6–7

Baudrillard, Jean, 194n55

Beauvoir, Simone de, on modern housewife in *The Second Sex*, 12–13, 14, 58, 79–80, 89, 93, 154, 155, 161

Bentley, Richard, 128–30

Berger, Harry, Jr., 62–63

Berger, John, 136–37

Best, Stephen, 7, 110, 168n26, 168n27

Bierlaire, Franz, 60, 169n31

Blair, Ann, 60, 166n11, 169n31

Blake, William, 83

Bloch, R. Howard, 109–10

Bodin, Jean, 186n7

Boland, Eavan, 156, 203n14

Botzheim, John, 16

Boyer, Anne, 152–53, 155

Bracciolini, Poggio, 7

bread, 44

Browne, Thomas, 191n21

Bruns, Gerald L., 22

Budé, Guillaume, 51

Burckhardt, Jacob, 6–7

Caedmon, 202n65

Calhoun, Alison, 93

Callaghan, Dympna, 117–18

Campana, Joseph, 67–68, 71–72, 74

Carruthers, Mary, 202n65

Printed in Great Britain
by Amazon